THE PROCESS OF COMMUNICATION

The Process of Communication

AN INTRODUCTION TO THEORY AND PRACTICE

David K. Berlo

MICHIGAN STATE UNIVERSITY

Holt, Rinehart and Winston, Inc.

New York • Chicago • San Francisco • Atlanta • Dallas
Montreal • Toronto • London • Sydney

Copyright © 1960
by Holt, Rinehart and Winston, Inc.
Library of Congress Catalog Card Number: 60–7981
ISBN 0–03–55686–4
Printed in the United States of America
012   008   232221

Preface

THIS is a book about the way people communicate with each other. Essentially, it is concerned with the scope and purpose of communication, the factors involved in the process, and the role of language in human behavior. It is about people's behaviors and the relationships between the talker and the listener, the writer and the reader, the performer and the audience. It explores the complex nature of the communication process. It identifies and describes factors affecting communication and its results. It attempts an approach to the process that will increase understanding and effectiveness, and yet avoid distortion or oversimplification.

The basis of this behavioral approach to human communication is interdisciplinary. It relies on relevant research in experimental and social psychology, sociology, linguistics, anthropology, and philosophy, together with the significant studies in mass communication and other applied communication fields. The central concepts of the book, particularly the core concepts of *meaning,* are developed multidimensionally, using whatever disciplines and subject-matter specialties are relevant.

This book is not intended as an abstract or review of what is known about communication, or as an attempt to construct a comprehensive theory. As its title indicates, it is intended as a theoretic introduction to the process, a beginning point for the interested reader. Its language is therefore as direct and nontechnical as possible. All terms used are explained in the text, and all models discussed are illustrated.

Each chapter refers to other books and articles that can provide more information and a more technical discussion. Questions are provided at the end of each chapter, and are intended to help the reader interpret the content of the chapter in terms of his own

v

experience. A bibliography of recommended reading and an index are provided to add to the book's usefulness.

It is hoped that the book will be of interest and value to readers who are engaged in or preparing for professional communication work in the public media or elsewhere. In addition, the book is intended for participants in communication seminars and training programs in government and industry, and for college students about to begin the systematic study of communication process and practice, whether oral or visual or both.

Most of the chapters have been developed and revised through use in the Seminars on Communication offered by the United States International Cooperation Administration, in courses offered by the Department of General Communication Arts at Michigan State University, and in workshops and training programs in industry and agriculture, particularly those of the National Project in Agricultural Communications. I am especially indebted to the American Association of Land-Grant Colleges and State Universities for permission to use materials which were developed for the association, and on which it holds the copyrights.

It is impossible to acknowledge adequately, or even to recognize, the influence one's colleagues have upon one's work. The writings and teaching of Charles E. Osgood and Wilbur Schramm have permeated my own thinking beyond recognition. I also owe a special debt to the work of Charles Morris and George Herbert Mead, and to others whose writings are cited specifically as they appear in the text.

The National Project in Agricultural Communications provided financial support for several chapters, and its Associate Director, Mr. Francis Byrnes, served as a sympathetic but demanding critic and editor. My colleagues in the Department of General Communication Arts at Michigan State have provided continuous advice and suggestion; in particular, Professors Erwin Bettinghaus, Hideya Kumata, and Malcolm MacLean, Junior, have read and criticized many of the chapters.

I am grateful to another colleague, Professor John Ball, for a substantive review of the entire manuscript and for a constant pressure to implement the concept of process in a discussion of communication. Mr. Glendon Drake labored over the index, and Mrs. Shirley Sherman maintained eternal vigilance against error in the preparation of many drafts. Acknowledgment goes also to the many students, graduate and undergraduate, who served as receivers and critics of preliminary drafts and who provided the frank appraisal or feedback necessary to clarity of style.

An encompassing debt is owed my wife and children, who provide that combination of skepticism, confidence, patience, and balance essential to a man who vacillates between exorbitant enthusiasm (when an idea works) and irrational irritability (when it doesn't).

East Lansing, Michigan   D. B.
February 1960

Contents

THE PROCESS OF COMMUNICATION

CHAPTER 1

Communication

SCOPE AND PURPOSE

THERE is research evidence to indicate that the average American spends about 70 per cent of his active hours communicating verbally—listening, speaking, reading, and writing, in that order. In other words, each of us spends about 10 or 11 hours a day, every day, performing verbal communication behaviors.

Language is only one of the codes we use to express our ideas. Birdwhistell[1] and others have studied communication involving nonverbal gestures: facial expressions, movements of the hands and arms. Through use of infra-red cameras and other devices such as the "wiggle-meter," researchers have observed the gross bodily movements of people attending movies or television, and have found that audiences communicate their interest by these bodily movements. Hall, in his book *The Silent Language*,[2] talks about other kinds of signals people use to express their attitudes; e.g., how many minutes late a man can arrive for an appointment without communicating disrespect, or how far apart people stand in order to

[1] Ray Birdwhistell, "Kinesics and communication." *Explorations*, No. 3, 1954. University of Toronto Press.
[2] Edward T. Hall, *The Silent Language*. Doubleday, 1959.

communicate acquaintanceship rather than friendship, etc. Stage designers and advertising copywriters use color, size, and distance as signals in communication. In short, anything to which people can attach meanings may be and is used in communication. Communication behavior is tremendously broad in scope.

People can communicate on many levels, for many reasons, with many people, in many ways. Ruesch and Bateson have prepared a hypothetical example of the kinds of communication that a typical man, Mister A, might use in an average day.

In the morning when Mr. A enters his office he reads his incoming mail (written communication). In sorting his mail he encounters a number of pamphlets which are designed to describe the merits of various business machines (pictorial communication). Through the open window the faint noise of a radio is heard, as the voice of an announcer clearly praises the quality of a brand of toothpaste (spoken communication).

When his secretary enters the room she gives him a cheerful "good morning," which he acknowledges with a friendly nod of his head (gestural communication) while he continues with his conversation on the telephone (spoken communication) with a business associate. Later in the morning he dictates a number of letters to his secretary, then he holds a committee meeting (group communication), where he gathers the advice of his associates. In this meeting a number of new governmental regulations (mass communication) and their effect upon the policies of the firm are discussed. Later in the meeting a resolution to the employees of the firm concerning the annual bonus (mass and group communication) is considered.

After the committee has adjourned, Mr. A, engaged in thoughts concerning unfinished business (communication with self), slowly crosses the street to his restaurant for lunch. On the way he sees his friend Mr. B, who in a great hurry enters the same luncheon place (communication through action), and Mr. A decides to sit by himself rather than to join his friend, who will probably gulp down his coffee and hurry on (communication with self). While waiting, Mr. A studies the menu (communication through printed word) but the odor of a juicy steak deflects his gaze (chemical communication); it is so appetizing that he orders one himself.

After lunch he decides to buy a pair of gloves. He enters a men's store and with the tips of his fingers carefully examines the various qualities of leather (communication through touch). After leisurely concluding the purchase, he decides to take the afternoon off and to escort his son on a promised trip to the zoo. On the way there, John, watching his father drive through the streets, asks him why he always stops at a red light and why he does not stop at a green light (communication by visual symbol). As they approach the zoo, an ambulance screams down the street, and Mr. A pulls over to the side of the road and stops (communication by sound). As they sit there he explains to his son that the church across the street is the oldest in the state, built many years ago, and still standing as a landmark in the community (communication through material culture).

After paying admission to the zoo (communication through action), they leisurely stroll over to visit the elephants. Here John laughs at the antics of an elephant who sprays water through his trunk at one of the spectators (communication through action), sending him into near flight. Later on in the afternoon Mr. A yields to the pressure of his son, and they enter a movie house to see a cartoon (communication through pictures). Arriving home, Mr. A dresses in order to attend a formal dinner and theater performance (communication through the arts).[3]

As Ruesch and Bateson remind us, this example in no way enumerates all our communication behaviors. It illustrates only some of the social situations in which communication occurs, and some of its elements or ingredients.

The word "communication" has become popular. It is used currently to label relationship problems between labor and management, among countries, among people generally. Some uses of the communication label refer to a different way of viewing these problems; others merely change the name of the same problems that existed yesterday.

The word "communication" has become popular within the uni-

[3] Jurgen Ruesch and Gregory Bateson, *Communication.* W. W. Norton & Co., Inc., pp. 22-23. Reprinted by permission of the publishers.

versity as well. Some universities have initiated a "communication" department or college to administer the new kind of interdisciplinary approach that has been described. Again, others have simply put the new label on existing departments and traditional ways of viewing things.

Outside the academic field, the technological revolution in communication has created or developed a greater need for competence in communication. Newspapers, magazines, oratory, the stage have long been a market for the professional communicator. The market has now been increased by needs for advertising copywriters, public relations counselors, producer-directors in radio, television, and films, audio-visual experts, and the like.

Another group of professionals is responsible for assessing the impact or effectiveness of various kinds of communication. Opinion and attitude researchers, marketing researchers, the pollster, the surveyor—all play roles in what might be called the communication industry.

It is easy to point out the differences among an advertising copywriter, an audio-visual expert, and a public-opinion pollster. At the same time, one basic process underlies the work of all such professionals and binds them together in a significant way. Each is responsible for the creation, delivery, or assessment of impact of messages that are intended to have an effect on one or more audiences.

We can define the field of the professional communicator even more broadly than we have. Many social commentators call this the age of symbol-manipulation. In our grandfather's day, most people earned their living by manipulating *things,* not by manipulating *symbols.* Men got ahead if they could forge a better horseshoe, harvest a better crop, build a better mousetrap. Communication was, of course, important then, too, but it was less relevant to a man's career.

Times have changed and are still changing. In industry, the technological revolution and the self-development of the working force have led to greater reliance on symbols and less reliance on things. For one thing, industry has become socially self-conscious.

The public looks on industry today as a social institution—with a social responsibility. Labor has organized and has pointed out weaknesses and deficiencies in industrial management. These developments have forced the creation of industrial departments of public relations and public information; departments of industrial relations and employee relations. The industrial departments have their counterparts in labor. All of them can be called communication departments. Their major task is the construction and dissemination of messages designed to "tell" management's or labor's stories.

Industry has changed in other ways. With the diffusion of technical skills, the product of one company has become so similar to the product of competing companies that often we cannot tell one from the other. In this context, companies must create brand name differences for equivalent products. The result is an increasing emphasis on "brand images" as a sales technique, requiring the construction and delivery of messages that give psychological value to a product. Soap is soap—but "Zest" is very different from "Dial."

An even more important development is that industrial production itself has become more symbol-oriented, more communication-minded. Fifty or seventy-five years ago, the manager of an industrial organization knew every operation performed in his shop. He could explain each technique, perform most of the tasks. With the development of automation and massive industry, we have witnessed the rise of the professional "manager"; the man who reaches the top of the industrial ladder, not because of what he can do with things, but because of what he can do with people—through communication.

Not long ago, I toured a large industrial plant with the president of the company. As we left his office and entered the plant full of flashing lights, huge pieces of relatively unattended machinery, long automated assembly lines, he turned to me and said, "I'm not too sure what happens, but here at this end we put in metal, and down there at that end, it comes out as refrigerators." This man did not receive his six-figure salary because of his knowledge of refrigerators; he was paid to direct and coordinate human behavior.

Anyone familiar with modern industrial management, at any level, is aware that most of the working day is spent in "talking," giving information to subordinates, receiving information from top management and transmitting it to them, meeting with colleagues to discuss schedules, interviewing employees to avoid grievances and increase efficiency, reading and writing memos to coordinate many departments into a single work unit. As automation develops, even the machine operator will spend more time manipulating symbols and less time manipulating machines.

The accelerated pace of research has made it more difficult for scientific, technical, and operating personnel to keep abreast of recent developments. There are significant time lags between the time when a research study is completed and the time when the results find their way into a book. There are expensive gaps between the uncovering of scientific knowledge by the researcher in his laboratory and the use of that knowledge by people in the field. These gaps have produced new communication professions: the scientific popularizer, the technical writer, people who interpret writers at one level for readers at another.

Certainly, modern government has become increasingly communication-oriented. The public administrator, the executive, can be said to live in a world of words. Mere preservation of the written material issued and received by the United States government in any one year costs more money than did the entire original United States budget. The mammoth problems of interrelationship among governmental agencies, the need for the right hand to know what the left hand is doing, the obligation to accumulate, interpret, and disseminate information to the public require the attention of a great number of governmental employees. All governmental agencies employ people to supervise communication, both internal and external. Even then, consultants are called from outside government to streamline communication channels, to eliminate communication waste, to improve communication efficiency.

The international aspect of both government and industry has become and is becoming communication-oriented. Again, the technological and philosophical revolutions of the twentieth century are responsible. In our grandfathers' day, Americans had little interest in, or understanding or acceptance of, people from other countries. We did not see any stake for us internationally. Times have indeed changed—and will change even more in the coming decades. The United States sees its stake now in the rest of the world—not just for curiosity's sake, but for survival.

If we are to maintain a position of world leadership, we must first make ourselves understood by—and understand—other peoples of the world. In our technical assistance program, each United States mission abroad has a team of communications officers. In the Department of State, each embassy has a staff of Public Affairs officers, charged with communicating and receiving information. We must construct messages which present the position of this country in ways that are consistent with the psychological, social, and cultural systems of our foreign audiences. We must do this in the context of people who are quite different from us. These are, in large part, communication problems.

These are some examples of the practical roles of communication. Many others could be listed. A basic assumption of the communication discipline is that an understanding of the process, the determinants, and the effects of communication improve a man's basic ability to handle the communication problems that he faces on his job, regardless of the kind of work in which he is engaged.

Demonstrably, communication concerns are broad in scope and have permeated much of human activity. The question still remains, what is all of this about? What are we doing when we devote such a significant part of our available energy to the production, interpretation, and reception of messages? What do we get out of it? What are we trying to accomplish through the process of communication?

The Purpose of Communication

Aristotle defined the study of rhetoric (communication) as the search for "all the available means of persuasion."[4] He discussed other purposes that a speaker might have; nevertheless, he clearly

---

[4] W. Rhys Roberts, "Rhetorica," in *The Works of Aristotle* (W. D. Ross, ed.). Oxford University Press, 1946, Volume XI, p. 6.

implied that the prime goal of communication was persuasion, an attempt to sway other men to the speaker's point of view. This view of communicative purpose remained popular until late in the eighteenth century, although emphasis switched from the methods of persuasion to what constituted the "good man" in the speaking situation.

In the seventeenth century a school of thought known as faculty psychology was developed. Faculty psychology made a clear distinction between the soul and the mind, attributing separate faculties to each.

By late in the eighteenth century, the concepts of faculty psychology had invaded rhetoric. The mind-soul dualism was interpreted as a basis for two independent purposes for communication. One purpose was intellectual or cognitive in nature; the other was emotional. One appealed to the mind, the other to the soul.

By this theory, one purpose of communication was informative—an appeal to the mind. A second was persuasive—an appeal to the soul, the emotions. A third was entertainment, and it was argued that we could classify the intentions of the communicator, and the supporting material he used, within these categories.[5]

Faculty psychology is no longer supported by psychologists, but its remnants still exist in the definition of communicative intent. Some people still distinguish between training in argumentation (appeal to the mind, using rational proof, logical argument) and training in persuasion (apparently reduced to appeal to the body, using irrational proof, illogical argument).

There undoubtedly is some merit in looking at communicative intent in this way. Some would argue that it is useful in the classroom. There is basis for the argument, however, that we need to revise and refine this concept of purpose, though we may not want to abandon it completely.

For one thing, contemporary theory about human behavior finds it useful to abandon the mind-body dichotomy. Behaviorists tend to take the position that the organism can be analyzed more fruit-

[5] See, for example, George Campbell, *The Philosophy of Rhetoric* (new edition). New York, 1951, pp. 23-24.

fully by no longer thinking about these entities as operating unto themselves. In following this belief, the behavioral communication theorist is very close to the classical Aristotelian position, refined in the light of later research and thinking.

One criticism of the concept of a three-fold division of purpose concerns the nature of language. As will be argued later, there is reason to believe that all use of language has a persuásive dimension, that one cannot communicate at all without some attempt to persuade, in one way or another.

The inform-persuade-entertain distinction has led to confusion in another way. There has been a tendency to interpret these purposes as exclusive: one is not giving information when he is entertaining, one is not entertaining when he is persuading, and so on. Clearly, this is not so. Yet the distinction is frequently made.

For example, it is popular today to distinguish between education (inform), propaganda (persuade), and entertainment (entertain). In the public media, we try to distinguish between educational programs and entertainment programs—without providing any reasonable basis for such distinction. Some professional communicators in the press and in education state that they are not trying to persuade people, they "merely give them information." Others view the entertainment industry as something independent of persuasion and ignore the effects their messages might be having on the levels of knowledge, thought processes, and attitudes of their audiences. The theatre, for example, is a distinguished vehicle of communication, with a considerable tradition and heritage. Many people would classify the theatre as an "entertainment" vehicle. Yet countless examples could be given of plays that were intended to have, and did have, significant effects on an audience, other than "entertainment."

The inform-persuade-entertain distinction causes difficulty if we assume that these can be considered as independent purposes of communication. They also cause difficulty because the terms are so abstract that our meanings often are broad, indefinite, and vague. We find difficulty in relating them directly to experience, in "knowing one when we see one."

A final criticism of this approach to defining purpose is that it often is not behavior-centered, but message-centered. Too often we look to the *message* (speech, manuscript, play, advertisement) in order to determine communicative purpose. *From a behaviorist's point of view, it is more useful to define purpose as the goal of a creator or receiver of a message, rather than as the property of the message itself.*

It is difficult to look at a given set of content and determine whether it is informative or persuasive, what effect it will have on a receiver, and what intention the source had in producing it. This can be illustrated by our present confusion in education when we try to define the "humanities," the "arts," or the "sciences" in terms of content, rather than intent or effects. We may find that we can relate certain characteristics of a message to certain intentions or effects, but it seems more useful to place purpose in the source and receiver, rather than in the message.

In summary, it has been suggested that we need to re-analyze the purposes of communication. In doing this, we should employ at least four criteria for our definition of purpose. Communication purpose must be specified in such a way that it is:

1. not logically contradictory or inconsistent with itself;
2. behavior-centered; that is, expressed in terms of human behaviors;
3. specific enough for us to be able to relate it to actual communication behavior;
4. consistent with the ways in which people do communicate.

In approaching a concept of communicative purpose, let us analyze briefly the development of the human organism. At birth, we are totally helpless creatures. We have no control over our own behavior, over the behavior of others, over the physical environment in which we find ourselves. We are at the mercy of any force interested in affecting us; we ourselves are powerless to affect anything or anyone intentionally.

Soon after birth, the physiological prerequisites for self-control develop. We can move our head, then our arms, then our legs—

at will. We can form sounds and we learn that some of these sounds elicit desirable behaviors from others—we are fed, clothed, kept warm, etc. Within nine months to a year, we can move our entire bodies (within limits) at will. We can approach desirable things, avoid undesirable ones. We can begin to *affect,* as well as be affected; determine our environment, as well as be determined by it.

In the second year, we begin to master a verbal language. We find that certain sounds and sound sequences affect other people, sometimes in ways we want, sometimes in ways we do not want. By trial, error, and imitation we learn to talk, to ask questions, to make requests. By the end of the sixth or seventh year, we learn to read, to extend our environment, our understanding. As schooling continues, we learn the processes of reasoning. We learn to make decisions in certain ways, and not in other ways. We analyze other people, and the nature of the physical world. Eventually, we begin to abstract ourselves from our environment, to analyze ourselves, as if we were someone else.

All of this experience requires communication. We give and take orders, make requests, comply with the requests of others. We learn about facts, how things are made, destroyed, changed. As we mature, we begin to study communication systems themselves: social organizations, economic relationships, cultural values, all constructed by man using communication behaviors as a tool.

Correspondingly, we enter into active participation in man-made organizations: the family, peer groups, the church, the community. We attend to the public media. We interact with other people. Communication is the basis of this interaction, of these relationships between man and man. Why do we learn about these things? Why do we communicate about them? What are our purposes?

Our basic purpose is to alter the original relationship between our own organism and the environment in which we found ourselves. More specifically, our basic purpose is to reduce the probability that we are solely a target of external forces, and increase the probability that we exert force ourselves. Our basic purpose in communication is to become an affecting agent, to affect others, our physical environment, and ourselves, to become a determining agent, to have a vote in how things are. *In short, we communicate to influence—to affect with intent.* In analyzing communication, in trying to improve our own communication ability, the first question we need to ask is, what did the communicator intend to have happen as a result of his message? What was he trying to accomplish, in terms of influencing his environment? As a result of his communication, what did he want people to believe, to be able to do, to say? In psychological terms, what response was he trying to obtain?

Much of our discussion will attempt to increase our meaning of the term "response." Let it suffice now to say that all communication behavior has as its purpose, its goal, the production of a response. When we learn to phrase our purposes in terms of specific responses from those attending to our messages, we have taken the first step toward efficient and effective communication.

This kind of formulation of communicative purpose clearly is similar to the classical statement of Aristotle. It may appear to belabor the obvious. Yet it seems to be one of the most difficult concepts for people to understand and act upon. A major task of the communication consultant is getting people to analyze their purposes for communicating and to specify them in terms of responses they want to obtain. Too often we lose sight of our purposes for communicating. Often, we phrase them in such a way that we cannot tell whether we are accomplishing them or not.

Much of the work of the psychoanalyst consists in getting his patient to specify his own objectives. Then the therapist tries to help the patient determine if he is behaving in ways that increase or reduce his chances of success. In studying public speaking or report writing, advertising copywriting or acting, the student will have difficulty in deciding what he will or will not communicate, until he specifies the effects he wants on his audience, in terms of the response he wants the audience to make.

We have said that the purpose of communication is to affect, to influence. Yet the present discussion implies that man "does not know" or "forgets" his purpose. This does not mean that there is one *proper* purpose, and that man should be aware of it. What it does imply is that there is a purpose in communicating, but that we often are not conscious of it in our own behavior.

We can hardly keep from communicating, with or without awareness of purpose. Since infancy, we have learned and practiced both verbal and nonverbal techniques for affecting or manipulating our environment. These behavior patterns become so ingrained, so habitual, that we often do not realize how continually we try to manipulate. In fact, our value system may develop in such a way that we do not like to admit that we are "manipulators," even in the sense that we have used the word. All that is suggested here is that we need to concentrate our attention on an analysis of purpose, if we are to check our behavior against it to determine whether we are behaving in such a way as to be effective.

Too often, writers think that their job is to *write* technical reports rather than to *affect the behavior* of their readers. Television producers and theatrical directors forget that their original purpose was to affect an audience—they get too busy "putting on plays" or "filling time with programs." Teachers forget about the influence they wanted to exert on students and concentrate on "covering the material" or "filling fifty minutes three times a week." Presidents of civic and professional organizations forget they are trying to influence or affect their members—they are too busy "having meetings" or "completing programs." Agricultural extension workers forget they are trying to affect farmers and homemakers—they get too busy "giving out information" or "reporting research."

How can we diagnose these apparent breakdowns in communication, this failure to affect the receiver in ways that were intended? An answer to this has some basis in research and experience, but any opinion here is still speculative and in need of further evidence to substantiate it. One opinion is that these communication breakdowns can be attributed to one or both of two causes: *inefficiency* or *misperception*.

Communication behavior, we have seen, becomes habitual. Once we have learned to perform these behaviors, they can be done easily, with little effort. We can write, direct, teach, conduct meetings, or give speeches, and never question whether it was worth the effort. It has become a habit, just as routine as tying shoes or driving a car.

When our behavior becomes habitual, it often becomes inefficient. We have a hazy idea of our purpose, but we are never forced to specify it in detail or check ourselves to see if we are accomplishing it. There may be better, shorter ways of doing what we are doing, but we do not think about it. This inefficiency may be one reason for our inability to specify purpose if someone asks us to.

The second reason assumes that someone, either the source himself or an observer, misperceives the response the source intends to produce. Many writers are not trying to affect their readers—they are trying to keep their jobs and to elicit the response from their supervisors and colleagues, "He gets a lot of things done." Many producers, teachers, extension workers, supervisors are not trying to affect their apparent audiences. They are trying to win the approval of their peers, to get colleagues to say, "He's one of us, he conforms to the way we do things around here." Some presidents or other group leaders are not trying to influence the thinking of their groups, except to get them to say, "Let's re-elect this man, he knows how to run a meeting." The actual purpose of communication may not be what it is perceived to be, even by the person performing it. We have said that the purpose of communication is to affect. This is not the only question we need to answer. The questions remain, affect whom, and how?

Dimensions of Purpose

THE "WHO" OF PURPOSE

Any human communication situation involves the *production* of a message by someone, and the *receipt* of that message by someone. When someone writes, someone must read it; when someone paints, someone must view it; when someone speaks, someone must hear it. Any analysis of communicative purpose, or of success in achieving the response intended, needs to raise and answer the question, for whom was this intended?

For example, we often communicate with ourselves; that is, we both produce and receive the same message. A colleague of mine has a friend in Italy who writes poetry. All of her poetry is written in English. When he asked her why, she replied that she wanted to make sure that no one else read it—she had written it to herself. If we wished to analyze the "effectiveness" of this woman's poetry, it would be ridiculous to have others read it and ascertain their responses. She wrote it to affect only herself; she was her own intended receiver.

In most of the communication we analyze, we presume an audience other than the message producer. When a poet submits his poetry to a publisher, when a speaker agrees to meet with an assembled audience, when an actor utilizes the airwaves, when someone mails the letter he wrote, we presume he intends to affect behavior other than his own. The communicator intends to affect the responses of a *particular* person (or group of persons) other than himself. However, his message may be received by the person for whom it was intended, or by persons for whom it was not intended, or both.

This distinction between intended and unintended receivers of communication is important in at least two ways. First, the communicator may affect people in ways he did not intend by forgetting that his message may be received by people other than those to whom he sent it. For example, an individual may make derogatory comments to a friend about a third person. His purpose may be to have his friend avoid this person or not recommend him for a job. Suppose the third person also receives these comments. He was not the intended receiver of the message. If he did receive it, however, and if it was in writing, he might sue the original communicator for libel. This distinction serves as a basis for our concern with quoting people "in context" (in the situation experienced by the receiver for whom the message was intended).

The second reason for the distinction between intended and nonintended receivers is related to criticism of communication. One can find numerous examples of criticism of a communicator as "not having accomplished his purpose." Two cautions need to be applied. One we have discussed earlier: the critic needs to ascertain the communicator's purpose before he can make this kind of judgment. The second caution concerns intended and nonintended receivers. The critic may or may not be a member of the intended audience for the message. If he is, we can accept his criticism (at least for his own behavior). If he is not, he cannot use his own response as a criterion for saying that the communicator did not accomplish his purpose. He can observe the behaviors of other people for whom the communicator did intend his message. Only on this basis can he make a valid criticism of the success or failure of the communicator to accomplish his purpose.

One dimension of any analysis of communicative purpose is the discovery of the intended receiver for the message. The communicator may intend his message for himself or for others. Others who receive it may or may not be those for whom it was intended. In producing, receiving, or criticizing any communication, a determination of the communicator's purpose must be phrased in the following terms: How did the communicator intend to affect whom? *Purpose and audience are not separable. All communication behavior has as its purpose the eliciting of a specific response from a specific person (or group of persons).*

We have talked about purpose primarily from the vantage point of the person initiating the communication. This has been merely for convenience. In any communication situation, there are at least two sets of desired responses: (1) the response sought by the person producing the message, and (2) the response sought by the person receiving the message. Readers as well as writers have purposes; audiences as well as performers have purposes.

The analysis of any communication situation must take into account both points of view: how did the communication source intend to affect the person receiving the message, and how did the receiver intend to affect himself or others (including the source)?

We cannot say that the effects of all communication are those that were intended; receivers do not always respond in accord with the purpose of the source.

When the purposes of the source and receiver are incompatible, communication breaks down. When they are independent, or complementary, communication can continue. In any case, both the communication source and the critic need to ask the reason for the receiver's approaching the communication experience. Why do people read newspapers, why do they attend the theatre, why do they enroll for classes?

In summary, we have described one dimension of communicative purpose: the determination of the receiver intended by the source, a decision on whether a given receiver is or is not an intended receiver, and an analysis of the receiver's own purpose in engaging in communication. Given that communication occurs because someone desires to affect behavior, we must ask:

1. Who was the intended receiver?
2. What purpose did the receiver, intended or nonintended, have in engaging in communication?

The "How" of Purpose

Given a decision on the target of communication—the "who" of purpose—the question remains, how does the source or receiver intend to affect behavior, what kind of effect does he want to produce? This question itself needs to be analyzed from at least two points of view.

We can place any communication purpose somewhere along a continuum, bounded at one end by what we can refer to as "consummatory purpose" and at the other by "instrumental purpose."[6] Position along this continuum is determined by the answer to the following question: To what extent is the purpose of this message

[6] See Leon Festinger, "Informal social communication," *Psychological Review*, 57:271–292, 1950.

accomplished entirely at the moment of its consumption, or to what extent is its consumption only instrumental in producing further behavior?

Schramm makes this distinction in another way when he talks about "immediate reward" as compared to "delayed reward."[7] He suggests that individuals are rewarded immediately on receiving or producing some kinds of messages. For example, an artist may compose a piece of music and be satisfied in the composing process. He may present his composition to an audience, intending that they should share his satisfaction. These are both examples of highly *consummatory* purposes.

On the other hand, he may compose and present his music, not intending to produce this response primarily, but hoping that he can compose something that people will like well enough to buy. In this case, he is using his composition for an *instrumental* purpose —the favorable response produced in his audience is instrumental in producing further behavior on their part—buying a record, hiring him to compose or present something else, donating to a political cause, and so on.

In the communication industries, one can find considerable friction among producers, generated by differences of the consummatory-instrumental variety. For example, a radio program director, a graphic artist in an advertising agency, the author of a book, often intend to produce consummatory effects in their audiences— they are satisfied if people receive and enjoy their messages. On the other hand, the radio sales manager, the advertising account executive, and the book publisher usually have more instrumental intentions—they want to sell goods. This difference in point of view, if not understood by both parties, can—and often does—create considerable tension.

The receiver of a message also can have primarily consummatory or instrumental purposes in receiving a message. He may read about crime, view certain television programs, engage in casual con-

---

[7] Wilbur Schramm, "The nature of news," *Journalism Quarterly*, 26:259–269, 1949.

versations, for consummatory reasons, in order to receive immediate rewards by feeling satisfied with himself, relaxing or reducing tension, and so on. On the other hand, he may read about certain things so that he may tell others about them later and be perceived as "well-informed." He may study techniques or principles, so that he may solve problems he faces on the job or in his personal life. In these cases, his purpose is instrumental—his rewards from the communication are delayed until he can use what he has received as a tool in doing something else.

Again, friction or dissatisfaction between the communication source and receiver may occur because of difference or misunderstanding of purpose. In education, the teacher often presents factual material or the results of his thinking with a consummatory purpose. He may not even be talking to the student, but merely enjoying hearing his own ideas. More often, however, he intends that the student will respond favorably to the consumption of his message— will enjoy "knowing" for "knowledge's" sake. The student, on the other hand, may not be interested in any message unless he sees an instrumental value in it—sees that he can "do something" with it later. This kind of communication situation usually produces judgments by the teacher that students are "apathetic" and lack "curiosity," while the students complain that the professor is not "practical," that he is "dull," or that his course is a "bore."

Any given message can have many purposes, some highly consummatory, others highly instrumental, for both the source and receiver. A play may be intended to produce the "I liked it" response from the audience and at the same time be intended to change the audience's future behavior with regard to a social or political issue. A listener may attend a public debate because he enjoys the pageantry of the situation and at the same time want to obtain information which will help him make a decision in a coming election. An employee may laugh at the boss's joke because he enjoys it, and he may also want to keep his job or get a promotion.

There is also ample evidence that the purposes of the source and receiver may be different, and yet each may accomplish what he intended. A reader may buy a popular magazine because he enjoys reading the stories (receiver's purpose) and may eventually begin buying products (source's purpose) because they were advertised in that magazine. An audience may view a television drama merely for relaxation, but because of it they may behave differently the following week toward people who are mentally ill.

A great number of similar illustrations could be drawn, but those given should be sufficient to demonstrate the utility of the consummatory-instrumental idea in analyzing communication purpose. In any situation, from the point of view of the source or receiver of communication, purposes may be placed on this kind of continuum. At one end are purposes which are satisfied entirely in the consumption of the message alone. On the other end are purposes which are satisfied only after the response to the message has been used as an instrument to produce other responses.

We have talked about two dimensions of communication purpose. First, we need to determine the "who-ness" of purpose. We need to distinguish among the communication source, his intended receiver, and the nonintended receivers who actually do receive the message. For each, we need to ask: does he participate primarily to affect himself or others, or both? This question needs a specific answer, in terms of the behavior the message is intended to produce, before we can continue any kind of analysis of purpose.

Second, we have talked about the need to place purposes on a consummatory-instrumental continuum. The purposes of both the source and the receiver can be located along this continuum: is the purpose satisfied by consumption of the message, or must the behavior produced by the message be itself used later as an instrument to elicit further behavior?

One problem remains: specification of the classes of response that are desired, of the kinds of effects intended. The categories of response-types could, of course, include all the behaviors available to man. This fact makes it extremely difficult to develop categories which are both consistent and useful in describing communicative intent; yet the need for such a set of categories is obvious.

Suggestions for Thought and Discussion

1. Keep a communication diary for one day, starting when you get up and continuing through the entire day. Keep a record of whom you communicate with, how long you spend at it, and what your purpose is. At the end of the day, sit down and analyze how you spent your communication time. Ask yourself the following questions:

   a. What were my most frequent purposes in communicating?
   b. How successful was I in accomplishing these purposes?
   c. How many different kinds of purposes did I have?
   d. What were the most frequent purposes that I would guess other people had in communicating with me?
   e. How many different kinds of communication did I participate in?
   f. How much time did I spend in *not* communicating?

2. In this chapter, it was suggested that the sole purpose of communication is to affect; in other words, that we communicate only to affect our environment and ourselves. What is your opinion of this thesis? Can you find examples in which communication seems to have other purposes? What are the implications of this thesis for a democratic society?

3. What do you mean by "education" as compared with "entertainment?" How do you distinguish between these two terms? If we avoid an inform-entertain distinction and accept the idea that all communication intends to affect, how can we make a distinction between these two terms—or can we?

4. The development of automation and of a technological society increases the emphasis placed on communication ability, and decreases the emphasis placed on thing-manipulation. What implications does this have for your own career, your own educational plans, the kind of work which you will be doing? What implications does this have for the kind of educational system that is needed today—and tomorrow?

5. Try to find examples of communication situations in which the source of communication failed to accomplish what you believe to have been his purpose. Try to analyze why this happened. To what extent did he seem conscious of his purpose? Use yourself as an

example. Try to analyze your purpose for a particular communication situation.

6. It has been said that both a source and a receiver of communication have purposes in engaging in communication. What are the purposes of an audience in a theatre? Why do people watch television? Why do they read the newspapers? Speculate on what people get out of this kind of activity, why they make the decision to engage in it.

CHAPTER 2

A Model of the Communication Process

EVERY communication situation differs in some ways from every other one, yet we can attempt to isolate certain elements that all communication situations have in common. It is these ingredients and their interrelationships that we consider when we try to construct a general model of communication.

We attach the word "process" to our discussion of communication. The concept of process is itself complex. If we begin to discuss a model of the communication process without a common meaning for the word "process," our discussion might result in distorted views about communication.

The Concept of Process

At least one dictionary defines "process" as "any phenomenon which shows a continuous change in time," or "any continuous operation or treatment." Five hundred years before the birth of Christ, Heraclitus pointed out the importance of the concept of process when he stated that a man can never step in the same river twice; the man is different and so is the river. Thomas Wolfe's novel of the 1940's, *You Can't Go Home Again,* makes the same point.

If we accept the concept of process, we view events and relationships as dynamic, on-going, ever-changing, continuous. When we label something as a process, we also mean that it does not have *a* beginning, *an* end, a fixed sequence of events. It is not static, at rest. It is moving. The ingredients within a process interact; each affects all of the others.

The concept of process is inextricably woven into the contemporary view of science and physical reality. In fact, the development of a process viewpoint in the physical sciences brought about one of the twentieth-century revolutions that we mentioned earlier. If we analyze the work of physical scientists up to and including Isaac Newton, we do not find a comprehensive analysis of process. It was believed that the world could be divided into "things" and "processes." It was believed also that things *existed*, that they were static entities, that their existence was independent of the existence or operations of other "things."

The crisis and revolution in scientific philosophy brought about by the work of Einstein, Russell, Whitehead, and others denied both of these beliefs in two ways. First, the concept of relativity suggested that any given object or event could only be analyzed or described in light of other events that were related to it, other operations involved in observing it. Second, the availability of more powerful observational techniques led to the demonstration that something as static or stable as a table, a chair, could be looked on as a constantly changing phenomenon, acting upon and being acted upon by all other objects in its environment, changing as the person who observed it changes. The traditional division between things was questioned. The traditional distinction between things and processes was broken down. An entirely different way of looking at the world had to be developed—a process view of reality.

Communication theory reflects a process point of view. A communication theorist rejects the possibility that nature consists of events or ingredients that are separable from all other events. He argues that you cannot talk about *the* beginning or *the* end of communication or say that a particular idea came from one specific source, that communication occurs in only one way, and so on.

The basis for the concept of process is the belief that the structure of physical reality can not be *discovered* by man; it must be *created* by man. In "constructing" reality, the theorist chooses to organize his perceptions in one way or another. He may choose to say that we can call certain things "elements" or "ingredients." In doing this, he realizes that he has not discovered anything, he has created a set of tools which may or may not be useful in analyzing or describing the world. He recognizes that certain things may precede others, but that in many cases the order of precedence will vary from situation to situation. This is not to say that we can place no order on events. The dynamic of process has limitations; nevertheless, there is more than one dynamic that can be developed for nearly any combination of events.

When we try to talk or write about a process, such as communication, we face at least two problems. First, we must arrest the dynamic of the process, in the same way that we arrest motion when we take a still picture with a camera. We can make useful observations from photographs, but we err if we forget that the camera is not a complete reproduction of the objects photographed. The interrelationships among elements are obliterated, the fluidity of motion, the dynamics, are arrested. The picture is a representation of the event, it is not the event. As Hayakawa has put it, the word is not the thing, it is merely a map that we can use to guide us in exploring the territories of the world.

A second problem in describing a process derives from the necessity for the use of language. Language itself, as used by people over time, is a process. It, too, is changing, on-going; however, the process quality of language is lost when we write it. Marks on paper are a recording of language, a picture of language. They are fixed, permanent, static. Even spoken language, over a short period of time, is relatively static.

In using language to describe a process, we must choose certain words, we must freeze the physical world in a certain way. Furthermore, we must put some words first, others last. Western languages go from left to right, top to bottom. All languages go from front to back, beginning to end—even though we are aware that the process we are describing may not have a left and right, a top and a bottom, a beginning and an end.

We have no alternative if we are to analyze and communicate about a process. The important point is that we must remember that we are not including everything in our discussion. The things we talk about do not have to exist in exactly the ways we talk about them, and they certainly do not have to operate in the order in which we talk about them. Objects which we separate may not always be separable, and they never operate independently—each affects and interacts with the others. This may appear obvious, but it is easy to overlook or forget the limitations that are necessarily placed on any discussion of a process.

To illustrate the point, let us take an example other than communication. Education is a process. In discussing education, we can list certain ingredients. We have students, teachers, books, classroom lectures, libraries, discussion, meditation, thought, etc. We can order the ingredients. We can say that, in education, a teacher lectures to students (50 minutes at a time, three days a week, for x years). We can say that a student reads books (6 books, 119 books, any number of books). We can say that the library has 100,000 volumes, or 1,000,000 volumes, or 6,000,000 volumes. We can say that students will hold x discussion sessions, spend y hours meditating, and write z papers or examinations.

When we put all this together, we can say that if all of these ingredients are available and have been used, the student has received "an education." We *can* say this, but if we do we have forgotten the concept of process, the dynamics of education. As any good cook knows, it is the mixing process, the blending, that makes a good cake; ingredients are necessary, but not sufficient.

For an example in the communication field, take the theatre. What is "theatre"? Again, we can list ingredients: a playwright, a play, directors, actors, stage hands, audiences, scenery, lighting, an auditorium. Add them, and the total is theatre? Definitely not. Again, it is the blending, the dynamic interrelationships among the ingredients developed in the process that determine whether we have what we would call "theatre."

We need to remember that the dynamic of movement which relates the ingredients is vital. The concept of dynamic also implies that factors that we may overlook in any single listing of the ingredients also determine what is produced.

The dynamic of theatre is in part related to whether the play is produced for an audience before or after they have eaten dinner, or whether they had a heavy or a light meal, whether they enjoyed it or disliked it. The dynamic of education is in part determined by whether the student has just come from another situation in which he learned something which still excites him or whether he is fresh and has an "uncluttered" mind, whether he is taking an elective course he chose himself or a required one, whether his classmates make comments which stimulate him, or whether he has only his own thinking to help him, and so on.

Much of the scientific research in communication attempts to isolate factors which do or do not make a difference in the development of the process. Obviously, all the ingredients have not been determined—in fact, there is considerable basis for doubt as to whether they ever will be determined.

In any case, we need constantly to remember that our discussion of a process is incomplete, with a forced order and possibly a distorted perspective. Discussion is useful, it can lead to greater insight about a process. But it is not a complete picture, it can never reproduce the process itself. We cannot list all the ingredients nor talk adequately about how they affect each other. We can provide some suggestions, some hints about both the ingredients and the dynamic of the process.

There have been approaches to analyzing communication that have not been process-oriented. Such approaches might be labeled as "hypodermic needle" concepts of how communication works, or "click-click; push-pull" points of view. Such descriptions of communication are restricted to saying that first the communicator does A, then he does B, then C happens, and so on.

Much of the early discussion of the effects of the mass media of communication were of the "hypodermic-needle" variety. Critics as well as advocates of the print or electronic media (radio, TV) talked about how these media would affect the American public. Their concept of effects implied that a radio broadcast or a television program could be viewed as a hypodermic needle. If we would just stick these messages in the minds of the public, learning or entertainment or greater participation in civic affairs would be produced. The research conducted on the effects of the media indicates otherwise; whether or not these sources of communication are effective depends on a complex of factors, some of which the media can control and some of which they cannot.

Much of the debate over the effects of comic books on children, the effects of the movies, advertising, or political campaigns on the public is of this variety. Critics and commentators often overlook the effect of children on the contents of the comics, the effect of the public on movies, etc. It certainly is true that newspapers affect public opinion, but a process point of view argues that it is equally true that public opinion affects the newspapers.

With the concept of process established in our minds, we can profit from an analysis of the ingredients of communication, the elements that seem necessary (if not sufficient) for communication to occur. We want to look at elements such as *who* is communicating, *why* he is communicating, and *to whom* he is communicating. We want to look at communication behaviors: *messages* which are produced, *what* people are trying to communicate. We want to look at style, how people *treat* their messages. We want to examine the means of communication, the *channels* that people use to get their messages to their listeners, their readers. In short, we want to list the elements in the communication process that we must take into account when (a) we initiate communication, (b) we respond to communication, or (c) we serve as communication observers or analysts.

The Ingredients of Communication

The concern with communication has produced many attempts to develop models of the process—descriptions, listing of ingredients. Of course, these models differ. None can be said to be "right," or "true." Some may be more useful than others, some may correspond more than others to the current state of knowledge about communication.

In the *Rhetoric,* Aristotle said that we have to look at three communication ingredients; the speaker, the speech, and the audience. He meant that each of these elements is necessary to communication and that we can organize our study of the process under the three headings of (1) the person who speaks, (2) the speech that he produces, and (3) the person who listens.[1]

Most of our current communication models are similar to Aristotle's, though somewhat more complex. One of the most-used contemporary models was developed in 1947 by Claude Shannon, a mathematician, and explained to the nonmathematician by Warren Weaver.[2] Shannon and Weaver were not even talking about human communication. They were talking about electronic communication. In fact, Shannon worked for the Bell Telephone Laboratory. Yet behavioral scientists have found the Shannon-Weaver model useful in describing human communication.

The Shannon-Weaver model certainly is consistent with Aristotle's position. Shannon and Weaver said that the ingredients in communication include (1) a source, (2) a transmitter, (3) a signal, (4) a receiver, and (5) a destination. If we translate the source into the speaker, the signal into the speech, and the destination into the listener, we have the Aristotelian model, plus two added ingredients, a transmitter which sends out the source's message, and a receiver which catches the message for the destination.

There are other models of the communication process, developed by Schramm,[3] Westley and MacLean,[4] Fearing,[5] Johnson,[6] and

[1] W. Rhys Roberts, "Rhetorica," in *The Works of Aristotle* (W. D. Ross, ed.). Oxford University Press, 1946, Volume XI, p. 14.

[2] Claude Shannon and Warren Weaver, *The Mathematical Theory of Communication.* University of Illinois Press, 1949, p. 5.

[3] Wilbur Schramm, "How communication works," in *The Process and Effects of Mass Communication* (Wilbur Schramm, ed.). University of Illinois Press, 1954, pp. 3–26.

[4] Bruce Westley and Malcolm MacLean, Jr., "A conceptual model for communication resarch," *Journalism Quarterly,* 34:31–38, 1957.

[5] Franklin Fearing, "Toward a psychological theory of human communication," *Journal of Personality,* 22:71–78, 1953.

[6] Wendell Johnson, "The fateful process of Mister A talking to Mister B," in *How Successful Executives Handle People.* Harvard Business Review, 1953, p. 50.

others. The suggested readings at the end of the book list several of these. A comparison will indicate the great similarities among them. They differ partly in terminology, partly in the addition or subtraction of one or two elements, partly in the differences in the point of view of the disciplines from which they emerged.

In developing the model presented here, I have tried to be consistent with current theory and research in the behavioral sciences. It has been changed many times in the past few years, as a result of using it with students in the classroom, with adults in extension courses, and with workshops and seminars in industry, agriculture, and government. It is similar to other communication models and is presented only because people have found it a useful scheme for talking about communication in many different communication situations.

A Communication Model

We can say that all human communication has some *source*, some person or group of persons with a purpose, a reason for engaging in communication. Given a source, with ideas, needs, intentions, information, and a purpose for communicating, a second ingredient is necessary. The purpose of the source has to be expressed in the form of a *message*. In human communication, a message is behavior available in physical form—the translation of ideas, purposes, and intentions into a code, a systematic set of symbols.

How do the source's purposes get translated into a code, a language? This requires a third communication ingredient, an *encoder*. The communication encoder is responsible for taking the ideas of the source and putting them in a code, expressing the source's purpose in the form of a message. In person-to-person communication, the encoding function is performed by the motor skills of the source —his vocal mechanisms (which produce the oral word, cries, musical notes, etc.), the muscle systems in the hand (which produce the written word, pictures, etc.), the muscle systems elsewhere in the body (which produce gestures of the face or arms, posture, etc.).

When we talk about more complex communication situations, we often separate the source from the encoder. For example, we can look at a sales manager as a source and his salesmen as encoders: people who produce messages for the consumer which translate the intentions or purposes of the manager.

For the present, we shall restrict our model to the minimum complexity. We have a communication source with purpose and an encoder who translates or expresses this purpose in the form of a message. We are ready for a fourth ingredient, the *channel*.

We can look at channels in several ways. Communication theory presents at least three meanings for the word "channel." For the moment, it is enough to say that a channel is a medium, a carrier of messages. It is correct to say that messages can exist only in *some* channel; however, the *choice* of channels often is an important factor in the effectiveness of communication.

We have introduced a communication *source,* an *encoder,* a *message,* and a *channel.* If we stop here, no communication has taken place. For communication to occur, there must be somebody at the other end of the channel. If we have a purpose, encode a message, and put it into one or another channel, we have done only part of the job. When we talk, somebody must listen; when we write, somebody must read. The person or persons at the other end can be called the communication *receiver,* the target of communication.

Communication sources and receivers must be similar systems. If they are not similar, communication cannot occur. We can go one step further and say that the source and the receiver may be (and often are) the same person; the source may communicate with himself—he listens to what he says, he reads what he writes, he thinks. In psychological terms, the source intends to produce a stimulus. The receiver responds to that stimulus if communication occurs; if he does not respond, communication has not occurred.

We now have all the basic communication ingredients except one. Just as a source needs an encoder to translate his purposes into a message, to express purpose in a code, the receiver needs a *decoder* to retranslate, to decode the message and put it into a form that the receiver can use. We said that in person-to-person communication the encoder would be the set of motor skills of the source. By the same token, we can look at the decoder as the set of sensory skills of the receiver. In one- or two-person communication situations, the decoder can be thought of as the senses.

These, then, are the ingredients that we will include in our discussion of a model of the communication process:

1. the communication source;
2. the encoder;
3. the message;
4. the channel;
5. the decoder;
6. the communication receiver.

We will mention many other communication factors; however, we will return to these six ingredients again and again, as we talk about communication at various levels of complexity.

The Parts of the Model

What do we mean by a source, an encoder, and so on? Our preliminary discussion has given us the beginnings of a meaning for each of these terms—but only the beginnings. At this point, precise definitions of each term might not be as useful as a set of examples which include all the ingredients.

Let us start with a common communication situation: two people talking. Suppose it is Friday morning. We find Joe and Mary in the local coffee shop. There is a picnic scheduled for Sunday afternoon. Suddenly, Joe realizes that Mary is *the* girl to take on the picnic. Joe decides to ask her for a Sunday afternoon date. Joe is now ready to act as a communication source—he has a purpose: to get Mary to agree to accompany him on Sunday. (He may have other purposes as well, but they are not our concern.)

Joe wants to produce a message. His central nervous system orders his speech mechanism to construct a message to express his purpose. The speech mechanism, serving as an encoder, produces the following message: "Mary, will you go to the picnic with me on Sunday?"

The message is transmitted via sound waves through air, so that Mary can receive it. This is the channel. Mary's hearing mechanism serves as a decoder. She hears Joe's message, decodes the message into a nervous impulse, and sends it to her central nervous system. Mary's central nervous system responds to the message. It decides that Friday is too late to ask for a Sunday date. Mary intends to refuse the date, and sends an order to her speech mechanism. The message is produced: "Thanks, Joe, but no thanks." Or something somewhat more polite.

This is a very elementary and oversimplified treatment of the nature of the communication process, but it includes, at least superficially, all six ingredients we have introduced. Let us try another example.

Take the communication situation in which you are now engaged: reading this chapter. In this communication situation, I served as the source. I had a purpose in producing this manuscript —this message. My writing mechanisms served as an encoder (of course, typewriters, typists, and printing presses also served as encoders). The message includes the words on this page, and the way that the words are arranged. The message is transmitted to you through the medium of a book, by means of light waves. Your eye is the decoder. It receives the message, decodes it, retranslates it into a nervous impulse, and sends it to your central nervous system. Your central nervous system is the receiver. As you read, you will make responses to the book.

Let us take another example, and look at it more closely. Suppose Bill and John are at the dinner table. Bill has a problem. He is ready to eat a sandwich. He likes salt on a sandwich. The salt is at John's end of the table. Bill wants the salt. What does he do? He could reach from his end of the table to John's end and get the salt himself; however, this not only would be rude, it would be work. More likely, Bill asks John to pass the salt. Being a congenial sort of fellow, John passes Bill the salt. Bill puts it on his sandwich. All is well.

Again, what has happened, in terms of our communication model? Bill's central nervous system served as a communication source. He had a need, *salt on sandwich*. He had an intention, a purpose, to get John to pass him the salt. Bill relayed this purpose as a nervous impulse to his encoder, his speech mechanism. His encoder translated and expressed his purpose in code—English—and produced a message. The message: "Pass me the salt, please."

Bill transmitted this message via sound waves, through the air, in such a way that John could receive the message. John's hearing mechanism caught the message, decoded it, and sent it on to John's central nervous system. John had meaning for the message, responded to it, and passed Bill the salt. Mission accomplished.

This is communication. These are elementary examples, but even here communication is quite complex. The process we have just described occurs in only a small fraction of the time it took to talk about it—and we oversimplified our description at that. What were some of the things that could have gone wrong?

Suppose Bill did not have a clear idea of his purpose. He knew he needed something for his sandwich but he did not know what he needed. How could he have instructed his encoder to transmit a message?

Suppose Bill did not like John, or thought that John was inferior to him. This information might get through to his encoder, and the message might come out something like "Hey, you, gimme the salt —now." John might pass the salt—or he might say, "Get it yourself."

Suppose Bill was a new clerk in the company, and John was a Vice-President. Bill might not feel that he should start any communication with John—and Bill eats a sandwich without salt.

Suppose wires get crossed between Bill's nervous system and his encoder, and he produces an embarrassing message such as "Sass me the palt." Suppose his encoder is deficient, and it substitutes an "m" for an "s"; the message becomes "Pass me the malt." Either John gives Bill something Bill doesn't want or he doesn't give him anything at all.

Suppose the coffee shop is crowded and noisy. John does not hear Bill because the communication channel is overloaded. Result —John does not respond, and Bill never eats with John again. Finally, suppose John and Bill come from different cultures. In John's culture people do not eat salt on meat, or John might even disapprove of anyone using salt on meat. Result—he might not understand Bill, or he might not think as well of him.

These are only a few examples of the kinds of things that can go wrong, even in a simple two-person communication situation. You might like to return to our example of Joe asking Mary for a date or of your reading of this manuscript. What kinds of things could have happened at one or another stage of the process to cause those two communication situations to break down?

Our examples have been confined to relatively uncomplicated communication situations. The model is equally useful in describing the communication behavior of a complex organization. In such a situation, the encoding and decoding functions often are separable from source and receiver functions. Correspondingly, certain people in the organization occupy roles as both sources and receivers.

Take a large-city newspaper as an example. The operation of the newspaper involves a complex network of communication. The newspaper hires people whose prime job is decoding—reporters who observe one or more kinds of events in the world and relay them to the "central nervous system" of the paper, the "desk" or "slot" or central control office.

When these messages are received, some decision is reached by the editorial staff. As a result of these decisions, orders are given from the control desk to produce or not produce a given message in the paper. Again, the encoding function becomes specialized. The paper employs rewrite men, proofreaders, linotype operators, pressmen, delivery boys. They all are responsible for one or another part of the encoding and channeling functions, getting the message out of the control office on to the pages of the newspaper, and thence to a different set of receivers, the reading public.

The communication model can be used to describe the personal behavior of any member of the newspaper staff. At the same time, it can be applied at a different level of analysis, and used to describe the workings of the organization as a communication network.

Within the paper, elaborate subdivisions of communication responsibility are made. Some people decode only certain kinds of messages: police work, society behavior, sports, etc. Others are assigned to a more general beat. Some people do not feed information into the paper, but are responsible solely for encoding messages which get this information back out. Still others neither decode nor encode (at the network analysis level), but are responsible for receiver-source behaviors; in other words, for making decisions about the messages they receive and giving orders about messages they want sent out.

The newspaper is one example of a communication network. Others might include the behaviors of any information organization, the operations of the Department of State, and the structure of a large industrial organization. Communication analysis can be performed on communicative institutions or on a specific person. The model is equally applicable to both. It represents a point of view, a way of looking at behavior, whether the behavior is individual or institutional.

The examples given have several implications for further discussion. One is the varying nature of communication purposes. To a large extent, the modern newspaper is not an "original" source of communication. It specializes in interpreting information it receives from one set of sources and transmitting this information, as interpreted, to another set of receivers. It works as an intermediary in communication.

At the same time, through the editorial page, the newspaper does originate messages, does transmit "original" information to its reading audience. It both originates and interprets. One of the canons of responsible journalism is the requirement that the newspaper keep these two functions separate—that it avoid originating material while pretending to be interpreting material received from outside its own system.

There are other examples of the originator-interpreter distinction. The New York Stock Exchange is a good illustration. The operation of the market can be analyzed as an intricate communication network, in which the behaviors allowed to people performing various roles are explicitly defined and rigorously enforced. Some brokers on the floor are primarily encoders. They transmit the intentions of the main office or of customers who may live far from the exchange itself. Other brokers are both encoders and decoders. They transmit their employer's purposes and decode messages from others about the state of the market, the price of a particular stock. They send these messages to their office, where a decision is made. Still others are allowed to make decisions by themselves. They may buy or sell on their own initiative, for their firms or their personal holdings.

A second implication of the examples given concerns the way in which we should interpret the concepts of source, encoder, decoder, and receiver. These should not be viewed as separate things or entities or people. They are the names of behaviors which have to be performed for communication to occur. More than one person may be involved in the same behavior-form (multiple sources, encoders, etc.). One person may perform more than one set of behaviors. The same person may be both a source and a receiver, even simultaneously. The same person may—and usually does—both encode and decode messages. This illustrates the earlier point that the ingredients of communication, or of any process, are not separable, cannot be divided into independent or nonoverlapping entities.

The examples also can be used to illustrate the principle of relativity referred to earlier. At one level of analysis, we can describe a reporter as a decoder. At another, he is both a source and a receiver and performs both encoding and decoding behaviors. What we call him depends upon our own purposes, how we view him, in what context we place him, and so on.

Finally, the examples demonstrate the meaning of process, the interrelationship of the ingredients of communication. Within the newspaper, we cannot order communication events as (1) reporting, (2) decision-making by the central office on the value of messages received, (3) orders to put certain articles in the paper, and (4) encoding of those articles. It is hard to say which comes first.

Clearly, the reporter is affected by what he believes his editors want him to report, by the deadlines he faces in order to meet the requirements of the encoding process, etc. The central office is limited by what it receives from its reporters. It also is affected by what it believes to be the editorial policy of the publisher, his political beliefs, the space available in the paper, the time and costs of encoding, etc. And, of course, all employees are affected at all times by their assumptions as to the purposes of the reader who eventually will consume the paper. What they believe the reader wants affects what they report, what they interpret, and what they encode.

The communication of news is a process. All the ingredients of the process affect each other. A dynamic peculiar to that specific process is developed. A journalism student can quickly become familiar with the ingredients of journalism: events, typewriters, articles, city desks, printing presses, distribution systems, etc. It is the dynamic which is hard to learn, and which usually has to be experienced before it is understood.

The ingredients discussed are essential to communication. Whether we talk about communication in terms of one person, two persons, or an institutional network, the functions labeled as source, encoder, decoder, and receiver have to be performed. Messages always are involved and must exist in some channel. How they go together, in what order, and with what kinds of interrelationships depend on the situation, the nature of the specific process under study, the dynamic developed.

It is useful to use these ingredients to talk about communication. It is dangerous to assume that one comes first, one last, or that they are independent of each other. This denies the concept of process, and communication is a process. The importance of process might best be typified by the traditional argument of the relative priority of chickens and eggs. One useful deterrent to forgetting about interrelationships within a process is to remember the following definition: a chicken is what an egg makes in order to reproduce itself.

Suggestions for Thought and Discussion

1. The concept of process is central to an understanding of the process of communication. What is your meaning for the term "process"? Find examples of a process. Can you describe a process through the use of language? What do you do to a process when you talk about it? What is left out, if anything? Find examples of something which is not a process. How can you determine what is a process and what is not? What importance is there in making this distinction? How does a concept of process affect the way in which we view the world?

2. Select an example of an institution in your own field of interest. Try to describe the behaviors of the institution from the point of view of the communication model presented in this chapter. Can you include all the institutional behaviors? What utility is there in describing the institution in communication terms? What dangers are there in such a description?

3. What is the difference between a communication source and a communication receiver? What do they have in common?

4. In this chapter a distinction was made between a source and an encoder. Within your own experience, can you find examples in which one person performed one of these functions and another person performed the second one? In analyzing political communication, or the work of the public relations counselor, how can we distinguish between source and encoder functions? What responsibility do people have to tell us whether they actually constructed their own messages, or whether they were only delivering messages that someone had constructed for them?

CHAPTER 3

The Fidelity of Communication

DETERMINANTS OF EFFECT

GIVEN a purpose for communicating, a response which is to be elicited, a communicator hopes that his communication will have high fidelity. By fidelity, we mean that he will get what he wants. A high-fidelity encoder is one that expresses the meaning of the source perfectly. A high-fidelity decoder is one that translates a message for the receiver with complete accuracy. In analyzing communication, we are interested in determining what increases or reduces the fidelity of the process.

Shannon and Weaver, in talking about the fidelity of electronic communication, introduced the concept of *noise*.[1] We are used to thinking of noise as sound that is distracting—as messages that interfere with other messages. The Shannon-Weaver concept is similar to this common meaning. They defined noise as factors that distort the quality of a signal. We can broaden our meaning of noise to include factors in each of the ingredients of communication that can reduce effectiveness.

Noise and fidelity are two sides of the same coin. Eliminating

---

[1] Claude Shannon and Warren Weaver, *The Mathematical Theory of Communication*. University of Illinois Press, 1949, p. 6.

noise increases fidelity; the production of noise reduces fidelity. Some of the literature in communication talks about noise, some about fidelity. The same problem is being discussed, regardless of label. As a student once remarked on an examination, "Noise is what you had when the communication didn't work, and fidelity is what you had when it did."

The basic concern related to noise and fidelity is the isolation of those factors within each of the ingredients of communication which determine the *effectiveness* of communication. When we analyze these ingredients, what factors do we have to take into account? What determines the ways in which each of the ingredients operates in a given situation?

We have listed six basic elements of communication: source, encoder, message, channel, decoder, receiver. When we are talking about person-to-person communication, the source and encoder can be grouped together, as can the receiver and decoder. In this truncated version of the model, some source encodes a message and places it in a channel so that it can be decoded by a receiver. What are the factors in the source, receiver, message, and channel which determine communication effectiveness, the fidelity of the process?

The Source-Encoder

A communication source, after determining the way in which he desires to affect his receiver, encodes a message intended to produce the desired response. There are at least four kinds of factors *within the source* which can increase fidelity. They are his (a) communication skills, (b) attitudes, (c) knowledge level, and (d) position within a social-cultural system.

COMMUNICATION SKILLS

There are five verbal communication skills. Two of these are encoding skills: writing and speaking. Two of them are decoding skills: reading and listening. The fifth is crucial to both encoding and decoding: thought or reasoning. Thought is essential not only to coding—thought is involved in purpose itself.

Obviously, there are other encoding skills, such as painting, drawing, and gesturing; however, what we say about writing and speaking can be generalized to the other encoding skills as well.

As source-encoders, our communication-skill levels determine our communication fidelity in two ways. First, they affect our ability to analyze our own purposes and intentions, our ability to say something when we communicate. Second, they affect our ability to encode messages which express what we intend.

Let us discuss the latter first. For the moment, let us assume that we already have a well-thought-out intention, a specific purpose for communicating with someone else. To encode a message which expresses this purpose, we must possess the necessary encoding skills.

If we are to write our message, we need to have a vocabulary adequate to express our ideas. We do not want to use words that merely reveal that we have "been educated." We do want to use words that express our meaning most clearly. We need to know how to spell the words in our vocabulary—so that our reader can decode them easily. Again, we do not spell "properly" merely to comply with *laws* of spelling, but to encode a message that has a good chance of being decoded accurately. Given a vocabulary, we have to understand how to put our words together most effectively— we have to be good practicing grammarians. We have to arrange our words so that our meaning is clear.

If we are speaking, we need all of these skills—and more. Writing utilizes some channels. Speaking utilizes others. In speaking we need to know how to pronounce our words, how to gesture, how to interpret the messages we get from our listeners, and how to alter our own messages as we go along.

We shall not discuss the methods and techniques of good writing and speaking here. There are adequate sources of the principles and techniques of effective oral and written communication elsewhere, in standard texts in such fields as Speech, Journalism, and English. Instead, let us dwell for a moment on the other communication skill—thought.

Let us *not* assume that we already have a well-thought-out purpose for communicating. Rather, let us look at the communication skill, thought, that produces well "thought-out" purposes. All of us would agree that our communication skills, our facility in handling the language code, affect our ability to encode thoughts that we have. Our language facility, our communication ability does more—it actually affects the thoughts themselves. More specifically, *the words we can command, and the way that we put them together affect* (a) *what we think about,* (b) *how we think, and* (c) *whether we are thinking at all.*

Philosophers and psychologists have long debated the question, what are the ingredients of thought; i.e., what tools does man need before he can think? We can get agreement that thought is a process involving mixing ingredients to produce conclusions. Communication theorists are interested in the same question as the philosophers and psychologists: What are the thought units that are mixed in the process?

Plato introduced the notion that thought requires mental symbols —images which man carries around with him.[2] He argued that when we want to think about the physical world, our thought units actually are small visual replicas of the objects they represent, received and kept intact by the retina of the eye. In the light of existing knowledge about the physiology of perception, Plato's specific theory is naive, but we have to remember that man knew little scientifically about the nature of perception when Plato was writing. There still is merit in the general principle.

Until early in this century, most theorists took the position that thought required some kind of image, pictorial or otherwise, though there was debate as to the nature of the image. In the early 1900's, some psychologists took the position that thought does not require images at all.[3] To date, this debate has not been resolved scientifically. Actually, the imageless-thought theory is not subject to precise scientific test. In any case, this kind of argument is primarily of

[2] Plato, *The Timaeus and the Critias* (Thomas Taylor, trans.). Pantheon Books, 1944, pp. 162 ff.
[3] M. Wertheimer, *Productive Thinking*. Harper & Brothers, 1945.

academic and theoretic interest; for most of our behaviors, the question *can* be resolved. We can agree that thought involves a manipulation of symbols, of thought units—at least most of the time for most people. We can go further, and agree with earlier philosophers that thought usually is tied directly to experiences— to specific, concrete objects. In other words, as one of them, Berkeley, testified, when we think of "man" we are forced to think of "a white, or a black, or a tawny, a straight, or a crooked, a tall, or a low, or a middle-sized man."[4] We also can agree with Berkeley that it is difficult, if not impossible to think without using thought units which are tied to our experiences.

The question remains, what are the major sets of symbols that are available to us? What are our units of thought? I am suggesting that *the major units of thought are units of language,* that we have difficulty in thinking about an object, a process, any construct for which we have no name, no label, no words. For example, if you have no word to name the white stuff that falls on the ground in the winter which English-speaking people call "snow," you might have trouble thinking about snow. On the other hand, if you have five or six different words to refer to different kinds of "snow," as some Eskimo languages have, you will be more likely to notice five or six different kinds of snow, and you will be better able to separate five or six kinds of snow when you think about snow.

The theory that man's language affects his perception and his thinking was hypothesized by Sapir and Whorf.[5] In essence, the Sapir-Whorf hypothesis states that a person's language will in part determine what the person sees, what he thinks about, and the methods he uses to think and to arrive at decisions. As yet, we have no conclusive evidence as to the general applicability of this suggestion. There is some evidence that the hypothesis has merit. We are likely to think about things we have experienced and for which

[4] G. Berkeley, *A Treatise Concerning the Principles of Human Knowledge.* Dublin, 1710.

[5] Benjamin L. Whorf, "The relation of habitual thought and behavior to language," in *Language, Thought and Reality.* Massachusetts Institute of Technology, The Technology Press, 1956, pp. 134–159.

we have names that we can manipulate. *Naming is essential to thinking.* The names we have at our disposal, and the ways in which we name, affect what and how we think.

The linguistic facility of a communication source is an important factor in the communication process. As sources of communication, we are limited in our ability to express our purposes if we do not have the communication skills necessary to encode accurate messages. Second, our communication-skill deficiencies limit the ideas that are available to us and limit our ability to manipulate these ideas—to think.

So much for the first factor, communication skills. What else do we need to consider in analyzing the source-encoder in the communication process?

ATTITUDES

A second factor is the source's attitudes. The attitudes of a communication source affect the ways in which he communicates. Unfortunately, the word "attitude" is not easy to define. In fact, social scientists have had (and still have) considerable difficulty in determining what they mean by "attitude."

For our purposes, we might attempt to define an attitude in this way: Given a man, Mister A, and an object x, which might be another person, Mister A himself, or any other object. We can say that Mister A has an attitude toward x if Mister A has some predisposition, some tendency, some desire to either approach or avoid x. In different words, we can say that Mister A has an attitude toward x if he tends to like or dislike x, to want or not want to associate himself with x, to identify or disassociate himself from x.

If Mister A likes to be with x, to talk with x, to be seen with x, we might infer that A has a *favorable* attitude toward x. On the other hand, if Mister A tries to avoid x, tends to "vote x down," so to speak, we might infer that A has an unfavorable attitude toward x.

With this superficial meaning for the word "attitude," we can ask the question: How do the attitudes of the source affect communication?

ATTITUDE TOWARD SELF. We can argue that the source's attitudes affect communication in at least three ways. First, his attitudes toward himself are important. Recalling our example of Joe asking Mary for a date on Sunday, let us assume that Joe had a negative attitude toward himself; that he did not believe that a girl like Mary (or any girl) would want to spend Sunday with him. This kind of self-evaluation quite probably would affect the kind of message that Joe creates. All of us have encountered the "you don't want to spend Sunday with me, do you?" kind of individual, or the salesman who drives his supervisor to drink because he continually says to the customer, "You didn't want to buy anything else, did you?"

On the other hand, let us assume that Joe had a highly favorable attitude toward himself, that it was inconceivable to him that Mary (or any other girl) would not be thrilled to spend Sunday with him. There is *testimony*, all from males, that this kind of attitude toward self leads to success in dating. The *evidence* indicates that this kind of boy does *not* maintain a high batting average with the opposite sex. In any case, I think we would agree that Joe's attitudes toward himself would affect the way in which he communicated.

The student who suffers "stage-fright" in a public-speaking course, the employee who avoids a promotion because he distrusts his own ability to handle increased responsibility, the writer who just "can't get started" in his writing are all illustrations of the impact of self-attitudes on communication. Much of the success of self-confidence courses such as Dale Carnegie's can be attributed to the increase in self-confidence that such training gives to its participants. The whole complex of variables that go together to comprise the individual's "personality" are related to the concept of self-attitude in communication.

ATTITUDE TOWARD SUBJECT MATTER. Attitude toward self is not

the only attitude which affects the source's communication behavior. A second factor is his attitude toward his subject matter. When you read an article or a book, when you listen to a teacher or a lecturer, a salesman or an actor, you get an impression of the writer's or speaker's attitude toward his subject matter. His attitudes quite often come through in his messages. Of course, there are exceptions. Some communicators can hide (avoid encoding) their attitudes toward their subject matter. For the most part, however, subject matter attitudes come through. Many industrial firms will not hire salesmen unless the firms are convinced that the salesmen believe in the product—have favorable attitudes toward it. Almost any top-notch salesman will tell you that he cannot sell a product unless he believes in it himself.

Deficiencies in attitude toward subject matter are apparent in the work of many professional writers. A reporter, a technical writer receives assignments to write about many different things. If he does not believe in the value of his subject matter, it is difficult for him to communicate effectively about it.

ATTITUDE TOWARD RECEIVER. There is a third kind of attitude that affects the source's communication behavior—his attitude toward his receiver, the other fellow in the process. Let us return to the communication situation in which Bill asked John to pass the salt. Suppose that Bill had an unfavorable attitude toward John. Suppose that Bill felt that John really did not belong at the same table with him, that John was far beneath Bill's social level, that John was not good enough to eat with him. This kind of negative attitude toward the receiver affects the source's message, and affects how people will respond to the source's message. If John realizes that Bill does not like him, he may pass the salt or he may not—but it is fairly certain that John will not pass Bill very many things. Eventually, he would not even want to pass the time of day.

The source's attitudes toward his receiver affect communication. When readers or listeners realize that the writer or speaker really likes them, they are much less critical of his messages, much more likely to accept what he says. Aristotle called this perceived characteristic of the speaker *ethos,* a quality in the speaker that is personally appealing to the listener.[6] The concept of *ethos* includes many behaviors other than a favorable attitude; however, the source's attitudes toward his receiver are an important determinant of his effectiveness.

We have mentioned three of the kinds of attitudes held by sources of communication which affect the communication process. We could have listed others. The source's attitudes toward any person or object relevant to the communication situation will affect his communication behavior. The three types of attitude mentioned are relevant to most communication situations: the source's attitude toward (a) himself, (b) his subject matter, and (c) his receiver. Let us turn to the third factor in the source-encoder that can affect the fidelity of communication.

KNOWLEDGE LEVEL

It is obvious that the amount of knowledge a source has about his subject matter will affect his message. One cannot communicate what one does not know; one cannot communicate with maximum effectiveness content material that one does not understand. On the other hand, if the source knows "too much," if he is overspecialized, he might err in that his particular communication skills are employed in so technical a manner that his receiver cannot understand him.

This dilemma is represented by the oft-heard argument over how much a teacher needs to know in order to teach. Some argue that he does not need to know anything, he merely needs to know how to teach. Others argue that he does not have to know anything about teaching; if he knows his subject matter thoroughly, he will be able to transmit this knowledge effectively. Clearly, both positions are fallacious when stated this way. The source needs to know his subject matter. He also needs to know how to teach it effectively.

Knowledge of the communication process itself affects source

[6] W. Rhys Roberts, "Rhetorica," in *The Works of Aristotle* (W. D. Ross, ed.). Oxford University Press, 1946, Volume XI, p. 7.

behavior. What and how the source communicates depends on his ability to conduct the kind of analysis we have been describing. In other words, his communication behavior is affected by how much he knows about his own attitudes, the characteristics of his receiver, the ways in which he can produce or treat messages, the kinds of choices he can make about communication channels, etc. Knowledge *of* communication affects communication *behavior*.

SOCIAL-CULTURAL SYSTEM

No source communicates as a free agent, without being influenced by his position in a social-cultural system. We need, of course, to take into account the personal factors in the source: his communication skills, his attitudes, his knowledge. But we need to know more than this. We need to know the kind of social system in which he is operating. We need to know where he fits in that social system, the roles he fulfills, the functions he is required to perform, the prestige that he and other people attach to him. We need to know the cultural context in which he communicates, the cultural beliefs and values that are dominant for him, the accepted forms of behavior that are acceptable or not acceptable, required or not required in his culture. We need to know about his own expectations and the expectations others have about him.

We will devote an entire chapter to the importance of a culturally determined set of social systems. We can illustrate the nature of our later discussion by pointing out that all the groups to which a source belongs, all the values and standards which he has learned, his own perceptions of his "place" in the world, his position in his own social class, his rank—all these things will affect the source's communication behavior.

People in differing social classes communicate differently. People from different cultural backgrounds communicate differently. Social and cultural systems partly determine the word choices which people make, the purposes they have for communicating, the meanings they attach to certain words, their choice of receivers, the channels they use for this or that kind of message, etc. An American does not communicate in the same way that an Indonesian does. Japanese and Germans may encode the same messages to express widely differing purposes, or they may encode quite different messages to express the same purposes.

We have said that a source's position in a social and cultural context will affect his general communication behavior. It is also true that the source fulfills many roles, and that he has changing perceptions or images of the social and cultural position of his receiver. These perceptions affect his communication behavior. For example, a captain in the Army may talk one way when he is speaking to a group of sergeants, and another when he is speaking to a group of colonels. A labor union leader may talk one way to management in private, and another way when he talks about management to the members of his union. A corporation vice-president may talk one way to his secretary and quite differently to his wife or the company president.

In summary, we have said that there are at least four kinds of factors that operate on a communication source-encoder. Each affects his communication behavior, his purpose, his encoding mechanisms, his messages. Each affects the way in which his receiver will respond to his messages. Factors in the source include:

1. communication skills;
2. attitudes;
3. knowledge level;
4. social-cultural system.

When we serve as sources of communication, when we observe other people behaving as source-encoders, we need to take each of these four factors into account if we are to understand why a communication source behaves as he does, and why he is or is not effective in communicating his purposes to other people.

The Decoder-Receiver

The decoder-receiver is a second ingredient in our model. We already have talked at some length about the decoder-receiver, when we talked about the source-encoder. The person at one end of the communication process and the person at the other end are quite similar. In fact, when we engage in intrapersonal communication, the source and the receiver are the same person.

This is one of the things we meant when we spoke of the difficulties of talking about a process. It might appear as if there is a beginning of communication—the source—and an end of communication—the receiver. This is not the case. It only appears so because we have to structure a model to talk about it.

It is useful to talk about sources and receivers separately, for analytic purposes. It is not meaningful to assume that these are independent functions, independent kinds of behavior. Calling an individual a source implies that we have stopped the dynamic of the process at one point; calling him a receiver implies that we have merely used a different cutting point.

He who is a source at one moment has been a receiver. The messages he produces are determined by the messages he has received, the forces imposing on him prior to the moment of encoding. The same is so for the receiver. He too can be looked on as a source. During a given communication situation, he often behaves as both a source and a receiver. Certainly, he will perform source behaviors in the future, which will be affected more or less by the messages sent to him as a receiver.

With this point of view in mind, we can talk about the decoder-receiver in terms of his *communication skills*. If the receiver does not have the ability to listen, to read, to think, he will not be able to receive and decode the messages that the source-encoder has transmitted.

We can talk about the receiver in terms of his *attitudes*. How he decodes a message is in part determined by his attitudes toward himself, toward the source, toward the content of the message. All the things that we said about the attitudes of the source apply to the receiver as well.

We can talk about the receiver in terms of his *knowledge-level*. If he does not know the code, he cannot understand the message. If he does not know anything about the content of a message, he probably cannot understand it either. If he does not understand the nature of the communication process itself, the chances are good that he will misperceive messages, make incorrect inferences about the purposes or intentions of the source, fail to operate in what may be his own best self-interest.

Finally, we can talk about the receiver in terms of his *culture* and his position in a *social system*. His own social status, his group memberships, his customary modes of behavior affect the ways in which he receives and interprets messages.

One other point can be made about the importance of the receiver in communication. If we limit our discussion to *effective* communication, the *receiver is the most important link in the communication process*. If the source does not reach the receiver with his message, he might as well have talked to himself. One of the most important emphases of communication theory is a concern with the fellow at the far end of the communication chain—the receiver.

When we write, it is the reader who is important. When we speak, it is the listener who is important. This concern with the receiver is a guiding principle for any communication source. The receiver always has to be kept in mind when the source makes decisions with respect to each of the communication factors we have discussed.

When the source chooses a code for his message, he must choose one which is known to his receiver. When the source selects content in order to reflect his purpose, he selects content that will be meaningful to his receiver. When he treats the message in any way, part of his treatment is determined by his analysis of his receiver's communication (decoding) skills, his attitudes, his knowledge, and his place in a social-cultural context. The only justification for the existence of a source, for the occurrence of communication, is the receiver, the target at whom everything is aimed.

As implied, both the source and receiver can be analyzed in terms of their communication skills, attitudes, knowledge levels, cultural contexts, and places in multiple social systems. What may not have been implied is the *interdependence* of the source and receiver in such an analysis. We can gather information about a source, about a receiver. This is helpful; however, many of the key determinants of communication involve the *relationships* between source and receiver characteristics.

It can be argued, for example, that the communication skills of the source are important in enabling him to develop and encode a purpose. The communication skills of the receiver are important in enabling him to decode and make decisions about a message. But the relationship between the skill level of the source and receiver is a vital determinant of fidelity. A given source may have a high level of skill not shared by one receiver, but shared by another. We cannot predict the success of the source from his skill level alone— we have to consider it in relationship to the levels of particular receivers.

The distinction being made here is an important one for all our discussion. In theorizing about communication, it is useful to distinguish between what might be called *monadic* and *dyadic* approaches to analysis. If we define a concept monadically, we define it in terms of one person, one object, without reference to a relationship among people or objects. On the other hand, a dyadic definition emphasizes relationships and de-emphasizes one-person characteristics.

For example, we can define leadership in terms of the characteristics of a leader: he is intelligent, he has a warm personality, he is aggressive, etc. This is a monadic definition. A dyadic definition of leadership is based on a relationship between at least two people: one person cannot lead unless another is led, and leadership has to involve related behaviors of both the person leading and the person led.

A dyadic definition of leadership might be of the following order: if an individual makes statements of the order "we should do this" or "let's do that," and if a second individual then makes statements of the order "OK," or "I agree," or "that's a good idea," then leadership—a relationship between these two sets of behaviors—is present.

A great portion of communication theory must be dyadic in nature. Our discussion and analysis must be phrased in terms of the relationships between communication ingredients, rather than in terms of the values of a particular ingredient for a given person. This is not to say that individual characteristics are not important. They are, but usually in the context of their relationship to other factors with which they operate conjunctively.

The Message

We have discussed the source and the receiver. Let us turn to a third ingredient and ask what the factors are in the *message* which affect fidelity.

We defined a message as the actual physical product of the source-encoder. When we speak, the speech is the message. When we write, the writing is the message. When we paint, the picture is the message. When we gesture, the movements of our arms, the expressions on our faces are the message.

At least three factors need to be taken into account in the message: (1) the message code, (2) the message content, and (3) the message treatment. In discussing code, content, and treatment as message factors, we can talk about two things: (a) the elements in each, and (b) the way in which the elements are structured.

ELEMENTS AND STRUCTURE

What do we mean by "elements" and "structure"? It is not easy to define these two words because they are not independent or fixed in their meanings for us. We cannot have either without the other, and we change our referents for the words as we shift from one level of analysis to another.

Anything that exists for man, that is known to man, exists and is known in some form. We cannot talk about anything without imposing some structure on it, without naming it, putting it in some form. Man can perceive the world as what William James referred to as a "blooming, buzzing confusion." But man cannot operate in the world, cannot talk about the world until he structures it in some way.

When we learn to distinguish and to name objects, we isolate units and label them as object *elements*. Then we put these units together in some way—we place them in a *structure*.

Let us look at an example or two of the way we define elements and structure. The basic elements of a language are sounds. We group these sounds into what we call phonemes, then into higher-level sound groups, called morphemes. Eventually we attempt to make some kind of notations for these sound groups, using the letters of our inadequate alphabet to do this.

Take a written word in English such as *fish*. We can say that letters of the English alphabet are elements of a recorded language and that we can structure these elements in certain ways to form words. In the word *fish*, the elements are the letters *f, i, s,* and *h*. Each letter is an element. Each letter can be separated from all other letters. We can put these letters together in many ways: we can structure them as *fshi*. We can structure them as *hsif*. We can structure them as *fish*. Each combination of these elements is a structure. Some combinations we call words, others we do not. Some are more useful to us than others, but all such combinations involve the structuring of elements.

Clearly, we cannot talk about two or more letters of the alphabet without putting them in some structure, some form. One letter must come first, one must come last. The word *fish* names the structure that exists when we combine the alphabet elements *f, i, s,* and *h* in a way that is meaningful to us as users of English.

Let us look at another example, a tree. The word *tree* names the structure that exists when we combine certain elements in certain ways. One way of looking at the elements of a tree is to look at such things as the trunk, the leaves, the bark, the limbs. When these elements go together in certain ways, we say we have a tree. When they go together in other ways, we say we do not have a tree.

Elements and structure go together, yet we sometimes try to draw dichotomies between them. We may debate which is more important in art, form (structure) or substance (elements). We may debate which is more important in communication, having good ideas (elements) or having good organization (structure). These are meaningless chicken-or-the-egg arguments; you cannot have one without the other. Neither can be said to exist separately.

The Level of Discussion

We said earlier that we shift our meanings for elements and structure as we shift the level of discussion. What do we mean by this? Take our example of the word *fish*. Suppose we have a sentence, "some fish can swim." In this context we might look on the word *fish* as an element in the sentence. The sentence has three other word-elements: *some, can,* and *swim*. The word *sentence* is the name of a certain method of structuring these word elements. We have shifted our level of analysis by broadening our perspective.

We can do the same thing with a word such as *tree*. We looked on *tree* as the name for a particular combination of elements such as bark, limbs, and so on. Let us widen our discussion level and talk about a forest. What is an element of a forest? A tree. In other words, *forest* is now the name of a structure, and *tree* names an element in the structure.

We can shift our discussion down as well as up. We can talk about the limb of a tree as the name of a structure, and words like *sap, veins,* etc., as names for elements in that structure. We can take a letter like *f* as the name of a structure and talk about things such as positions of the tongue, positions of the lips, etc., as elements of the structure.

The point is related to our earlier discussion of process. There is no fixed unit to which we can refer at all times as an element and no fixed sequencing of units to which we can refer at all times as structure. What we look on as elements and structure will depend on our purpose, our level of analysis.

It is correct to say that anything that exists contains elements. It also is correct to say that any set of elements has to be combined in some structure. We cannot have one without the other, but the distinction between elements and structure is useful when we talk about many things—including messages.

Our level of analysis varies to fit our purpose; however, whenever we analyze the message in communication, we can look at its code, its content, and its treatment. In looking at these three elements in a message structure, we can consider both elements and structure of the code, elements and structure of the content, and elements and structure of the treatment.

MESSAGE CODE

Let us look at what we mean by code. A code can be defined as any group of symbols that can be structured in a way that is meaningful to some person. Languages are codes. The English language is a code: it contains elements (sounds, letters, words, etc.) that are arranged in certain meaningful orders, and not in other orders.

Anything is a code which has a group of elements (a vocabulary) and a set of procedures for combining those elements meaningfully (a syntax). If we want to know whether a set of symbols is a code, we have to isolate its vocabulary, and check to see if there are systematic ways (structures) for combining the elements.

In the same way, if we want to learn a code, to "break a code," we look for the elements that appear, and we look for consistent ways in which the elements are structured. This kind of talent is useful in military intelligence; it is useful when we try to reconstruct "dead" languages, languages which are no longer used, but of which we have a record.

We said that languages such as English or German are codes. We use other codes in communication. Music is a code: it has a vocabulary (notes), and it has a syntax: procedures for combining notes into a structure that will be meaningful to the listener. If we are to understand music, we need to learn the code.

All music in the Western world uses pretty much the same vocabulary—and it is a limited vocabulary. Musical tastes, distinctions as to types of music, rest primarily on differences in syntax—differences in the ways in which notes are combined. People who say they do not like "classical music" may simply not know the code, not understand its structure. People who say they do not like "rock and roll" or "progressive jazz" or "Dixieland" or "pop music" may know the code—but not consider it "proper."

Painting involves a code. The painter has a vocabulary, elements that he uses. He combines these elements and produces a structure. Any amateur painter has almost the same vocabulary as did Van Gogh or Renoir—it is the quality of the structure of painting that distinguishes one painter from another. For that matter, any amateur musician has almost the same vocabulary as did Beethoven, Bach, or Bartok. Again, it is the syntax that separates one composer from another.

Dance requires a code. Any art form that communicates, that is concerned with meaning, requires a code. We can speak of the code of radio-television production, of advertising layout and copy, of headline writing. In each of these message situations, the communicator has a set of elements, and various alternatives for combining them. To be a good dancer, a good producer, a good copywriter is (in part) to know the available vocabulary and to be able to structure the vocabulary in the most effective way.

As yet, we have little systematic knowledge of the syntax and vocabulary of some forms of modern dance, of radio-TV production, of layout and design. There is no recorded grammar for these codes. The experts in these fields still have difficulty in telling us what their structuring procedures are, or even what their vocabulary is. This may not affect their own artistic behavior, but it does make it difficult to teach newcomers to the profession to analyze the characteristics of message production, to measure the effects of their messages.

Some message producers, source-encoders, might argue that we shouldn't study the code system in fields such as dance, radio-TV, advertising. They would argue that these fields are artistic. I can find no rationale for this position. It is ridiculous to think that a Beethoven would not be interested in knowing more about counterpoint, that a Van Gogh would not be interested in knowing more about compositions of color.

If our meaning for the word "art" is "without system," or "without knowledge of what we do," then we can defend ignorance of the code in certain fields by calling the fields artistic. On the other hand, if our meaning for "art" is "the attempt to structure certain elements in a way that will best express our purpose" or "have the most effect on the receiver" or "have the intended meaning for the receiver," then it seems to me that we need to study the vocabulary and syntax of all art forms.

Whenever we encode a message, we must make certain decisions about the code we will use. We must decide (a) which code, (b) what elements of the code, and (c) what method of structuring the elements of the code we will select. Second, when we analyze communication behavior, messages, we need to include the source's decisions about the code in our analysis. It is for these reasons that we include code as part of our analysis of structure.

MESSAGE CONTENT

We can define content as the material in the message that was selected by the source to express his purpose. In this book, my message content includes the assertions that I make, the information that I present, the inferences that I draw, and the judgments that I propose.

Content, like code, has both elements and structure. If you try to present three pieces of information, you have to present them in some order. One has to come first, one last. If you have five assertions to make, you must structure them—you must impose one or another order on them. Each assertion can be considered as a content element (of course, each assertion is itself the result of a structuring of lower-level elements). The ways you choose to arrange assertions in part determine the structure of the content.

MESSAGE TREATMENT

We have listed code and content as factors in a message. In talking about each, we suggested that the source-encoder has choices available to him. In encoding a message, the source can choose one or another code, he can choose one or another set of elements from within the code, he can choose one or another method of arranging his code elements.

In presenting a message to express his purpose, the source can select one or another piece of information, one or another set of assertions, one or another set of evidence. He can arrange his content in one or another form. He can repeat some of it. He can summarize all of it at the end. He can leave some of it out and let his receiver fill it in for him if the receiver wants to.

In the selection of elements and structure of both code and content, the source has many decisions to make, many availabilities to choose from. In making these choices, he demonstrates his style of communicating—he treats his message in certain ways. *In short, we can define the treatment of a message as the decisions which the communication source makes in selecting and arranging both codes and content.*

In preparing copy for the newspaper, the journalist treats his message in many ways. He selects content that he thinks will be interesting to his reader. He selects words from the code that he thinks his reader will understand; he structures his assertions, his information, in the way that he thinks his reader would prefer to receive them.

Given his code and content choices, he will vary type size to let his reader know that he considers some things to be more important than other things. He will put some stories on page 1 and others on page 11. All these decisions are treatment decisions. They are ways in which the source chooses to encode his message by selecting certain elements of code and content and presenting them in one or another treatment, one or another style.

When a radio newscaster is preparing his program, he has research evidence that indicates that listeners are more likely to remember news items when they are indexed for him by use of such phrases as "now hear this" or "this is important" or "bulletin." When the newscaster uses these indices, he is treating his message to better accomplish his purposes.

In general, message treatment refers to the decisions the source makes as to how he should deliver his message—the choices he should make with respect to both code and content, and with respect to the method of delivering code and content.

What determines message treatment? On what bases do communication sources make treatment decisions? First, the personality and other individual characteristics of the source determine the treatment he will give a message. This factor is typified by statements such as "style is the man." Each of us has distinctive encoding patterns. Each of us selects certain code, content, and treatment elements and rejects others. Each of us arranges our message elements in certain ways and not in others. Our own communication skills, attitudes, knowledge, culture, and position in social systems dictate certain choices on our part.

We often try to identify an individual on the basis of his characteristic message behaviors. We talk of the style of Hemingway, of Steinbeck, of Brando, of Gary Cooper, of Tennessee Williams, of Roosevelt. When we say that "this message sounds like so and so" or "in this play or movie, so and so played himself—as usual," we are saying that we can identify sources by analyzing their messages. We observe the code, content, and treatment choices that were made in the message and make an assumption as to who encoded it. Occasionally, these predictions become quite interesting. For example, there has long been a debate over whether Shakespeare or Bacon or Marlowe wrote "Shakespeare." There have been attempts, not too conclusive, to demonstrate authorship of these works by analyzing message treatment, style. The assumption underlying these attempts is that a particular individual communicates in a way that is distinctive to him, that can be detected by analyzing any messages which he has produced.

When we decode messages, we make inferences as to the source's purpose, his communication skills, his attitudes toward us, his knowledge, his status. We try to estimate what kind of person would have produced this kind of message. We often decide what the source's purpose was, what kind of "personality" he has, what objects he values or believes in, what he thinks is worthless.

We can and do make all these kinds of inferences from observing the treatment that the source gives to his content and code. There is danger in making inferences about the source from an analysis of his messages. Even if we are skilled in the factors that affect communication, we often will err in the inferences that we make. If we are not skilled, we will err consistently.

It is a good idea to proceed with extreme caution, particularly when we make inferences about the *intentions* of the source, based on our decoding of a few of his messages. In fact, people who continually impute purposes to a source from listening to or reading messages that the source produced are exhibiting some of the symptoms that are characteristic of a serious mental illness.

Let us turn to another important determinant of treatment: the receiver. To communicate is to seek a response from a receiver. Any communication source communicates in order to get his receiver to do something, to know something, to accept something.

As sources, we need to keep the receiver in mind at all times. We choose codes that our receiver can understand. We select elements from the code that will appeal to him, that are easy for him to decode. We structure these elements to minimize the effort required to decode and interpret the message. We choose content that will be convincing to the receiver, that will be pertinent to his interest, his needs. Finally, we treat the message generally in order to achieve the maximum possible effect—to accomplish our purpose.

We cannot detail the principles of message treatment that improve the effectiveness of communication. At various points, we will discuss some of them; however, several books would be required to summarize what is known about the relationship between various message treatments and the effects of those messages on the receiver.

In summary, we have listed three factors that are pertinent to the message produced by the source-encoder: the code, the content, and the treatment. In communicating, in analyzing the communication of others, we need to focus our attention on the set of symbols (the code) that the source used to produce his message. We analyze content: what were the ideas expressed or the information reported? We analyze treatment: in what ways did the source-encoder make code and content choices, for wnat reasons, and with what effect?

For an analysis of all three factors (code, content, treatment), we need to select certain units, certain elements. We need to determine which elements were chosen and which were rejected. We need to determine which element structures were utilized and which were avoided. Our choice of element and structure levels will be determined by the purpose and level of our analysis.

The Channel

It might be accurate to say that no one word in communication theory has been as used and abused as the word "channel." We use it to mean many different things. We need to look at three meanings at least for channel.

Let us start with an analogy. Suppose that I am on one side of a wide lake with steep banks, and you are on the other side. I have a package for you. I want to get the package from where I am to where you are. What do I need in order to get the package to you?

First, I need a *boat* to carry the package. Second, I need some way to put my package in the boat. I need a *boat dock* to connect me with the boat. At the other side, you need some way to get the package out of the boat. You too need a boat-dock to connect you. Finally, I need some *water*. I need something which will serve as a carrier for the boat—some medium through which the boat can travel. If we both have boat-docks that are in good working order, if we have a boat in good working order that we can use as a vehicle to carry the package, and if we have some water that will support the boat, I can get my package from where I am to where you are. If we do not have all three of these things, we cannot get in touch with each other.

In communication theory, we refer to the analogues of all three of these things (boat-docks, boats, and water) and we call all of them channels. Suppose you and I want to talk to each other. In order to do this we each need to have encoding and decoding apparatus which will enable us to translate internal electrical (nervous) impulses into some external physical message. I need to be able to speak, you need to be able to hear. *My speaking mechanism and your hearing mechanism are analogous to boat-docks.*

The oral message that I produce has to come to you in some *message-vehicle*. The vehicles which carry oral messages are sound waves. *Sound waves are analogous to our boats.*

Finally, the sound waves themselves need something to support them, a wave carrier. We need a *vehicle-carrier*. Usually, in human communication at least, sound waves are supported by air. *Air is analogous to our water.*

These then are the three major meanings of the word "channel" in communication: modes of encoding and decoding messages (boat-docks), message-vehicles (boats), and vehicle-carriers (water). We need not concern ourselves at great length about the vehicle-carrier meaning of channel. This is the concern of the engineer, the physicist, the biologist, the chemist. This leaves the other two meanings we have for the word. Let us look first at the "boat" meaning— message-vehicles.

One approach to the "boat" meaning of channels is to consider light waves, sound waves, etc., as message-vehicles. Again, this is outside our present field of interest. It is the concern of communication engineers, men who work on the problems of transmitting messages by applying principles or theories of light and sound. More typically, we look on the *public media* of communication as message-vehicles: radio, telephone, telegraph, newspapers, films, magazines, the stage, the public platform, etc. Of course, each of these media can be examined as an entire communication system. Any radio station, any advertising agency employs sources, encoders, decoders, etc. We have discussed this aspect of the media. For now, we can look at the media as message-vehicles, as boats that we can hire or build to carry our messages for us.

In communicating, the source has to choose a channel. He has to choose some vehicle in which to carry his message. Suppose you are a national advertiser. Should you transmit your messages over TV, newspapers, direct mail, or magazines? Once you have chosen a particular medium, you still need to make selections. If you want

TV, do you want NBC, CBS, or ABC? Do you want network TV or local TV? If you choose magazines, do you want *Life, The Saturday Evening Post?* Or do you want *Vogue, Popular Mechanics, Better Homes and Gardens?*

These kinds of questions are channel questions, message-vehicle questions. In advertising, and in political campaigns, a large group of people devote all their time to just such questions. We refer to these people as media buyers, channel purchasers. Media buyers operate by choosing the "best" message-vehicle or combination of message-vehicles. This is a complicated process. A lot of things determine media selection. Selection is limited by (a) what is available, (b) how much money can be spent, and (c) what the source's preferences are. Other determinants of channel selection are (a) which channels are received by the most people (at the lowest cost), (b) which channels have the most impact, (c) which channels are most adaptable to the kind of purpose which the source has, and (d) which channels are most adaptable to the content of the message.

We have voluminous answers to the first question, which channels are received by the most people (at the lowest cost). Findings of audience head-counters such as Hooper, Neilsen, and Gallup are available. Circulation figures for newspapers and magazines are available. We have little or no systematic knowledge about the other three questions. True, there are agencies that attempt to measure the impact of messages over various channels, the level of readership of newspapers, the probability that people can recall magazine ads, the amount of return from direct mail, etc. These facts, however, are of dubious value in predicting *affect*.

There are people who have acquired considerable ability to pick and choose among channels. Yet, just as in the case of the code of radio-TV producers, the language of copy or layout, we have scant scientific evidence as to the relative merits of one or another message-vehicle. This is a virgin field for research—the next ten years should produce a significant increment in our knowledge about the possibilities of the available public media of communication. As yet, we know little.

We have mentioned the public media of communication as the "boats" of communication; the vehicles which carry our messages. There is a third meaning for channels—the "boat-dock" meaning. When we are concerned with an examination of the human communication process, we might consider channels of communication in the sense of boat-docks.

As source-encoders, we have to decide how we will channel messages so our receiver can decode them—can see, hear, touch, and even occasionally taste and smell them. In other words, we can look on channels of communication as the motor skills possessed by the encoder and the sensory skills possessed by the decoder.

For simplicity's sake, we will restrict our use of the term to the decoding skills. In short, we can define a communication channel psychologically as the senses through which a decoder-receiver can perceive a message which has been encoded and transmitted by a source-encoder.

At this point, you might understandably be confused about one thing. Earlier, we defined a decoder as the sense mechanisms of the receiver. We defined the decoder in person-to-person communication as the sense of hearing, seeing, touching, etc. In our present discussion, we provided as one definition of "channel" the senses of the decoder—again, seeing, hearing, touching, etc. In other words, we have talked about an individual's sense mechanisms as both channels and decoders.

Let us return to our analogy and refer to the term "boat-dock." Suppose you were asked to say whether a boat-dock is part of the land or the water. It is connected to both—in fact it is the connecting link between land and water. We can say that the boat-dock *primarily* is part of the land, or we can say that the boat-dock *primarily* is part of the water. According to our purpose, we sometimes might say one thing and sometimes another.

We have the same problem when we talk about the sense mechanisms. We can look on them as part of the receiver or as part of the channel. We sometimes will do one, and sometimes the other. To avoid confusion, all that is necessary is for us to remember that there are boat-docks and that you cannot get from land to water without them. In communication, messages cannot become connected to receivers without being sensed by the receiver. You may prefer to call the senses "channels" or "decoders." In any case, it is not the name that is vital—it is the function. Channels couple the source and the receiver, enabling them to communicate.

In communicating, we have to decide which channels we will use. Should we encode a message so that it can be seen, can be touched, can be heard, and so on? How do we make this decision? Unfortunately, research in this area is of recent origin and has not given us much useful information as yet.

The fact is that we usually do not pick one channel over another for any good reason. We do not think about it. For example, if an office manager wants to communicate something to his staff, should he communicate his message in such a way that the staff can hear it or see it, should he call a meeting and talk to the staff, or should he write a memo? In education, we usually fail to analyze teaching from a communication channel point of view. For example, we do not often raise such questions as:

1. What kinds of messages should be transmitted orally in the classroom?
2. What kinds of messages should be transmitted visually, through books?
3. What kinds of messages should be transmitted visually, but nonverbally, through pictures, rather than words?
4. What kinds of messages should be transmitted physically, through touch, by having students actually perform certain tasks, examine and manipulate certain objects, etc.?

These are all channel questions. Clearly, we cannot discuss or make decisions about the selection of channels independently of our decisions on message. The content, the code, the treatment of a message are related to our choice of channels. At the same time, knowledge of our receiver is related to choice of channels: can the receiver decode better by ear, by eye, by touch? Finally, the source himself is related to the channel he selects. Is the source a better communicator when he speaks, when he writes, when he demonstrates something physically?

We cannot isolate the ingredients one at a time when we are making communication decisions—all the ingredients of communication are interlocked and are interdependent. Again, communication is a process. All we are suggesting now is that all messages must be transmitted through a channel and that the choice of channel is important in determining the efficiency and effectiveness of communication.

Of course, we do have some knowledge about channel selection, about the boat-dock. For example, we know that two channels are usually better than one, that a receiver will be more likely to decode a message accurately if he can see it and hear it at the same time. We know, too, that the receiver cannot retain as much oral information as he can visual, other things being equal. We know, therefore, that it is more effective to transmit "hard" content visually rather than orally. Yet, we actually know very little about "boat-dock" channels that can help us in making decisions about message transmission. This too is an area that will require a great deal of further research.

One final point before we leave a discussion of channels. It should be apparent that our meanings for *channel* as a boat and as a boat-dock are not independent. Only certain kinds of boats can use certain kinds of boat-docks. Other boats require more elaborate, or at least different, docking points. The same is true for the vehicles of communication.

We can organize the vehicles of communication under the categories we use to talk about boat-dock channels; i.e., the senses. Radio is a vehicle. Messages transmitted by radio are channeled so that they may be heard. Television is a vehicle that enables us to channel messages so that they may be both heard and seen. Newspapers can be seen—and touched as well. And so on. The meaning of channel as a message-vehicle and the meaning of channel as the decoding skills of the receiver are themselves interrelated. We need to take both meanings into account when we communicate and when we analyze the communication processes of others.

We have spent some time presenting an elementary model of the process of communication. We have introduced several terms to refer to the ingredients of communication. We have discussed some of the factors that decrease the fidelity of communication, that produce noise. As we continue our discussion, we can return to the model and try to place our discussions in its context. Next, we will talk about communication in a personal context—about the learning process in communication, about some of the principles of effective communication. We will try to explain and define what we mean by a social system and a cultural context, the context in which communication occurs. We will analyze messages, talk about meaning in communication, and examine in more detail what we mean by code, content, and treatment. Finally, we will talk about some of the choices which the communication source has to make when he communicates.

Before concluding our discussion of the communication model, another reminder of the caution we should use in talking about a process is in order. It is all too easy to look at this or any other communication model as a "click-click—push-pull" system. This is not the way communication works. All the communication ingredients and factors that we have mentioned and discussed are intertwined. When we engage in communication as a process, we cannot pull any one of them out—or the whole structure collapses.

When we want to analyze the communication process, to take it apart, we have to talk about sources, or messages, or channels, or receivers—but we must remember what we are doing. We are distorting the process. We have to, but we do not want to trick ourselves into believing that communication occurs "by the numbers."

With this in mind, it is useful to analyze the source's and the receiver's communication skills, their attitudes, their levels of knowledge, their roles in multiple social systems, and the cultural context in which their communication behaviors occur.

In analyzing messages, we can focus on various elements or

structures in choice of code, content, or treatment. We can look at channels in at least three ways: as coupling mechanisms, as vehicles, or as vehicle-carriers.

Suggestions for Thought and Discussion

1. In this chapter it was suggested that language affects thought. We can only think about things that we have named. The ways in which we think are determined in part by the ways in which our language is structured. What are the implications of this suggestion for the following areas:

   a. communication among people from nations in which different languages are spoken;
   b. communication between people of widely different educational levels;
   c. development of critical thinking in the child;
   d. correction of fallacious thinking in adults.

2. Examine your own communication experience. Can you find an example of communication which was affected by the source's attitudes toward himself? toward his subject matter? toward his receiver?

3. Is it correct to say that knowledge increases communication ability? Can a person know too much to be able to communicate what he knows effectively? Why do you answer the way that you do? What is the optimum relationship between knowledge and ability to communicate that knowledge?

4. What is the distinction between monadic and dyadic approaches to analysis? In your own vocabulary, can you find words which you use to refer to monadic characteristics? Do you have words which you use to refer to dyadic relationships? When should a particular concept be defined monadically? dyadically?

5. What are the implications of the discussion of elements and structure? How can we know reality? How can we determine what is real and what is not? How can we be sure that we are operating at the most desirable level of analysis in choosing elements and structure?

6. Discuss the question of the relative importance of form and content. In the musical arts, which is more important? In painting? In writing? In speaking? How can we distinguish between form and content? Which is more important: having something to say or saying it well?

7. What is the relationship between the intent of a message and the content of a message?

8. List as many of the media of communication as you can. Can these media be classified under the boat-docks meaning of channel discussed in this chapter? What are the advantages and disadvantages of talking about communication channels as human senses rather than as media such as television, magazines, etc.?

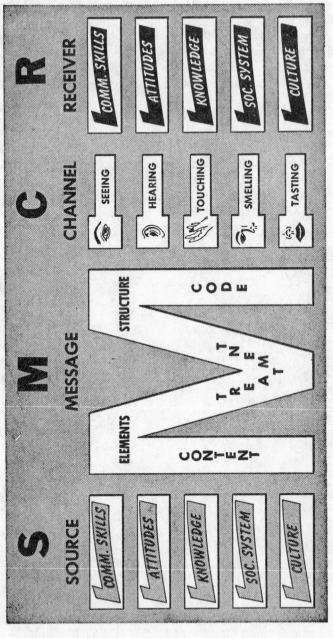

A model of the ingredients in communication.

CHAPTER 4

Learning

COMMUNICATION IN A
PERSONAL CONTEXT

THE Source-Message-Channel-Receiver model of the communication process emphasizes the importance of a thorough understanding of human behavior as a prerequisite to communication analysis. If communication is intended to affect behavior, we need to understand the variables and processes underlying behavior and behavior change. Although we separate the source from the receiver in our communication model, anything we learn about one applies to the other—the source and receiver are corresponding systems. Both are human organisms who exist in similar states. An analysis of behavior from a communication point of view applies equally to communication sources and receivers.

There is more than one approach to the analysis of behavior. If we separate psychology from sociology, we primarily are separating a personal from a social approach to behavior. Stated differently, a psychological or personal approach to behavior looks for individualistic characteristics of the organism, for what goes on between the time an individual is exposed to a message and the time he responds to it. A sociological or group approach to behavior is more likely to emphasize relationships among people as determinants of behavior; e.g., how does the presence or absence of one person or group of persons affect the behavior of another person or group. A third discipline, social psychology, has developed in an attempt to bridge these interests and to relate personal and social factors that go into the communication process.

In this and the following two chapters, we shall analyze communication behavior from each of these three vantage points. It should be emphasized that they are not discrete, independent points of view. Each interacts with the others. All three are approaches to the same thing; an explanation of how, why, when, with whom, and with what consequences man behaves.

To talk about communication in a personal context is to talk in part about how people learn. Recognizing that learning is a process, we can take it apart and talk about the ingredients in learning and the relationships among them—retaining all the hesitancies and qualifications needed in any static discussion of a process.

There are differences of opinion among learning theorists on many points, agreements on others. This chapter presents only one point of view. There are others. Learning theory and research has not developed to the point where there can be agreement that all learning occurs one way and not another. The position here reflects particularly the work of learning theorists such as Hull,[1] Tolman,[2] and Osgood.[3]

STIMULUS AND RESPONSE

Our discussion of learning will use the terms "stimulus" and "response" frequently. Before we begin, it might simplify matters to develop an explicit meaning for both terms, as well as for the concept of learning itself. We can define a *stimulus* as any event which an individual is capable of sensing. In other words *a stimulus*

[1] Clark L. Hull, *Principles of Behavior*. Appleton-Century-Crofts, 1943.
[2] E. C. Tolman, *Purposive Behavior in Animals and Man*. Appleton-Century-Crofts, 1932.
[3] Charles E. Osgood, *Method and Theory in Experimental Psychology*. Oxford University Press, 1953, pp. 299–727.

is anything that a person can receive through one of his senses, anything which can produce sensation in the human organism. If x exists, and if the human organism can sense it (see it, hear it, touch it, etc.), then x is a stimulus.

We can define the term *response* in terms of a stimulus. Given an individual who has perceived a stimulus, *a response is anything that the individual does as a result of perceiving the stimulus.* A response is a reaction of the individual organism to a stimulus, behavior that is elicited by a stimulus.

The organism can and does receive a great variety of stimuli. As a result of exposure to a stimulus, the organism can and does produce an equally great variety of responses. Suppose your hand were to come in contact with a hot stove. You would jerk your hand away. In this example, the hot stove can be called the stimulus. One response to the stimulus is the removal of your hand. Suppose a friend gives you a piece of chocolate cake. You might salivate, you might smile, you might say "thank you," you might smack your lips, you might "feel good inside," you might wrap part of the cake in a piece of paper to save it for a cakeless day. In addition, your digestive system would go into action, your stomach would contract, etc. In this example, the cake can be called the stimulus. All your behaviors that are elicited by your perception of the cake can be called responses.

This will be our general meaning for the terms *stimulus* and *response.* As was suggested in the earlier discussion of elements and structure, we can define stimuli and responses at many levels. We can talk about cake in the mouth as a stimulus. We can talk about cake in an uncut stage as a stimulus. We can talk about cake in your friend's hand as a stimulus. We can even talk about the word *cake* as a stimulus. The same is true for responses. We can talk about something as specific as the contraction of your stomach muscles as a response. We can talk about something as general as your "good feeling inside" as a response.

The level at which we choose to talk about stimuli and responses is determined by our interests. If we were biochemists, we might want to talk about specific chemical changes in the body as responses to the cake. If we were testing the probable success of a new cake mix, we might be willing to settle for a phrase like "I like it," or "the cake gives me a good feeling inside" as responses.

We need to distinguish between two broad categories of response behavior. We can label one category as "*overt* responses," and the other category as "*covert* responses." An *overt* response is one that is observable, detectable, public. A *covert* response is one that occurs within the organism, that is not readily observable or detectable, that is private.

The labels of "overt" and "covert" also are not fixed or permanent. A response that is covert to the layman may be overt to the physician, the clinical psychologist, the biochemist. A response which is covert today may be overt tomorrow, as we develop better instruments of observation or detection. Yet, we shall find it useful to distinguish between these two broad response classes when we discuss learning and communication.

THE MEANING OF LEARNING

We have suggested the meanings that we will have for the terms stimulus and response. The third term that requires definition is *learning*. We can define learning as *a change in the stable relationship between* (a) *a stimulus that the individual organism perceives and* (b) *a response that the organism makes, either covertly or overtly.*

We can provide a more specific definition of learning by describing two possible situations. First, let us take Mister O, an individual who in the past has made response X to simulus A. In other words, when A is perceived by Mister O, he performs X behavior. Suppose a different stimulus, B, is presented to Mister O. If O begins to perceive B and to make some of the same responses to B that he used to make to A (namely, to do X), we can say that O has learned. In other words, if an individual transfers a response he made to one stimulus (covert or overt) to a different stimulus, we can say that he has learned.

For the second illustration; suppose that Mister O in the past has made response X to stimulus A. Suppose that when A is presented again, Mister O no longer responds with X, but he begins to respond with Y—he makes a different response (covert or overt). If O begins to make a different response to A, we can say that O has learned. More generally, if an individual begins to make a different response to a stimulus he has responded to before, we can say that he has learned.

In summary, we can define learning in this way: Given an individual who responds to a stimulus; learning occurs if the individual either (1) continues to make some of the same responses, but to a different stimulus, (2) makes a different response to the same stimulus.

This is related to communication in that the communication objective of the source often is a change in the behavior of the receiver. The source wants the receiver to change, to learn. We communicate in order to get our receivers to respond in different ways to old stimuli, or to respond in old ways to different stimuli.

Suppose you are running for political office. The voters have never been exposed to you as a stimulus. You want them to elect you, to mark x for you on the ballot. The voters have responded with an x before—it is an old response to them. They have never marked an x for you. You want them to transfer their old response, marking x, to a different stimulus—you. This is a communication situation, with a learning objective.

Take another example. Suppose you are the advertising manager for a given product. Your product has been on sale for some time. People have not bought it. In learning theory terms, people have perceived your product (a stimulus), and have responded to it by saying, "No, thank you." Your objective is to get the consumer to change his response to the stimulus: you want him to change his response to your product from "No, thank you" to "I want it." This too is a communication-learning situation.

As communicators, we often have purposes that involve learning by our receivers. We want them either to change their responses to an existing stimulus or to transfer existing responses to a changed stimulus. When this is our objective, we need to understand as much as we can about the principles of human learning, about the process that goes on in the organism between the time the individual perceives a stimulus and the time he responds to it.

Sometimes we do not need to change the stimulus-response relationships for our receivers. Our purpose may be merely to select a stimulus which previously has elicited the desired response. For example, a political party may select a candidate the voters have approved in the past. Even in this kind of situation, when we are not intending to produce learning, we need to understand the learning process so that we may know how to select and present our message.

As a final example, suppose that you are the advertising manager for a highly acceptable product. In other words, many people already are saying "I want it" about your product. In this situation, you may not be interested primarily in changing behaviors, in developing new stimulus-response connections. Your major purpose is to strengthen the existing stimulus-response relationship. Again, you need to understand the learning process if you are to be successful in accomplishing your objectives.

The Learning Process

We defined a stimulus as anything which the organism has the capacity to perceive, to sense. Obviously, a stimulus has to be presented to the organism before the organism can respond to it; therefore, the existence of a stimulus is the first requirement for learning.

If a stimulus is to affect the organism, the organism must have more than just the capacity to perceive it—the stimulus must actually be perceived. We can say, then, that the second step in the learning process is the perception of a stimulus by the organism—the focusing of one or more of the senses on some stimulus.

From our earlier discussion, it should be clear that some covert or overt response is essential to learning. When learning, the organism responds to the stimulus that it perceives. A response is necessary if we are to have learning. But this is not a sufficient condition. The organism is capable of producing many responses to stimuli without benefit of learning. For example, if a puff of air is blown across your eye (stimulus), you blink your eyelids (response). If food is put into your mouth (stimulus), you salivate (response). If you touch a hot stove (stimulus), you jerk your hand away (response). In each case, the response to the stimulus is reflexive. The organism has no control over the response—it just happens. Such stimulus-response (S-R) connections are built into the organism. We refer to such behavior as "wired-in" behavior, or reflexive behavior.

stimulus ➡ response

In the early development of psychology, some theorists thought that all human behavior could be explained with the simple S-R model used for reflexive behavior. Certain stimuli are presented—certain overt responses occur. Further research has indicated that this simple model is inadequate to explain much of human behavior. Man is a more complicated animal than a simple S-R diagram would indicate.

Wired-in behaviors are themselves not learned. Yet they are important to learning. They are the only responses available to the organism when he begins to learn. As small infants, we all possessed certain responses which we made to certain stimuli. To produce learning in our own children, we get them to make these responses (or some of them) to new stimuli. This is one of our illustrations of learning, the making of an old response to a new stimulus.

For learning to occur, for behavior to change, the original stimulus-response relationship has to be broken. Something has to happen between the time that the stimulus is perceived and the time that the response is made. The organism has to make certain decisions. The brain, the central nervous system, has to function. The stimulus has to be not only perceived, but *interpreted*. For learning to occur,

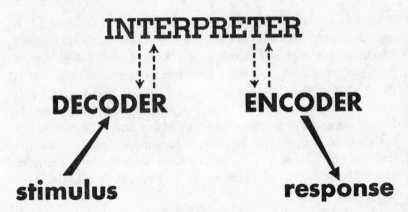

the organism often has to perceive a stimulus, interpret it, and respond to it. The organism has to interpret the stimuli it perceives, has to exert some control over the responses it makes.

In summary, we have said that the learning process involves first the presence of a stimulus: anything that the organism is capable of sensing. Second, the organism must actually sense the object, must perceive it. Third, the stimulus as perceived must be interpreted by the organism. Fourth, the organism must produce some response to the stimulus, as perceived and interpreted. At least one more condition is required before we say the organism has learned.

We said earlier that learning involves a changed stimulus-response relationship. When we use the term "relationship," we imply some permanence, some stability over time. In other words, we want more than a one-time response to a stimulus before we are willing to say that the response has been learned. We want the response to be made regularly, every time the stimulus is presented. When the organism changes its responses to an old stimulus, or attaches an old response to a different stimulus, permanence is not yet implied. The organism must decide whether it will continue to make this new response or to attach a response to this new stimulus.

The thing that the organism does is to observe the *consequences* of the response. It checks to see what happens to it as a result of the response. The first response that the organism makes is usually tentative, hesitant, cautious. We can look on first responses as *trial responses*—the organism tries a given response to see what happens. At this point, the organism observes the consequences of the trial response. *A trial response is retained if the organism perceives the consequences to be rewarding. A trial response is discarded if the organism does not perceive the consequences to be rewarding.*

We cannot say that a person has learned just because he makes a response once or twice. Learning does not occur until the response becomes *habitual,* until it is repeated whenever the stimulus is presented. The determinant of learning, of the development of habit, is *reward.* We repeat responses which are rewarded. We do not repeat responses which are not rewarded. In each case, we observe the consequences and decide if we benefit from the consequences of the response or if we suffer.

Learning usually is not a one-time process. Each of us continually receives stimuli, interprets them, responds to them, observes the consequences of the response, reinterprets, makes new responses, reinterprets, and so on. Gradually, as we receive the same stimulus over and over again, as we make the same response to the stimulus and observe the same rewarding consequences, an S-R relationship develops. We get in the *habit* of responding in a certain way to a certain stimulus.

We have now introduced all the ingredients of the learning process. They include:

1. Presentation of a stimulus;
2. Perception of the stimulus by the organism;
3. Interpretation of the stimulus;
4. Trial response to the stimulus;
5. Perception of the consequences of the trial response;
6. Re-interpretation of the consequences, and the making of further responses;
7. Development of a stable stimulus-response relationship—habit.

Once a habit has been developed we cease to interpret the stimulus any more. We begin to respond to it automatically, without

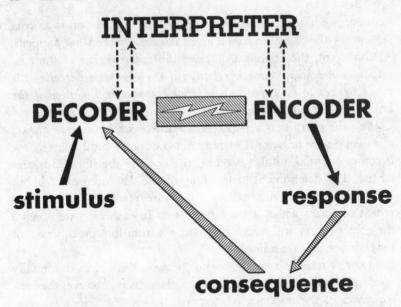

thought, without analysis. Although these S-R relationships have been learned, they become similar to the original wired-in relationships that controlled our behavior in infancy.

Let us look at one or two simple examples of habitual, noninterpretive S-R relationships. Suppose you hear the words "Jack and Jill." What response might you make? Probably, "went up the hill." Suppose you hear the words "Fourscore and." What response might you make? Probably, "seven years ago." You do not have to think about them—you just produce a response. At one time, you learned (perhaps painfully) that "went up the hill" comes after "Jack and Jill." You learned to make the "correct" response and you were rewarded for it. Eventually the S-R relationship became habitual; you did not have to think about it any more. The same is true for "fourscore and seven years ago," and many similar verbal connections.

We can look on this kind of behavior as "short-circuiting" within the organism. A stimulus does not travel over the entire nervous system—it jumps circuits and responses are produced. Much of our behavior is of the short-circuiting variety. We do not think about how to tie our shoes, put on our clothes, walk, eat, be well-mannered, etc. We have learned to respond automatically to some stimuli—our responses have become habitual. When we speak, we do not think about how to pronounce most of our words, about which word comes where in the sentence. Again, we have practiced speaking so many times that the responses have become habitual, although the original learning process may have been very time-consuming.

Much of man's behavior is habitual. People talk about man as a "creature of habit." This is true. The development of habits is essential to everyday living. We need to develop habits in order to reduce the effort required to make responses. If we had to think about everything we do, we would not get anything done. Habits are sometimes useful and sometimes dangerous. The argument over the relative utility or danger of habits is interesting, but not necessary to the present discussion. Habits are essential to human behavior, and need to be taken into account.

The notion of habit is related to that of communication. When we want to produce learning in a receiver, we must break some existing habit patterns and establish new ones. We must eliminate short-circuiting, force reinterpretation of a stimulus. Sometimes, of course, we do not want to produce learning. We only want to *utilize* an existing habit pattern. At other times we may want to *strengthen* a habit pattern which exists but is not strongly developed. All communication is related to the habits of the receiver, the ways in which he tends to respond to certain stimuli.

If we are concerned with communication, we need to understand the principles of habit development. What are some of the factors which determine the strength or weakness of habits? What are some of the things that affect the chances that an organism will make certain responses to a certain stimulus and will not make other responses?

Most of what we know has come from research with animals other than human; nevertheless, we do have some guiding principles which work with humans as well. We cannot present a detailed discussion of the determinants of habit strength in people. We can discuss a few of the major principles that are useful in analyzing habits as they are related to communication.

Determinants of Habit Strength[4]

We have taken the position that a habit is a relationship between a stimulus and the response which the individual makes to that stimulus and for which he has been rewarded. Assuming the existence of a stimulus that has been perceived, and a rewarded response that has been made to that stimulus, we can isolate at least five factors that affect the development of habit strength.

1. *Frequency of rewarded repetition.* The strength of a habit is determined in part by the total number of times that a particular S-R connection has been made and rewarded. *Each time a stimulus is presented, a response is made, and the response is rewarded, habit is strengthened.* The more repetitions, the stronger the habit—if the response is rewarded.

The notion of reward is vital here. If responses to a stimulus are not rewarded, the habit is not strengthened—it is weakened. In fact, if a stimulus is presented enough times, and the response to the stimulus is not rewarded, the S-R relationship is broken. The habit is extinguished. *Frequently rewarded S-R connections strengthen habit. Frequently nonrewarded S-R connections weaken habit.*

2. *Isolation of the S-R relationship.* The strength of a particular stimulus-response connection is determined in part by the extent to which the stimulus produces other responses, or to which other stimuli produce the same response. In other words, if the organism makes a particular response (X) to a given stimulus (A), the relationship between A and X will be strengthened if the organism does not give X as a response to other stimuli as well. The relationship will also be strengthened between A and X if the organism does not give other responses to A as well.

3. *Amount of reward.* We have said that a response to a stimulus

---

[4] Material in this section is adapted from Charles E. Osgood, *Method and Theory in Experimental Psychology.* Oxford University Press, 1953, pp. 328–336.

must be rewarded if the S-R relationship is to be strengthened. An organism can receive varying amounts of reward from a response. True, any reward strengthens the habit; however, *the greater the reward, the more the habit tends to be strengthened*. If S-R relationships are to develop, the response should be rewarded as much as possible.

4. *Time between response and reward.* We know that response must be rewarded if it is to be maintained. We also know that the amount of reward is important. Another factor is the time interval between response and reward.

When an individual responds, he perceives the consequences of his response. *The faster he perceives that the consequences of a response are rewarding, the more likely he is to retain the response.* In short, reward should be given as soon as possible—preferably immediately.

5. *Effort required to make the response.* Some responses require more energy than others. We can argue that man operates on what has been called a principle of least effort. By this we mean that man does not want to expend any more energy than he has to in order to achieve his goals. From this, it follows that *responses that are easy to make are more likely to be retained than are responses that are hard to make*—other things being equal. The less the effort required to make a response, the more likely that the response will be retained, and that the S-R connection will be strengthened.

In summary, we have suggested that learning occurs if and only if a stimulus is presented, perceived, interpreted, and responded to. In addition, the organism perceives the response to have some consequence. If the consequence is rewarding, the response is retained. If the consequence is not rewarding, the response is discarded. We have suggested five basic principles which strengthen S-R relationships, five determinants of the development of habits. They are:

1. Frequency of repetition of the S-R relationship;
2. Isolation of the S-R relationship from competing S-R connections;

3. Amount of reward;
4. Time between response and reward;
5. Effort required to make the response.

These are only five principles. There are many others. In fact, all the findings of scientific research pertinent to the process of human learning can be of use in analyzing communication. These five were selected because they are extremely important. Here is an illustration or two of how each can be used in analyzing the process of communication.

1. FREQUENCY. We use the concept of frequency in S-R connections whenever we try to learn a new skill, to perform a new task. We usually refer to the principle of frequency by the term "practice." We say that practice makes perfect. From our earlier discussion, we can see that practice does not necessarily make perfect. Only rewarded practice makes perfect—unrewarded practice makes for no practice at all in time. Yet it is true that continued practice which is rewarded does improve the S-R relationship.

Can you recall how you first learned to understand or speak English, or any language? Words or sentences in the language were said to you (a stimulus). You responded with other words, or by pointing to the objects named by the words, or by performing the behaviors called for by the sentence (a response). When you gave the "correct" response, your parents or your teacher smiled, patted you on the back, or gave you an "A." These were intended as rewards. When you gave the incorrect response, you were not rewarded. Gradually, you learned to make the correct responses, to develop the right habits.

This process was repeated—over and over again. If we forget the tremendous number of practice sessions involved in language learning, it becomes difficult to believe that a child could learn a language. To learn any language, you need constant practice—frequent repetition of stimuli (utterances in the language) and frequent rewarding of your correct responses.

Some of the best examples of the use of the principle of frequency in communication come from advertising. George Washington Hill, the late president of the American Tobacco Company (Lucky Strikes), made the principle of frequency famous in advertising. Today, the slogans of advertising are household words. Many people cannot name their senator or describe crucial issues of the day, but they know which car has "the forward look," which cigarette is "for the thinking man," which soap "makes you feel really clean."

Messages such as this, repeated frequently, increase the chances that we think of the sponsor's product (make the "right" response) when we want an automobile, a cigarette, a soap. We will be more likely to purchase at least one of these as a trial response. The primary mission of advertising is to get people to make a trial response.

Of course, advertising messages serve another function. True, they increase the chances that we will make a trial response, buying the product once. They also tell us what kinds of reward we will get from using the product. If we use one brand of cold cream, we will become engaged. If we buy one kind of car, we will feel young again. If we smoke one brand of cigarette, we will enjoy smoking again. Advertising attempts to structure our perceptions of the possible rewards to be gained from use of the product.

In communication, stimulus-response connections can be strengthened or weakened by use of the principle of repetition, of frequency. If we reward a response, we strengthen the habit. If we do not reward a response, we weaken the habit—eventually we extinguish it. In either case the frequency of presentation of the stimulus, with or without a rewarded response, affects the strength of a habit.

2. ISOLATION. At any given time, each of us usually has a choice of stimuli that can be perceived. We can attend to several different public media of communication, we can talk with people, we can think by ourselves, etc.

If a communication source can isolate the receiver, can restrict the messages which are available to the receiver, the source can increase the chances that the receiver will attend to the source's message rather than other messages. We can see examples of stimulus isolation in many totalitarian countries if we examine the government's control of the public media of communication. Governments may not allow private commercial media of communication to operate, to transmit messages which compete with the government's own messages. The government may censor stories in the newspaper, may control news content so that people in the country can only get one set of messages, one point of view about the news.

In our own country, some critics of the media have become concerned over the increased concentration of newspaper ownership in the hands of a few people. Increasing numbers of American cities have only one newspaper. Other newspapers do not reach the city in any quantity. The reasons for this in the U. S. are economic (profit margins) rather than political; nevertheless, *reduction of the available stimuli increases the effectiveness of the stimuli that remain.*

Some governments go to great lengths to eliminate competing stimuli. In Europe, many of the Soviet satellite governments "jam" the air against Radio Free Europe or the Voice of America. One of the most extreme illustrations of the use of stimulus elimination occurred during the communist occupation of Seoul, Korea, during the Korean War. Radio Seoul is one of the most powerful transmitters in Southeast Asia. When the Communists took the city of Seoul, they confiscated all radios in the city. Even though the Communists now had control of the chief transmitter, they rejected the power that this would give them over the South Korean people. They took radios away from the citizens of Seoul to keep the citizens from listening to other, clandestine stations on the side. The penalty for keeping a radio, for listening to any station was death. The communists preferred to abandon radio as a vehicle for presenting their messages, because they feared the effects of non-isolation.

3. REWARD LEVEL. We have said that responses must be rewarded if they are to be retained. We can add to this. The more reward we get from a response, the more likely that we will retain the response.

Suppose you are the foreman or personnel manager of an industrial plant. You want a particular worker to increase his productivity. When he makes the correct response (increases his output) you reward him—you give him a raise, you compliment him on his work, you publicly acknowledge his contribution, you promote him to a more important job. All these consequences of his response are intended to be rewarding to him. The bigger the raise, the more the reward. The more enthusiastic the compliment, the more the reward. The more public your acknowledgement of his contribution, the more the reward. The bigger the promotion, the more the reward.

This example illustrates one caution that needs to be applied. *Reward has to be defined in terms of the receiver*. In rewarding people, it sometimes is difficult to know what kinds of consequences they will find rewarding; however, once you have located the type of consequence which will serve as a reward, you can increase the strength of the S-R connection by increasing the reward level.

In our everyday interpersonal relations, we continually give or withhold rewards from other people—our supervisors, colleagues, subordinates, family, friends, etc. All of us recognize the importance of "giving credit where credit is due." We often fail to utilize the credit-giving situation. We provide the right kind of reward, but we do not provide enough of it.

4. REWARD DELAY. The presence of reward is vital to effective communication, as is the amount. So is the time lag. *When a communication receiver gets immediate rewards from his response, he is more likely to retain the response*. If his rewards are delayed, the response strength is less likely to increase.

Schramm has utilized the concept of response–reward time span in predicting the readership of news stories.[5] Schramm suggests that some material in the newspaper provides delayed reward for the reader. In this category, Schramm includes news about public affairs, science, social problems, etc. These are areas in which the

[5] Wilbur Schramm, "The nature of news," *Journalism Quarterly*, 26: 259–269, 1949

receiver often has an instrumental rather than a consummatory purpose. He learns these things because he hopes to use them later.

Schramm suggests that other kinds of news provide more immediate reward (consummatory purpose). In this category he includes news of crime, disasters, sports, society information, etc. Schramm found that people vary with respect to their response-reward span. Some people can wait longer for rewards than can others. Newspaper readers at low education levels were least likely to read material which provided delayed reward. People with a good deal of formal schooling were most likely to read material which provided delayed reward.

Delayed-reward material may actually increase the tensions of the reader for the moment, but the reader is undeterred because he believes that the reward will come eventually. It is important to point out that in the Schramm study college graduates and grade-school graduates both read more of the information which provided immediate rewards. They differed only in that college graduates also read a good deal of delayed-reward material.

Two important facts can be drawn from the research findings. First, material that provided immediate reward was more likely to be read by everybody. Second, delayed-reward material was read more by people of high education levels than it was by people who had not attended school as long.

Other things being equal, responses that are rewarded immediately are more likely to be strengthened than are responses that are rewarded less rapidly. We need to keep this in mind when we try to provide rewards for our communication receivers. Even if the final reward must be delayed, communication effectiveness is increased if a group of sub-goals (small immediate rewards) can be established for the receiver. If we work on a task which requires three years to complete, we should set up a group of small sub-tasks which can be completed in shorter lengths of time. Completion of these sub-tasks provides some reward, and these rewards sustain us until the entire task is completed.

5. RESPONSE EFFORT. *Other things being equal, the organism*

makes responses which require little effort and avoids responses which require much effort. When we communicate, we will be more effective if we can reduce the effort required by the receiver to make the desired response.

Again, we can find good examples of this in advertising communication. When you receive a piece of direct-mail advertising, it often includes a stamped self-addressed return envelope. Why is this? The communication source (the advertiser) knows that it is easier for you to respond if you do not have to find an envelope, address it, and put a stamp on it. He makes it easier for you to make the correct response. Experience indicates that more goods are sold when return envelopes are included. The reduction of effort increases the chances of the "right" response being made.

The same thing is true with many radio and TV commercials. One kind of commercial includes a statement such as "Send no money, just your name and address," or "don't bother to write, just pick up the phone and call Riverside 1-2-3-4." These messages are designed to reduce the effort required to make the correct response. Again, some research indicates that sales (correct responses) go up when the consumer does not have to pay his money right away or can merely telephone his response instead of writing a letter.

A third example comes from the field of public opinion research. When we conduct opinion research, we often mail questionnaires to people. We have learned two things. First, if we include a stamped return envelope, returns go up. Second, if we make the questionnaire shorter, if we permit the person to make check marks instead of writing sentences, returns go up. In fact, merely making the questionnaire *appear* to be shorter (easier) increases returns— even though it may be just as "hard" to complete as a longer questionnaire.

In summary, we have introduced five principles of effective communication that can be drawn from research evidence on the determinants of habit strength in the individual. In constructing messages, in receiving messages, or in analyzing other people's communication, we need to take into account:

1. The frequency of presentation of the message—with reward, and without reward.
2. The competition of a given stimulus or response with other stimuli and responses.
3. The amount of reward which was perceived as a consequence of the response.
4. The time lag between the making of the response and the reward which was received.
5. The amount of effort which the receiver perceived as necessary to make the desired response.

LEARNING AND REWARD

Throughout our discussion, we have used the term *reward* frequently. The concept of reward is central to habit strength, to communication effectiveness. Individuals do not respond unless they expect their responses to be rewarding, to have rewarding consequences. Reward determines the strength of our habits, the speed and extent of our learning.

We can go further than this. Even the selection and interpretation of a stimulus is related to our expectations of reward. We perceive and interpret stimuli when we believe that we can respond to them in ways that will be rewarding. If we do not have an expectation of reward, we often refuse to even select and interpret a stimulus.

For a better understanding of what is meant by reward, we can turn to Dewey's concept of "self-interest." Dewey argued that man only behaves in ways that he perceives to be in his own self-interest.[6] He does things he believes will help himself, and avoids doing things that he believes will hurt himself. Each of us approaches any communication situation with what we can call a "what's in this for me" attitude.

As communication sources or receivers, we want to meet our needs, satisfy our drives, accomplish our purposes. We have said that our major purpose is the desire to affect—to have influence

---

[6] John Dewey, *Human Nature and Conduct*. The Modern Library, 1930, pp. 134–139.

over self, others, and our physical environment. To understand the nature of reward, we need to specify in more detail the concept of affect.

Man's first perceptions of the world are vague, hazy, without form. From the beginning, he attempts to impose a structure on what he perceives; he tries to formalize, to organize his perceptions. Much of the theory about human behavior is based on the following assumption: man labors under physiological ("wired-in") tensions in the presence of ambiguity, formlessness. Apparently, his desire to affect is a desire to reduce his own tension by reducing ambiguity, reducing uncertainty about the nature of his environment.

As we discussed earlier, the ways in which man chooses to structure the world are determined in part by his own intelligence, his attitudes, his knowledge, the values that are transmitted to him through his culture, his membership in social organizations, etc. The method of structuring may differ from person to person. The need to impose a structure, to reduce ambiguity, is common to all men.

Man tries to affect by imposing structure, by giving meaning to his environment. In the absence of structure, he is tense. Increasing his uncertainty increases his tensions, reducing his uncertainty reduces his tensions. If we accept one further assumption, that man seeks a state of reduced physiological tension, it follows that he will seek situations which reduce uncertainty, and avoid situations which increase uncertainty.

These relationships of the concepts of certainty and tension underlie the theory of homeostasis in education, Osgood and Tannenbaum's theory of congruity in communication,[7] and Festinger's theory of cognitive dissonance-consonance in human behavior.[8] They also underlie the concept of reward.

We can go further than the mere assertion that man desires to

[7] Charles E. Osgood and Percy Tannenbaum, "Attitude change and the principle of congruity," in *Process and Effects of Mass Communication* (Wilbur Schramm, ed.). University of Illinois Press, 1954, pp. 251–260.

[8] Leon Festinger, *A Theory of Cognitive Dissonance.* Row, Peterson and Company, 1957.

impose structure. All of us are aware of the five senses that we discussed as communication channels: seeing, hearing, tasting, smelling, and touching. It can be argued that man has at least one more sense: the sense of balance.

Physiologically, the sense of balance permits us to adjust ourselves to our physical environment. Correspondingly, the psychological sense of balance produces the desire for a consistency of structure in our perceptions. In other words, man not only exerts influence by imposing structure on his environment; he also attempts to affect by making the various structures he imposes consistent with each other.

It is from this argument that we derive the concept of reward. Man perceives a response as rewarding to the extent that it helps him to develop a consistent structuring of his universe. He attends to those stimuli which he expects will be of use to him in structuring his environment and avoids those which he does not perceive to be of use.

Both Dewey's concept of "self-interest" and the concept of "reward" have been interpreted too narrowly by some theorists. When we say that man approaches a communication situation with a "what's in this for me" attitude, or with a "how will this develop my self-interests" attitude, we do not mean to restrict ourselves to a narrow hedonistic concept of pleasure vs. pain, although this too is important. What we "get" from a communication situation depends on our own values, the society and culture in which we operate, our neurological capacity for prolonged tension, the time tolerance we have that permits rewards to be "delayed."

What we have suggested is that the concept of reward needs to be looked on as the result of combining all the possibilities of affect that the receiver sees as a consequence of a particular response. Some of these consequences are immediate and obvious, others may be delayed and less apparent. One of the crucial dimensions of affect is the need of the organism to reduce his internal tension by developing a consistent structure for the environment in which he operates. In all cases, reward has to be defined in the context of the person making the response. What is rewarding for the source may or may not be rewarding for the receiver.

The consequences of a given response are not all of the "plus" variety. The same response may produce consequences that are "minus" as well. The taking of money that has been earned by another has "plus" factors (e.g., it reduces uncertainty about your financial security, it enables you to buy things you want). It also has "minus" factors (e.g., you may be arrested, you may have a feeling of guilt, you may lose the respect of people who are important to you). In a less serious vein, staying up all night playing poker with friends has plus factors in that your friends seem to like you for it, approve of your doing it. It also has minus factors in that your wife may disapprove, you may lose money you cannot afford to lose, your boss may fire you the next day for sleeping on the job. The field of ethics is concerned with the bases for decision in situations where any given choice of behavior has both plus and minus factors.

All these things need to be taken into account in determining reward. The determination of what things are "plus" and what things are "minus" is one of the major concerns of the behavioral sciences. In any communication situation, we select topics, treat messages, choose channels in part on the basis of the potential reward for the receiver. As communicators, we need to remember that *the response we want from a receiver must be rewarding to him or it will not be learned.*

We can look at reward as the result of adding all the plus and minus factors that are involved in the intended response. We emphasize plus factors in effective communication and we minimize minus factors. *As plus factors increase and minus factors decrease, communication becomes more effective.*

In summary, we have said that man's basic purpose in communicating is to affect, to influence himself, his social and physical environment. A response is rewarding if its consequences are perceived by the responder as increasing his influence, as being in his own self-interest. In addition to the obvious dimensions of influence, we have suggested that one of man's basic desires is to reduce uncertainty, to impose a structure on the world, and to make this structure consistent. When he does this, his internal tensions are reduced. When uncertainty is increased, tensions increase. The organism strives toward the reduction of tension, a state of internal balance.

For those interested in producing learning, this presents a paradox. We have said that the receiver strives toward a reduction of tension, an increase in certainty. Yet, learning requires a temporary increase in tension, a reduction in certainty. *The only time a stimulus-response relationship is altered is when the organism interprets the existing relationship as less rewarding than a possible alternative relationship.*

Learning requires the breaking of an existing stimulus-response relationship and the substitution of a new one. This *creates* tension within the receiver. The receiver does not welcome an increase in tension; he strives for *reduction* of tension. If this is so, how can people learn? How can communication produce a change in behavior?

In order to avoid this paradox, we need to distinguish between creative and uncreative tension. Any message intended to convince the receiver that his present stimulus-response relationships are inadequate will produce tension within the receiver. If the receiver can perceive that a new relationship may eventually produce greater certainty, allow him to have an even greater effect, he will tolerate the temporary reduction of certainty in the hope of greater certainty or affective potential in the future. If this occurs, we can label the tension as creative. If, however, the receiver does not perceive the possibility that a new relationship will be of more use to him, tension is still produced, but it is not creative. It does not produce learning. It produces avoidance of the message, rejection of the source, or mental imbalance on the part of the receiver. *Learning requires the production of tension, the reduction of certainty within the organism—but the tension must be creative if it is to be productive.*

What is reward? Let us assume a situation in which a receiver has related a given stimulus to a given response. He perceives his response to have certain consequences. Some of these consequences increase his ability to affect, others may reduce it. Some may increase his ability to structure his environment, to reduce uncertainty, others may not. The total of these plus and minus factors, as perceived by the receiver, determine the reward value of a given response.

How does reward operate in learning? Learning requires the breaking of a given stimulus-response relationship and the substitution of another one. The receiver interprets the consequences of each relationship and selects the one which he perceives as having the greater potential reward to him, within his own value system and intellectual ability to project.

In doing this, he increases his own psychological tension. If he does not perceive some possibility of increased reward from the new relationship, he will not consider it, but will continue to behave in the way to which he was accustomed. Learning requires the arousal of tension, the reduction of certainty—but the tension must be creative in that the receiver perceives the possibility of a later reduction of tension by creating a more consistent pattern of certainty, a more useful structure of reality.

Let us approach reward from another direction. One dictionary defines reward as "something given in return." Reward gives us greater power to affect, greater ability to structure the world. What do we give in return? The receiver gives *energy, work, time.* When we speak or listen, when we write or read, when we perform any communication task, we expend energy.

We have said that man operates to conserve his energy (the principle of least effort). The more energy required to make a response, the less likely is it that that response will be made—other things being equal. Required energy works as a deterrent to learning. Reward works as a stimulant to learning.

When we decide to perform or not perform a given communication behavior, we base our decision on the relationship between amount of reward and amount of energy required. As Cottrell points out in *Energy and Society*,[9] people and societies differ in the amount of energy available to them; therefore, they differ in the amount of learning or changes in behavior that they can tolerate. In any given situation, however, behavior change is determined by reward expected vs. energy required.

Schramm has developed this relationship as a predictor of attention paid to communication.[10] He defines the *fraction of selection* of a message, from the point of view of the receiver, as:

$$\text{Fraction of Selection} = \frac{\text{Expected Reward}}{\text{Expected Energy Required}}$$

This concept can be broadened to include more than the selection of a message. It applies to interpretation and learning as well. We decide to perform those behaviors which we expect will be "worth the effort." We decide not to perform behaviors when we believe they are "not worth the effort." We can define the *fraction of decision* as:

$$\text{Fraction of Decision} = \frac{\text{Expected Reward}}{\text{Expected Energy Required}}$$

The use of this fraction is helpful in practical communication situations. Although it is difficult, if not impossible, to put quantitative values in the fraction, the implication is of value. The greater the reward an individual perceives in making a response, the more energy he will expend (if he has it available) to make the response. As perceived reward decreases, required energy must also decrease if the response is to be made.

Communication effectiveness can be increased in one or both of two ways: increasing reward or reducing energy. The nature of reward is quite complex. It cannot be interpreted merely as a short-range material or physical benefit. Within the broad context of reward, however, the principle that "it is more blessed to give than

[9] Fred Cottrell, *Energy and Society*. McGraw-Hill, 1955.
[10] Wilbur Schramm, "How communication works," in *The Process and Effects of Mass Communication* (Wilbur Schramm, ed.). University of Illinois Press, 1954, p. 19.

to receive" needs to be re-assessed—man does not behave on this principle unless he gets more from the giving than he does from the receiving.

We can turn our attention from a discussion of the nature of learning and its implications for communication to a discussion of the relationship between the two processes themselves. In the following section, the thesis will be offered that our earlier model of the communication process encompasses the model of learning. We can look at learning in the same way that we look at communication.

Communication and Learning: The Similarity of Processes

We have discussed two models, one of communication and the other of learning. Clearly, an understanding of the process of learning has many implications for a theory of communication. It can be argued that the relationship extends beyond this, and that the model of learning is itself similar or equivalent to the model of communication. In order to test this thesis, we can compare the ingredients and relationships within each of the two models.

In our discussion of the communication process we said that communication requires six basic ingredients: a source, an encoder, a message, a channel, a decoder, and a receiver. The source encodes a message. The encoded message is transmitted in some channel. The message is decoded, and interpreted by the receiver.

In our discussion of the learning process, we said that learning requires five basic ingredients: a stimulus, perception of the stimulus by the organism, interpretation of the stimulus, a trial response, and a rewarding consequence of the trial response. A stimulus is perceived by the organism. The stimulus, as perceived, is interpreted by the organism. A response is made. The response is perceived as having consequences. If the consequences are rewarding, the organism retains the response. As he gets in the habit of making the same response to the stimulus, he develops an S-R relationship.

Basically, these are not two different processes. In large part, we can translate one of these process models into the other. The two models represent only a difference in point of view. A learning model usually starts with the decoding function, a communication model usually starts with a discussion of purpose. That is the primary distinction between the two, and it is not important theoretically. In order to demonstrate this, let us look at a sample communication situation.

Suppose you are writing a letter. First you have some idea, some purpose for writing. At this point you are operating as a communication source. Your central nervous system tells your writing mechanism to encode a message, a letter. The encoder produces a written message. But you do not send this message to the person to whom you are writing—you read it yourself first.

When you read your own letter, you are engaging in one form of intrapersonal (one-person) communication. Your decoder re-translates the message back into a nervous impulse, and sends it to your central nervous system. Your central nervous system responds to the decoded message—the central nervous system operates as a communication receiver.

All of the communication ingredients have been included, but the source, the encoder, the decoder, and the receiver are all contained in you. Only the message and the channel (the written letter) are external to you.

As a receiver, your central nervous system may be critical of the message. It may respond by disapproving of certain sentences, by not liking the way part of the letter was written. If this is the case, your central nervous system creates a new, corrected message. *Now it is operating as a source again.* The new message is sent to the encoder, a new message is produced. It too can be decoded by you, again sent to the central nervous system, and so on.

This kind of internal, intrapersonal communication goes on continually. Each of us has the capacity to operate as both a source and a receiver, as both an encoder and a decoder, at the same time. We can communicate with ourselves.

Using communication with self as an example, it is easy to demonstrate the relationships between the communication model and the learning model.

A *message* can be thought of as a *stimulus*. When you *decode* the message you are *perceiving* it as a stimulus. When you *encode* a new message, you are making an overt *response* to the stimulus, as perceived and interpreted. These three steps in the processes of learning and of communication are equivalent. Only one other set of steps in the two processes needs to be related.

We have said that learning requires *interpretation* of the perceived stimulus. We also have said that intrapersonal communication requires the organism to operate as both a *receiver* and a *source*. The important point is: *these two statements are equivalent.* Our meaning for the term "interpretation" is the same as our meaning for the phrase "operates as both a receiver and a source."

When you interpret a stimulus, you make a response to it (operate as a receiver). The response you make is *covert,* it is internal, it is nonobservable, at least with currently available observation techniques. We can only hypothesize that the organism responds internally (covertly) to a perceived stimulus, but this hypothesis seems sound theoretically.

Your internal covert response is part of interpretation, but not all of it. The organism also creates a new stimulus as it interprets (operates as a source). The internal response that the organism makes serves to stimulate the organism; it forces the organism to create a new message. *Interpretation includes the internal covert response which the organism makes to a perceived stimulus. Interpretation also includes the stimulus which the organism creates as a result of having made the internal response.* When we interpret a stimulus, we operate as communication receivers *and* as communication sources.

We now have related all the ingredients of the two processes. *The process of intrapersonal communication is equivalent to the process of human learning.* We perceive (decode). We interpret (serve as a receiver and as a source). We produce an overt response (encode). The stimuli we perceive and the responses we make are included in our meaning for the term "message." We can place the two models side by side. For each step in one model there is an analogous step in the other.

When we talk about learning, we usually start with the perception of a stimulus (decoding a message). When we talk about communication, we usually start with the intentions of a source (interpretation). Because of these differing starting points, we often overlook the fact that we are talking about communication when we analyze learning. Both are processes. Neither has a required beginning or a required end. Both are continuous, dynamic, ongoing.

When we remember that both learning and communication are processes, it is easier for us to see that they are equivalent. The six ingredients that are involved in learning have their analogues in the ingredients that are involved in communication.

Ingredients in Learning	*Ingredients in Communication*
1. Organism	1. Channel
2. Stimulus	2. Message
3. Perception of stimulus	3. Decoder
4. Interpretation of stimulus	4. Receiver-source
5. Overt response to stimulus	5. Encoder
6. Consequent of response	6. Feedback

FEEDBACK

We have introduced one new term, feedback. When an individual communicates with himself, the messages he encodes are *fed back* into his system by his decoder—this is what we call *feedback*.

We might better understand our meaning for the term feedback by looking at a public address communication system. You probably have experienced the situation in which somebody talked into a microphone, and what he said was transmitted by a loud-speaker. If the volume of the public address system was turned too high, or the loud-speaker was too close to the microphone, some of the sound was fed back into the microphone, came out again—and produced a loud noise.

Engineers refer to the re-entrance of the sound from the speaker to the microphone as feedback. We mean the same thing by the term. *If a communication source decodes the message that he encodes, if the message is put back into his system, we have feedback.*

There is one difference between the engineer's meaning and the communication man's meaning for feedback. In engineering, feedback often is a "bad" word—engineers try to avoid feedback. In human communication, feedback is a very "good" word. When we communicate, we constantly seek feedback. We constantly check up on ourselves, decode our own messages to make sure we encoded what we intended. We shall return to the term feedback frequently as we discuss communication effectiveness.

In summary, we have discussed some of the principles of habit strength in human learning which are translatable into principles of communication effectiveness. We also have tried to relate our general model of the communication process to a model of the learning process. We have suggested that learning *is* communication, that what we mean by the learning process is included in our model of the communication process.

Learning is the development of changed relationships between a stimulus that is perceived and interpreted, and a response that is made to it. Learning requires some permanence of a new S-R relationship. Learning involves the development of habits, of habitual responses to a stimulus.

As communicators, we often want to produce learning in our receivers. If we do not want to *produce* learning, we want to *utilize* existing habits in the receiver, to *strengthen* them, to create messages which *take them into account*. For these reasons, we need to understand the process of learning and to know the factors which determine the strength of habits, of S-R connections.

This chapter has discussed some of the basic principles of habit strength and tried to relate them to communication situations. By no means have we included all or even most of the available knowledge about the ways in which people learn. The references at the end of the book provide further information sources for the reader who desires to increase his understanding of principles of learning that are related to the effectiveness of communication.

Suggestions for Thought and Discussion

1. Select an example in which a source wants his receiver to learn—to change an S-R relationship. Specify the prior S-R relationship and the one which is to be substituted for it. On the basis of the principles of learning that have been discussed, suggest ways in which the source could increase the chances that the receiver would learn in the way intended.

2. What is the difference between a trial response and a response? Do they differ, or is the distinction merely a useful one for describing behavior? Are there responses other than trial responses? What implications are there in the statement that some responses are final responses, not trial responses?

3. Using the determinants of habit strength as a reference, find examples of messages that were deficient in producing learning. What suggestions could you give the communication source that he could use to increase learning? Limit your suggestions to applications of the determinants of habit strength.

4. Discuss the concept of reward. How is it useful in understanding the process and effects of communication? What dangers are there in our use of this concept? How can we protect ourselves from these dangers?

5. Discuss the similarities between the process of learning and the process of communication? Do you see any differences between them? Specify your answer in detail. What advantages are there in showing the relationships between these two processes? between any two processes?

6. Review the principles of learning in this chapter. Discuss the practical applications for your own communication that can be inferred from these principles. How confident can you be in using these principles in a practical situation? What limitations must be placed on them?

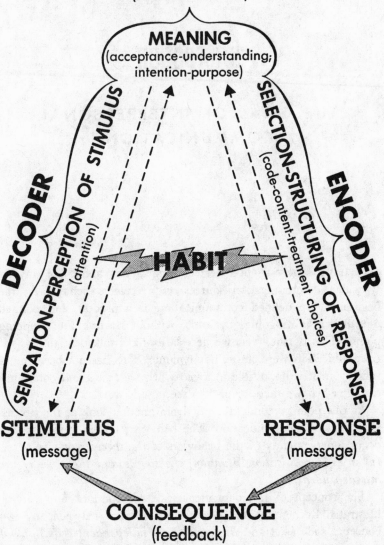

A model of the relationship between communication and meaning.

CHAPTER 5

Interaction

THE GOAL OF INTERPERSONAL COMMUNICATION

WE HAVE SPENT a good deal of time talking about the ways in which communication sources and receivers behave. At the beginning, we defined communication as a process, and pointed out that it is on-going, dynamic, without starting and stopping points. This is true. Yet, we necessarily have talked at times as if communication were static, nondynamic. This has not been intentional, but it is impossible to avoid when we *talk about* communication, when we take it apart to see how it works.

At this point, we might profit from another look at the process viewpoint of communication. The behaviors of the source do not occur independently of the behaviors of the receiver or vice versa. *In any communication situation, the source and the receiver are interdependent.*

The concept of interdependence is itself complex and can be illustrated by defining the possible relationships between any two concepts, such as A and B. A *and* B *are independent if and only if neither affects the other.* For example, the color of a person's hair (A) and his left- or right-handedness (B) are independent. They do not affect each other. Blondes are just as likely to be right-handed as they are left-handed. So are brunettes or red-heads. Right-handed people are just as likely to be blondes as they are to be brunettes or red-heads. The same is true for left-handed people. Neither affects the other.

There is a dependency relationship between A *and* B *if* A *affects* B *but* B *does not affect* A, *or vice-versa.* For example, the production of the ragweed flower (*A*) and the incidence of hay-fever (*B*) are dependently related. The presence of ragweed affects some people by producing hay-fever. Hay-fever is dependent on the existence of ragweed. Ragweed is not dependent on the existence of hay-fever. People who have hay-fever do not affect the existence of ragweed. *A* is not affected by *B*, but *B* is affected by *A;* therefore, *A* and *B* are dependently related.

Interdependence can be defined as *reciprocal* or *mutual* dependence. If *A* affects *B and B* affects *A,* then *A* and *B* are interdependent. For example, in this country the farmer and the grocer are interdependent. The food the farmer grows affects the product the grocer can sell. On the other hand, the sales of the grocer affect the kind and amount of crops the farmer will grow. Each is dependent on the other, each affects the other.

There are varying levels of interdependence among concepts or events. Maximum interdependence is found in concepts that we have referred to as dyadic. For example, the concepts of father and child are interdependent for their existence, neither can exist without the other. The same is true for husband-wife, leader-follower, supervisor-supervisee, etc. This can be called *definitional interdependence.* Dyadic concepts refer to relationships between events which cannot exist alone.

Communication between two or more people requires an interdependent relationship; however, the levels of communicative interdependence vary from situation to situation. How do these levels differ?

Levels of Communicative Interdependence

For purposes of discussion, we shall distinguish four levels of communicative interdependence. Again, it must be emphasized that we are distorting the process of communication when we do this. The four levels discussed are themselves not independent. Any communication situation probably includes some aspect of each; however, there are differences in emphasis from situation to situation.

If we remember that we are distinguishing among levels to point out differences in emphasis rather than differences in kind, we will not be misled. If we assume that communication at one level of interdependence is *not* related to the other levels, we will *not* be taking the process aspect of communication into account.

Definitional-Physical Interdependence

If we reflect for a moment, it becomes clear that the communication concepts of source and receiver are dyadic. They depend on each other for their very definition. You cannot define a source without defining a receiver. You cannot define a receiver without defining a source.

In addition to their definitional interdependence, the functions of the source and receiver are *physically* interdependent, although the functions may be performed at different points in time and space. When two people are communicating, they rely on the physical existence of the other for the production or reception of messages. Occasionally, this is the only kind of mutual interdependence involved to any appreciable extent. For example, let us look at the following hypothetical conversation between an industrial foreman (Harry) and a plant worker (John). John and Harry work in the same department. They meet when they get to work in the morning, and have the following "conversation":

JOHN: Harry, let me tell you about what happened last night at home . . .

HARRY: Fine, John. You know, things aren't going well on that experimental assembly job on the line . . .

JOHN: I came in last night, and everything hit me. The wife said that the kids had ruined some of the plants in the yard . . .

HARRY: If we don't get into full production pretty soon on that job, I don't see how . . .

JOHN: the plumbing stopped up in the basement . . .

HARRY: we can fulfill the contract we're working on.

JOHN: and the dog tried to bite the little boy down the street.

HARRY: Things are sure rough.

JOHN: They sure are.

This set of messages is exaggerated slightly to demonstrate a point, but most of us have heard conversations like this one, or even participated in a few. John and Harry were interdependent. Without the presence of the other, neither would have encoded the messages that he did; however, their major functions were to serve as receivers for the other's messages.

The kind of interdependence emphasized in this kind of situation is merely definitional-physical. The two communicators were not even reacting to each other's message. They were only waiting their turn to encode.

We probably would not want to label this "good" or "effective" communication. It *is* a frequent kind of communication.

When we communicate this way, we are not talking *to* each other, we are merely talking. We do not feel right in encoding certain messages unless we are in the presence of another. We cannot continue to do this when we are with another unless he puts up with it, or uses the situation for his own purposes. We are interdependent—but only because of the dyadic nature of the concepts of source and receiver.

ACTION-REACTION INTERDEPENDENCE

In explaining what is meant by action-reaction interdependence, we can use any of several servo-mechanisms as an illustration. For example, take the relationship between the modern furnace and the thermostat which we keep in our living rooms. We can look on thermostat-furnace behaviors as a communication relationship. Both the thermostat and the furnace serve as a source and a receiver. Each encodes messages, each receives messages from the other. Each affects the other. They are interdependent, and this relationship is more than mere physical interdependence. The responses that each make are determined by the responses of the other. We can describe the communication situation between the thermostat and the furnace as follows: The thermostat has an intention, a purpose: to maintain the temperature of the room at a specific level, such as 68°. As long as the temperature remains at that level, the thermostat is silent. It encodes no message. When the temperature drops below that level, the thermostat transmits a message to the furnace—"turn on." *The thermostat acts.*

When the furnace receives the message "turn on," it decodes it and *reacts* to the message. The furnace allows oil or gas to enter its chambers, it increases the force of the pilot, it produces heat. When the air at the top of the furnace reaches a certain level, such as 150°, another thermostat starts.

None of these messages are transmitted to the thermostat. They are internal (covert) responses of the furnace. When the blower starts, however, the furnace begins to transmit a message to the thermostat—heat. The thermostat receives this message (a reaction by the furnace), decodes it and decides that its original purpose has been accomplished. The room temperature is now at the desired level.

On making this decision, the thermostat reacts to the heat it received by encoding another message—"turn off." The furnace reacts to this message by reducing oil or gas flow, lowering the pilot, shutting off the blower, and stopping the transmission of heat. In time, the thermostat reacts to the absence of heat, decides the temperature has dropped below the desirable level, and encodes another message—"turn on." The cycle begins again. Continual communication occurs between the furnace and the thermostat. Each transmits messages, each receives messages. Each reacts to the messages it receives.

The thermostat-furnace relationship is illustrative of many communication situations. Take the earlier example of the dinner table discussion between Bill and John. Bill had a purpose, he wanted

John to pass him the salt. He encoded a message ("Pass me the salt, please.") He performed some *action*. John decoded the message and *reacted* to it. He responded by producing the salt. His action was taken as a result of decoding Bill's message.

When Bill perceived John's reaction, he reacted to it by reaching his hand out for the salt and saying "Thank you" to John. Each of these behaviors was dependent on the behavior preceding it. Bill acted, John reacted, Bill reacted, and so on. Bill and John were interdependent. Each was affected by the action of the other.

FEEDBACK. Communication terminology includes a term related to action-reaction interdependence to which we have already referred: "feedback." It is correct to say that the furnace reacted to the thermostat; however, if we analyze the situation from the thermostat's point of view, we can say that the reaction of the furnace was *fed back* to the thermostat. The thermostat can utilize the reaction of the furnace in determining its next message.

Feedback from the furnace was useful because it affected the next message that the thermostat produced. Without feedback from the furnace, the thermostat would not be able to determine whether it should tell the furnace to keep providing heat or to turn itself off. The thermostat needed feedback to ascertain whether it was being successful in its communication, whether it was having the desired effect.

The term "feedback" names a special aspect of receiver reaction. It names the use which the source can make of this reaction in determining its own success. For example, when Bill asked John to pass the salt, he could watch John to see if he did it. John's response was useful to Bill as feedback. It told him whether he had been successful in accomplishing his objective. If John did not pass the salt, Bill could have asked him again. If the furnace did not turn on, the thermostat would have repeated its message.

The source can use the reaction of the receiver as a check of his own effectiveness and a guide to his own future actions. The reaction of the receiver is a *consequence* of the response of the source. As a response consequence, it serves as feedback to the source.

Feedback provides the source with information concerning his success in accomplishing his objective. In doing this, it exerts control over future messages which the source encodes.

In the thermostat-furnace example, the reaction of each to the behavior of the other serves as feedback; however, these reactions can be utilized only in a limited way. The thermostat can repeat its message of "turn on" or "turn off." The furnace can repeat its message of "heat" or "no heat." No other alternative is available to either. Neither can communicate a different message, neither can alter the code, content, or treatment of its message. All feedback can do in this illustration is affect the repetition of a message.

In human communication, we can utilize feedback to a much greater extent. John's response to Bill was usable by Bill as feedback. It told him whether he had been successful or not. If John did not pass the salt, Bill could have changed his message, changed the code, the content, or the treatment. Bill could have changed channels and pointed. He could have changed receivers and asked someone else. He even could have changed his purpose and eaten his food without salt.

John also could get feedback. When he passed Bill the salt, he could observe Bill's response. If Bill smiled, and said "Thanks," or began to use the salt, that would be one thing. If Bill frowned, looked confused, said "What's that for," that would be another thing. All these responses could be used by John as feedback. *One consequence of a communication response is that it serves as feedback—to both the source and the receiver.*

In summary, communication often involves an action-reaction interdependence. The action of the source affects the reaction of the receiver, the reaction of the receiver affects the subsequent reaction of the source, etc. The source or the receiver can make use of the reactions of the other.

Reactions serve as feedback. They allow the source or receiver to check up on himself, to determine how well he is doing in accomplishing his purpose. Feedback also affects subsequent behavior, if the source and receiver are sensitive to it.

When a source receives feedback that is rewarding, he continues to produce the same kind of message. When he gets nonrewarding feedback, he eventually will change his message. In responding to a message, the receiver exerts control over the source. The kind of feedback he provides determines in part the next set of behaviors of the source. Speakers and audiences, actors and theatre-goers, sources and receivers generally can be interdependent through the mutual effects of their reactions on the other.

For example, suppose you are giving a talk, making a speech. At one point in your talk, you tell a joke. The audience is supposed to laugh. If they laugh, this can serve as feedback to you. It tells you that you were successful. It tells you to keep going, your messages are having an effect. On the other hand, suppose the audience does not laugh. Suppose it just sits. This, too, serves as feedback. It tells you that you are not getting what you want, your messages are not meeting with success. You might change your jokes, or stop telling jokes. *The audience exerts control over your future messages by the responses it makes*. These are fed back to you. You are dependent on the audience for feedback.

At the same time, members of the audience are dependent on feedback. If one person does not laugh at your jokes and all the other members of the audience do, these responses are fed back to the nonlaughing receiver. He begins to question his sense of humor —and often begins to laugh at succeeding jokes, whether they strike him as funny or not. Eventually, they may even begin to strike him as funny.

Communication sources and receivers are mutually interdependent, for existence and for feedback. Each of them continually exerts influence over himself and others by the kinds of responses that he makes to the messages he produces and receives. A newspaper affects its readers by selecting the news they are allowed to read. On the other hand, the readers also affect the newspaper (although probably not as much as some publishers would have us believe). If readers do not buy the paper (negative feedback), it may change its selection and presentation of news.

Advertisers control the reasons given to the public for buying this or that product. But the consumer affects the advertiser— through feedback. If the public buys more (positive feedback), the advertiser keeps his messages. If the public quits buying the product (negative feedback), the advertiser changes his messages—or the stockholders get a new advertising manager.

We can separate one communication situation from another by the ease with which feedback is obtained. Clearly, person-to-person communication permits maximum feedback. All available communication channels can operate. The source has an opportunity to change his message on the spot as a result of the feedback he gets. On the other hand, communication forms that we refer to as the public media (newspaper, television, magazines, etc.) have minimum opportunities for feedback. The source and the receiver are separated in time and space. They have little opportunity to get feedback from the responses of the other.

The difficulty of obtaining feedback for sources who use the public media has given rise to an entire industry: the public opinion pollster, the audience rating service, people who measure the amount of readership of a magazine, researchers who study the impact of advertising copy, organizations that interview receivers to check their responses to the source's message in an immediate and personal way. All these professionals attempt to provide feedback for a communication source. They are paid to help the source determine who is receiving his messages and what reactions are being made.

As communication receivers, we often overlook our affecting power on the source. In a competitive market, it is amazing how much influence ten letters to the manager of a television station can have on his future policy decisions. Our decisions to turn off the television set affect future program decisions; i.e., audience ratings serve as feedback. The battle of audience ratings is of great importance in the broadcasting industry. Major policy decisions are often made solely on the basis of feedback on how many people are listening to or viewing a given program.

Even in our own person-to-person communication situations, we overlook the importance of feedback. As students, we fail to realize the extent to which we can affect the teacher. When we indicate that we do not understand, he repeats, if he is sensitive to feedback. When we let him know we think he is a good teacher, he may become a better teacher. Any performer would testify that he gives a better performance when his audience reacts favorably, when they make responses which he can use as positive feedback.

We underestimate the value of feedback when we communicate with our friends and families. We neglect to tell them when we think they have done a good job or when we like them. These kinds of responses are useful to them as feedback. They affect future actions toward us.

Action-reaction relationships are significant in analyzing communication. Feedback is an important instrument of affect. The reactions of the receiver are useful to the source in analyzing his effectiveness. They also affect his subsequent behaviors because they serve as consequences of his prior responses. If the feedback is rewarding, he perseveres. If it is not rewarding, he changes his message to increase the chances of being successful.

An awareness and utilization of feedback increase the communication effectiveness of the individual. The ability to observe carefully the reactions others make to our messages is one of the characteristics of the person we designate as being good at "human relations," or "sensitive as a communicator."

It is true to say that one can find communication situations that fit this action-reaction level of interdependence between the source and the receiver. Granted, too, that it is useful to retain the action-reaction concept and the corresponding concept of communication feedback. Yet there are at least two possible pitfalls into which this kind of analysis can lead.

First, the concept of feedback usually is used to reflect a *source orientation* to communication, rather than a receiver orientation or a process orientation. When we talk about the receiver's responses as feedback for the source, we are observing communication situations from the point of view of the source. We are perceiving through his eyes, not as an external observer.

As we shall show, there are levels of interdependence higher than action-reaction. We do not have to look at the source-receiver relationship as a one-way relationship; however, the feedback concept emphasizes one-wayness, at the expense of a two-way analysis. When people are taught about feedback, they are likely to take a source orientation to communication. We talk about "getting feedback" to the source, or "using the receiver's behavior" as feedback for the source.

The term "feedback" implies a point of view. We have said that one individual makes a response, performs an act. This response is perceived by a second individual and responded to. We say that the second individual reacts to the original message. When we call this reaction "feedback," we are structuring it as if we were the original source. We are talking about a use we can make of a reaction, not the reaction itself. There is nothing inherently wrong with this kind of terminology. In fact, it is useful to think this way. Nevertheless, if we are not careful, we begin to think about all of the process from the source's point of view, and ignore the basic interdependence that produced the term "feedback" in the first place.

The second pitfall in the use of the action-reaction concept is concerned with our continuing reference to communication as a process. The terms "action" and "reaction" deny the concept of process. They imply that there is a beginning to communication (the act), a second event in communication (reaction), subsequent events, etc., with a final end. They imply an interdependence of events within the sequence, but they do not imply the kind of dynamic interdependence that is involved in the communication process.

People are not thermostats or furnaces. They have the capacity to make trial responses within the organism, to use symbols to anticipate how others will respond to their messages, to develop expectations about their own behavior and the behavior of others. The concept of *expectations* is crucial to human communication. It requires analysis at a third level of communication interdependence.

INTERDEPENDENCE OF EXPECTATIONS: EMPATHY

All human communication involves predictions by the source and receiver about how other people will respond to a message. Even in the minimal-interdependence situation that we have called physical interdependence, Bill and John had some expectations about each other. They made predictions about the language facility of the other, the length of time the other would tolerate listening rather than speaking, the social relationships that existed between them, etc. We can analyze expectations as a distinctive level of interdependence; however, to some extent this kind of interdependence is involved in all communication.

Every communicator carries around with him an image of his receiver. He takes his receiver (as he pictures him to be) into account when he produces a message. He anticipates the possible responses of his receiver and tries to predict them ahead of time. These images affect his own message behaviors. For example, the Madison Avenue advertiser has an image (accurate or inaccurate) of the American public. The Hollywood producer has an image of the movie-goer. Newspapers have expectations about how their readers will react to messages. Magazines can be distinguished on the basis of the images they have of their subscribers. Personnel managers have an image of the typical factory worker. Teachers have expectations about students.

The development of expectations of the receiver by the source has its counterpart in the development of expectations of the source by the receiver. Receivers have expectations about sources. When we observe the President, we expect him to behave in certain ways and not in others—because he is the President. Magazine readers have an image of the magazines they read. The public image of the *Ladies Home Journal* is not the same as the image of *Fortune, Playboy,* or *True Story*. We expect different messages from these magazines, different message treatments.

Communication receivers select and attend to messages in part because of their images of the sources and their expectations as to the kind of message these sources would produce. The public has an image of business corporations, labor union leaders, educators, doctors, etc. One of the major missions of the public relations expert is the development of expectations about his client. People in this profession are paid to manipulate the receiver's image of a company, a public figure, a product.

As sources and receivers, we have expectations about each other that affect our communication behaviors. Behavior is also affected by our images of *ourselves*. Our self-images influence the kinds of messages we create and the treatment we give our messages. Our expectations about our own behavior affect which messages we attend to. Subscribers to *Harper's* may have self-images different from those of subscribers to *The Reader's Digest*. Republicans have different expectations about their own behavior than do Democrats —at least in some behavioral areas.

As sources and receivers, we carry around images of ourselves and a set of expectations about other people. We use these expectations in encoding, decoding, and responding to messages. We take other people into account in framing messages. We frame messages to influence a receiver, but our expectations about the receiver influence us and our messages.

Some of the more interesting studies in communication analyze the images which individuals or communicative organizations have of their receivers, and how these expectations affect the source's behavior. For example, what image does Madison Avenue have of the typical Iowa farmer, of Madison Avenue itself? What image does the corporation executive have of himself, of the average factory worker, etc.? These are research questions, and important ones. Their answers can help us explain why people treat their messages as they do, because a source's expectations influence the way he communicates.

In approaching the concept of expectations, we can return to our basic model of the communication process. The communication source and receiver each possess certain communication skills, attitudes, and knowledges. Each exists within a social system and a cultural context. These affect how they will react to messages. Communication represents an attempt to couple these two individuals, these two psychological systems. Messages are used to accomplish this coupling of the organisms.

In one sense, messages are all that the organisms have available to them. By using messages, we come to "know" other men, to know ourselves. We believe that we can understand in part what is going on *within* another person. We develop expectations about what is going on within others and what will go on within ourselves. The basic question is, how do we develop these expectations?

To put it another way, we often make statements of the order, "I know John," or "He won't accept that argument—I know him inside and out." How do we come to "know" other people, inside and out? For that matter, how do we come to "know" ourselves? What is the process underlying our ability to develop expectations about others, to predict how they will behave before a situation arises?

Clearly, we frequently face decisions requiring this kind of knowledge. We decide whether we should promote Jones, whether we should marry Mary, whether we should recommend Bill for a responsible job. When we make these kinds of decisions, we operate on the assumption that we "know" Jones or Mary or Bill. We make decisions which imply that we understand people, that we can predict how they will behave.

When we say that we "know" somebody, we mean more than that we can recognize him physically when we see him. We mean that we can predict correctly that he will believe certain things and not others, he will behave in certain ways and not in others, he will react in certain ways and not in others.

When we say we "know" somebody, including ourselves, we are saying that we understand how he operates as a psychological entity—as a person with thoughts, feelings, emotions, etc. In making these predictions, we have physical behaviors as our basic data. Each of us perceives how others behave. We can observe these behaviors. They are overt, public. Expectations involve more than this. They involve the private behaviors of man, his covert responses, his internal states, his beliefs, his meanings. When we develop expectations, when we make predictions, we are assuming that we have skill in what the psychologists call *empathy—the ability to project ourselves into other people's personalities*. How do we develop empathic ability?

This is a basic question for students of communication. Unfortunately, there is no definitive answer to the question. In any complete sense, we are still without enough research evidence to substantiate one position or another. There are theories of empathy which are plausible—and at least consistent with research evidence. Tomorrow may provide an adequate answer—but we have to operate on what we know today. *We can define empathy as the process through which we arrive at expectations, anticipations of the internal psychological states of man.* How does this occur?

There are three major points of view on empathy. One school of thought argues that there is no such thing, that we cannot develop expectations. Supporters of this position for the most part are believers in a simple one-stage (S-R) theory of learning. This kind of learning theorist argues that all we have in communication is a set of messages. A message is produced by one person, and perceived by another. In other words, there are stimuli and responses. And that is that. We argued in Chapter 4 that a simple S-R theory of learning may account for nonhuman animal learning, but not for the more complex learning behaviors of man. By the same argument, a simple S-R theory of empathy does not seem to account for man's communication behavior.

We *do* develop expectations, we *do* have the ability to project ourselves into the internal states of others. We cannot accept the argument that empathy does not have meaning for us, that we cannot develop expectations and predictions. Some kind of *interpretive* process occurs.

The development of expectations requires a special kind of talent. We need to be able to think about objects that are not available. *Expectations require decisions about the not-here and the not-now.* In order to have expectations, to talk about the not-here and the not-now, we create arbitrary symbols to represent the objects that are not available. We need to be able to produce these symbols and manipulate them.

Man is distinguished from other animals in that he has developed both of these talents. He can receive and manipulate arbitrary symbols. He can produce these symbols to serve his purposes. Because of this, he can represent the nonavailable, the not-here and not-now. As Thorndike put it, the use of arbitrary symbols allows "humans to think *about* things, not merely to think things." Man clearly has these talents, although there are individual differences among people.

Some of our games involve this kind of skill, the development of empathic ability. Chess is an example. A successful chess-player cannot rely on action-reaction. He develops expectations about the consequences of his behavior, and operates under those expectations. He predicts how the other man will react—often several events in advance. He debates moving a pawn. He reasons, if I move this pawn, my opponent probably will take my knight with his bishop —but if he does that, then I will checkmate his king with my queen, etc.

The same thing occurs in contract bridge. The good bidder anticipates possible answering bids from his partner or opponents before he makes his own bid. He also predicts how others will play their hands. The inclusion of this kind of skill is what prevents bridge from becoming a mechanical game that can be described in books. We differ in empathic ability. Some of us are better predictors than others.

We can reject the argument that we have no meaning for the concept of empathy. All of us anticipate the future, we make predictions about the relationships between (a) certain behaviors on our parts, (b) subsequent behaviors of other people, and (c) subsequent behaviors of our own. We do more than act and react. We develop expectations about others which affect our actions—before we take them. This is what we mean by empathy.

Theories of Empathy

There are two popular theories about the basis for empathy. Both theories agree that the basic data of expectations are physical behaviors produced by man; i.e., messages. Both theories agree that man's predictions about the internal psychological states of man are based on observable physical behaviors. Both agree that man makes these predictions by using symbols to represent these physical behaviors and by manipulating these symbols. At this point, the two theories of empathy differ sharply. We can best discuss them separately.

INFERENCE THEORY OF EMPATHY[1]

An inference theory of empathy is psychologically oriented. It argues that man can observe his own physical behavior directly, and can relate his behavior symbolically to his own internal psychological states—his feelings, thoughts, emotions, etc. Through this process, man comes to have meanings (interpretations) for his own physical behavior. He develops a concept of *self*, by himself, based on his observations and interpretations of his own behavior.

Given a self-concept, he communicates with other people. He observes their physical behaviors. On the basis of his prior interpretations of himself, he makes *inferences* about the internal states of others. In other words, he argues to himself that if behavior on his part represented such and such a feeling, a similar behavior produced by somebody else would represent a similar feeling.

This view of empathy assumes that man has first-hand knowledge of himself and second-hand knowledge of other people. It argues that man has the ability to understand himself, through analysis of his own behaviors. From this analysis, man can make inferences about other people based on the similarities between their behavior and his own.

Let us take a simple example of this argument. Suppose you observe yourself making certain gestures; e.g., you repeatedly pound your hand on a table. You analyze how you felt when you performed this behavior. You conclude that you were angry, that you were upset. You discover a relationship between your overt behavior (table-pounding) and an internal state or feeling of anger. Then you observe somebody else pounding his hand on the table. From this behavior, you infer that he too is angry. You make assumptions

[1] The major source of this theory is Solomon Asch, *Social Psychology*, Prentice-Hall, 1952, pp. 139–169.

about his internal state from (a) observing his behavior, and (b) comparing his behavior with similar behavior on your part which reflected anger in you.

This is the position of an *inference* theory of empathy. What are its assumptions?

1. Man has first-hand evidence of his own internal states. He can only have second-hand evidence of other people's internal states.
2. Other people express a given internal state by performing the same behaviors that you perform to express the same state.
3. Man cannot understand internal states in other people which he has not experienced himself. Man cannot understand emotions which he has not felt, thoughts which he has not had, etc.

Let us take these assumptions one at a time. First, an inference theory of empathy says that man's first-hand knowledge is of himself. All other knowledge is second-hand. As we shall find, the other major view of empathy contradicts this assumption directly. From currently available research evidence, we cannot resolve this issue; the assumption can be neither accepted nor rejected.

There is considerable evidence that conflicts with the second assumption, that all people express the same purposes by the same behaviors, that all people mean the same things by the behaviors they perform. Many breakdowns in communication stem from this belief. We often assume that another person attaches the same meaning to a word that we do, that a smile by another person expresses the same internal state as does a smile by us, that other people see the world in the same way that we do—just because they perform many of the physical behaviors that we perform.

It is true that we often get our ideas about the internal states of other people by inferring them from our own internal states, as related to our own behavior. But in so doing, we often err. We often fail to "know" the internal workings of others when we assume they are the same as ours.

When we look at the success we have in predicting and anticipating the behavior of others, it seems likely that we need to add another approach to empathy to provide a complete explanation of our success. We need an approach which does not assume that man's first-hand knowledge is always of use. People are not the same.

There also is evidence that contradicts the third assumption of inference theory: that we cannot understand internal states which we have not experienced ourselves. Few theorists would dispute the point that man understands best those things which he has experienced himself. Yet we can find many examples of the understanding (at least in part) of emotions which have not been experienced. For instance, we can empathize with a mother who has just lost her baby. We can have expectations about how she will behave, what her internal states are, even though we have never lost a baby. We can empathize with people who are in a state of great happiness over their coming marriage, even though we have not been married ourselves. Experience increases our understanding, but it does not seem to be essential to understanding.

These are the essential arguments of an inference theory of empathy. There seems to be some merit in the arguments; however, inference theory does not seem to explain empathy in terms that are completely satisfying. We can turn our attention to the second point of view, popularized by Mead and usually considered to be a sociological point of view. Mead labeled his theory as *role-taking*.

ROLE-TAKING THEORY OF EMPATHY[2]

Let us not assume that man's first-hand knowledge is of himself, or even that man *has* a concept of self before he communicates with other people. We can examine some of the behaviors of man, and try to interpret their implications for empathy.

Let us look at the very young child, the infant. How does he behave, how does he develop his ability to empathize? The basic data that are observable to the infant are physical behaviors, message

[2] The major source of this theory is the work of George H. Mead. Much of the discussion is taken from George H. Mead, *Mind, Self and Society*. University of Chicago Press, 1934.

behaviors. The infant, like everyone else, can observe and produce physical behavior. The question is, how does the child develop interpretations of self and others, given observable physical behaviors?

Role-taking theorists argue that the new-born infant cannot distinguish himself from other people, cannot tell one person from another. In order to develop the concept of self, the infant must first look on himself as an object—must act toward himself as he acts toward other objects, other people. *In other words, the concept of self does not precede communication. It is developed through communication.*

The young child exhibits a good deal of imitative behavior. He observes other people's behavior. He tries to repeat the behavior as well as he can. Some of the behavior he imitates is behavior directed toward him. His mother makes sounds (speaks) in his presence. He begins to imitate the sounds. The father moves his face (smiles) in his presence. He begins to imitate these facial movements.

In imitating behaviors directed toward him, the infant begins to act toward himself as others act toward him, but he has no interpretation for these actions, no meaning for the actions. This is the beginning of role-taking, the beginning of the development of a concept of self. *In the first stage of role-taking, the infant actually plays other people's roles without interpretation.* He imitates the behavior of others. He is rewarded for these role-playing responses; therefore he retains them.

As the child develops, he increases his role-playing behavior. He increasingly acts toward himself in the same way that other people act toward him. At the same time, he learns to produce and manipulate a set of symbols, significant symbols, symbols for which he and other people have meanings. Equipped with a set of significant symbols, the infant can begin to understand the roles that he takes. He can understand how other people behave toward him. He can begin really to put himself in other people's shoes, to look at himself as other people do.

Those of you who have watched small children know what is meant by this. The child at age two or three will play by having a make-believe tea party. At the tea party, he will reprimand himself —produce messages such as "Todd, you mustn't do that or I'll send you up to bed," or "No, no, Sandy, that's not the way to sit at the table." When the child behaves like this, he is looking at himself as an object of behavior—as an external object. He is playing the role of the parent, putting himself in the shoes of the parent. *This is the second stage of role-taking, in which the infant plays other people's roles—with understanding.*

As the child matures, he engages in more complex role-playing. He begins to play games with several other people. In playing games, the child must take a large number of roles at the same time. In hide-and-seek, the child must put himself in the shoes of the person who is "it," must, simultaneously, take the roles of all the other children who are hiding.

It now becomes impossible physically to *play* all these roles. The child cannot imitate all the related behaviors. Through the use of symbols, however, he hypothesizes what it would be like to behave as the other children do. He infers their roles, he takes their roles in his own mind, rather than playing the roles physically. *This is the third stage of role-taking, in which the child begins to put himself in other people's shoes symbolically, rather than physically.*

By putting himself in the places of all the other children, the child develops expectations about his own behavior—about what is expected of him in this situation. He then behaves according to his expectations, as determined by *taking* the roles of others. If he has done a good job of role-taking, his behavior conforms to the expectations the others have, and they reward him, they let him play, they like him. If he has not done a good job of role-taking, his behavior does not conform to the expectations of the other children and he is not rewarded. He is rejected, punished.

As the child continues to participate in group activity, he takes the roles of many other people. In so doing, he looks on himself as a receiver, as an object of behavior. Gradually, he begins to *generalize* the roles of others. He starts to get a general concept of how other people behave, how they interpret, and how they act toward him. We can call this the concept of the generalized other. *The generalized other is an abstract role that is taken, the synthesis of what an individual learns of what is general or common to the individual roles of all other people in his group.*

Each of us develops a concept of the generalized other, based on our experiences in a specific social environment and in the successive roles of other people that we take. The generalized other provides us with a set of expectations as to how we should behave. This is our meaning for the concept of self. *Our self-concept is the set of expectations that we have as to how we should behave in a given situation.* How do we develop a self-concept? Through communication, through taking the roles of others, through acting toward ourselves as an object of communication, through the development of a generalized other.

Inference theory *assumes* a concept of self, and suggests that we empathize by using the self-concept to make inferences about the internal states of other people. Inference theory suggests that the self-concept determines how we empathize. Role-taking theory argues the other way around. It suggests that the concept of self does not determine empathy. Rather, communication produces the concept of self and role-taking allows for empathy. Both theories place great importance on the nature of language, significant symbols, in the process of empathy and the development of a concept of self.

Which are we to believe? How does man empathize? Here, we will take the position that *man utilizes both these approaches to empathy.* We can argue that man's first approach is through role-taking. Each of us takes roles of other people. Each of us develops a concept of the generalized other. The way that we look on ourselves, our definition of ourselves, is determined by our concept of the generalized other, the social context in which we exist, the expectations which we perceive others to have about our own behaviors.

As we develop and mature, we construct a concept of self. Then we operate on it. We now begin to make inferences about other people, based on our concept of self. We lessen our use of role-taking, and increase our use of inferences. We make the assumption that other people are like us, and that their behaviors reflect the same internal states that our behavior reflects. We do this until we do not find it rewarding.

When we empathize by making inferences and are not rewarded, we are forced to do one of two things. Either (1) we distort the behaviors of others that we perceive, and make them correspond to our expectations, or (2) we take another look at our images of ourselves, we redefine self, we return to role-taking.

If we take the first solution, distorting the world that we perceive, we become mentally ill, we have "delusions," we end up in an institution. This is not desirable. Yet we can predict that much of the problem of mental health is related to man's inability or unwillingness to change his own image of himself when he finds that it is not rewarded in his social environment.

What about the second alternative, a redefinition of self? To do this, we have to return to role-taking, we again have to take the role of others, to develop a new concept of the generalized other, a new set of expectations for our own behavior. In so doing, we redefine ourselves, change our behaviors accordingly, and again begin to make inferences about other people.

We often engage in role-playing when we are revising our role-taking or self concepts. Again, the mentally ill can use role-playing as a technique to increase their ability to make useful hypotheses about how others would react, and how they should react in a given situation.

As we play the role of another, we combine the inference and role-taking points of view. When we role-play, we actually perform certain behaviors. From these, we can infer our own internal states, we can make inferences from our own behavior which are pertinent to the behavior of another. We then can use these inferences in taking the role of another.

This process of role-taking, inference, role-taking, inference goes on continually. It is what we mean when we say that man is adjustable, adaptable, able to alter his behavior to fit the situation, the social environment in which he finds himself. He develops expectations by taking the roles of others, or by making inferences about himself, or both.

When do we often find it necessary to redefine self? When we enter a new social situation, a new group, a different social environment. For example, when a teen-ager enters the university, he finds himself in a new social situation. His inferences about other people are no longer valid. He makes false predictions, has hazy expectations. Often, he begins to ask himself who he really is.

What does the teen-ager begin to do? He reverts to role-playing, often at a primitive stage. He begins to imitate the behavior of others—without meaning. Gradually, he takes the roles of others (students, teachers, etc.) and is able to put himself in other people's shoes, to look at himself through their eyes. In so doing, he develops a new concept of the generalized other, a new set of expectations about his own behavior. He redefines self and begins to behave in accord with his new definition.

This kind of process is required of us many times in our lives. When we enter a new community, join a new group, travel to a different culture, our predictive power is weakened. We find it difficult to make inferences from self-knowledge. If we are to operate effectively in a changing social situation, we need to be able to take other people's roles, to redefine ourselves. In part, this is the mark of the adjusted man.

Interaction: The Goal of Human Communication

One necessary condition for human communication is an interdependent relationship between the source and the receiver. Each affects the other. At one level of analysis, communication involves only a physical interdependence; i.e., source and receiver are dyadic concepts, each requires the other for its very definition, each requires the other for its existence.

At a second level of complexity, interdependence can be analyzed as an action-reaction sequence. An initial message affects the response that is made to it, the response affects the subsequent response, etc. Responses affect subsequent responses because they are utilized by communicators as feedback—as information that helps them determine whether they are achieving the desired effect.

At a third level of complexity, communication analysis is concerned with empathic skills, the interdependence produced by expectations about how others will respond to a message. Empathy names the process in which we project ourselves into the internal states or personalities of others in order to predict how they will behave. We infer the internal states of others by comparing them to our own attitudes and predispositions.

At the same time, we engage in role-taking. We try to put ourselves in the other person's shoes, to perceive the world as he sees it. In doing this, we develop the concept of self that we use to make inferences about others. In communicating, we shift from inferences to role-taking as a basis for our predictions. The expectations of the source and receiver are interdependent. Each affects the other, each is in part developed by the other.

A final level of interdependent complexity is interaction. The term *interaction* names the process of reciprocal role-taking, the mutual performance of empathic behaviors. *If two individuals make inferences about their own roles and take the role of the other at the same time, and if their communication behavior depends on the reciprocal taking of roles, then they are communicating by interacting with each other.*

Interaction differs from action-reaction in that the acts of each participant in communication are interrelated with each other, they affect each other through the development of hypotheses about what these acts will be, how they fit the purposes of the source and receiver, etc.

The concept of interaction is central to an understanding of the concept of process in communication. Communication represents an attempt to couple two organisms, to bridge the gap between two individuals through the production and reception of messages which have meanings for both. At best, this is an impossible task. Interactive communication approaches this ideal.

When two people interact, they put themselves into each other's shoes, try to perceive the world as the other person perceives it, try to predict how the other will respond. Interaction involves reciprocal role-taking, the mutual employment of empathic skills. The goal of interaction is the merger of self and other, a complete ability to anticipate, predict, and behave in accordance with the joint needs of self and other.

We can define interaction as the ideal of communication, the goal of human communication. All communication is not interactional, or at least does not emphasize this level of interdependence. As we shall see in the following chapter, much of our social behavior involves attempts to find substitutes for interaction, to find less energy-consuming bases for communication.

We can communicate without interacting to any appreciable extent; however, to the extent that we are in an interactional situation, our effectiveness, our ability to affect and be affected by others increases. As interaction develops, expectations become perfectly interdependent. The concepts of source and receiver as separate entities become meaningless, and the concept of process becomes clear.

Suggestions for Thought and Discussion

1. Within the next twenty-four hours, try to find examples of communication which emphasize each of the four levels of communicative interdependence. Develop a method for determining which level is emphasized; i.e., how will you decide whether a given situation emphasizes one or another?
2. "The term 'feedback' implies a point of view." Discuss this thesis, emphasizing the advantages and disadvantages that a source can realize from using this concept in analyzing his own communication.
3. Think of somebody that you "know" quite well. List as many predictions as you can about his behavior. Think of different situations, and try to predict how he would react to each. Test some of these

by observing this person's behavior in different situations. Figure out how accurate you were in your predictions. In those cases where you predicted incorrectly, speculate on the reasons for your error.

4. There is an old proverb that says "you can tell a man by the company he keeps." Within the context of role-taking as a determiner of the self concept, discuss the implications of this proverb. Do you believe that it is valid? Defend your answer

CHAPTER 6

Social Systems

THE MATRIX OF COMMUNICATION

WE have established the thesis that man desires to affect his environment, his own development, the behavior of others. Man is not a self-sufficient animal. He must communicate with others to affect in ways that fit his purposes. In communicating, we must make predictions about how other people will behave. We develop expectations about others, and about ourselves. We can develop these expectations or predictions by increasing our empathic ability, our ability to project ourselves into the personality of another. We can attempt to interact with others. We have called interaction the goal of communication.

Given the appropriate skills and experience, communication can involve interaction, the reciprocity of role-taking. Role-taking, empathy, interaction are useful tools for improving the effectiveness of communication; however, they have at least two weaknesses.

First, role-taking or interaction requires the expenditure of large amounts of energy. It is a time-consuming operation continually to interpret the world from someone else's point of view. In entering unfamiliar social situations, we become physically tired as a result of this kind of effort. It is work to get to "know" people. The energy consumption by the individual is enormous; therefore, we would predict that he would try to conserve his energy, to find a way to make predictions by a less effortful method. *The first weakness in interaction as a basis for prediction is that it consumes too much energy.*

The second weakness in empathic predictions is that they have many prerequisites that often are not met. In other words, success in projecting ourselves into other people's personalities is complicated by factors affecting empathy. Maximum success in making predictions from role-taking rests on the assumptions that:

1. We are not communicating with very many people.
2. We have had prior experience with these people so that we have a basis for making our predictions about them.
3. We are sensitive to human behavior; that is, we have empathic skills.
4. We are motivated (willing to expend energy) to interact.

These are demanding assumptions that often are not tenable. For example, many communication situations are multi-personed. When we are part of a large organization of any type, we have to interact with sizable numbers of people. In group discussion, in communicating at conferences or meetings, we have to take several people into account at any given time. With the addition of each additional person to a communication situation, we increase the role-taking complexities. *As group size increases, empathic accuracy decreases.*

By the same token, we often are thrown into relatively unfamiliar communication situations. We communicate with people we have just met. We communicate with some people so infrequently that we do not have time to get acquainted with them personally. We are limited in the channels we have to communicate with people —such as letters or telephone calls. We continually change receivers, initiate and receive messages involving different people. The less our prior experience is with a given individual, the less able we are to empathize. *When prior communication is minimal, empathic accuracy decreases.*

There are individual differences among people in their ability to predict behavior, to develop accurate expectations about the internal states of others. We have little knowledge about the causes of these individual differences. We have adequate evidence that one person is better than another in predicting behavior. One person also may be better in predicting the behavior of some people than he is in predicting the behavior of others. This skill or sensitivity affects empathic accuracy. *When we are insensitive to the behavior of others, empathic accuracy decreases.*

Finally, empathy assumes motivation on the part of the person making the predictions. If we see rewards for ourselves in predicting accurately the internal states of others, we are willing to expend the energy to do so. If we do not see the rewards for ourselves, if it is not worth the effort, we are not motivated to interact. Many communication situations are not perceived as rewarding by one or more of the participants in it. Under these conditions, our willingness to empathize goes down, we conserve our energy for other things. *When we are not motivated in the communication situation, empathic accuracy decreases.*

Empathy is a useful approach to communication effectiveness. When empathic attempts are reciprocal, when we interact, we have reached the ideal communication situation. When the situation is appropriate, interaction probably is more effective than any other approach to communication. When the situation is not appropriate, we need other bases for our predictions.

A second kind of basis for the development of expectations about human behavior is found in the existence of social systems, organized human groups. *A knowledge of the composition and workings of a social system is useful in making predictions about how members of that system will behave in a given communication situation.*

Factors in Social Systems

As we have mentioned, man is not a self-sufficient animal. His goals, his objectives often cannot be obtained without the cooperation of other humans. He cannot get what he wants by himself. *He is interdependent with others in achieving his goals.* The interdependence of individual goals gives rise to the organization of human behaviors into a multiperson system. When two or more people are mutually dependent on the other, they have to find a way to relate their behaviors and their goals. *Social systems are the consequences of man's need to relate his behavior to the behaviors of others in order to accomplish his goals.*

In talking about a social system, we are concerned with both the elements and the structure of the system. At one level of analysis, the elements we choose are behaviors, responses that people make to a given stimulus. At the next higher level, we group these behaviors, we structure them into behavior-sets, behavior-categories. We have named these behavior-sets in earlier chapters without defining them. *We call them role-behaviors.* The term "role-behaviors" names a group of behaviors that have been sorted, collected, and associated with a person in a given position in the social system.

In talking about social systems, we structure these role-behaviors, we impose a relationship among one set of role-behaviors and another set. We *position* role-behavior sets, we arrange them in an order. Any given set of behaviors occupies a position in the social structure. *We call this the role-position.* In a system, each position bears some relationship to each other position.

Role-behaviors can be isolated without imposing positions on them. When we do not impose position, however, we do not refer to role-behaviors as being part of a social system. A social system is a collection of role-behaviors that have been assigned interdependent positions. Each set of behaviors is related to each other set of behaviors. Each position is related to each other position. Each is interdependent with all of the others.

The term "role" is used to name the combination of role-behaviors and role-positions. *We can define role as the name given to both a set of behaviors and a given position within a social system.* The names we give refer to both a set of behaviors and a position within a system: For example, we can talk about the role of the father. Fathers are elements of the social system we call the family. The term "father" refers to a set of behaviors that are performed in the family, and also to the position those behaviors occupy in the family. The father earns the income for the family, the father imposes discipline on the children, the father protects the family from external disturbances, the father settles disputes within the family, etc. When we make these kinds of statements about fathers, we are describing behaviors that occur, grouping them, and giving the group a name—"father."

The term "father" also refers to a position within the family structure, the social system of the family. The father has a given relationship with the mother, with the children, with outsiders, etc. If we look on a social system as a space, then each role occupies some position within that space, is related in a specific way to all other positions within that space.

Given an interdependent goal, the ways in which people develop roles within a system are attributable to two behavioral tendencies. When we are interdependent with others in achieving our goals, our behaviors tend to become *specialized* and *stratified*. In other words, two people who are co-relating their own behaviors organize their behaviors so that they do not duplicate each other. They divide the labor, they specialize the functions they perform.

The ways in which behaviors are stratified and specialized determine how role-behaviors will be grouped and roles defined; which behaviors will be grouped together under the same name, and which will be separated and put under another name.

Specialization produces the elements of the social system, role-behaviors. How is the structure produced? Role-behaviors become positioned within the system. Specific relationships are developed among roles. Roles are ranked, some role-behaviors are assigned more authority than others, some permit the exercise of more power than others, some are perceived as more valuable than others. In an office, we rank roles: the supervisor has a higher position or status than the clerical help, the engineer has a higher position or status than the janitor.

It is not easy to define the ways in which ranks are assigned to roles. For one thing, behavioral scientists have not concerned themselves especially with the ranking of positions in an emerging social system. For the most part, research has been concerned with analyzing existing social systems and observing how positions affect the system. In order to understand how positions are assigned in the first place, we have to return to our original discussion of goals.

As two or more people find that they are interdependent in reaching their goals, a social system develops. Functions are specialized, behaviors are grouped. Some of these behaviors are perceived as more important than others in the attainment of the goals. This perceived difference in importance may be a function of several things.

One set of role-behaviors may be more difficult to perform than another. For example, it takes more training to be an engineer than a janitor. There may be more people available to perform one set than another; there is a larger available supply of hospital attendants than there is of doctors. Two sets of behaviors may not be equally dependent on each other. One set may be more dependent on a second than the second is on the first; the parent produced the child, but the child did not produce the parent. There may be differences in our value or respect for one set of behaviors as compared to another; in a given system, men who work with their hands may receive more esteem than do men who work with paper and pencil, regardless of the particular task.

There are many possible reasons for the ways in which positions are allocated and ranks are assigned. We have suggested some possible bases, such as:

1. Difficulty of performance of a given role;
2. Availability of people competent to perform a given role;
3. Relative dependencies between two roles;
4. Values attached to behaviors associated with a given role.

We cannot provide an exhaustive or adequate set of reasons for the assignment of ranks. We can state that ranks are assigned to roles, that roles are positioned, that relationships develop among them. For most of our analyses, that is good enough. We usually are concerned with existing social systems rather than with emerging ones. It is interesting to speculate, however, on how the positions were assigned originally in systems to which we belong.

Within an existing system, ranking of positions is related to the concept of authority. The higher the rank, the greater the authority. Authority can be defined as a set of rights, prescribed for a given role position, which permits the occupant of that position to control the behaviors of others within the organization. The *designated* power to affect the operation of the system is related to the rank of position within the system. The *actual* power to affect may or may not correspond to the ranking or authority structure; i.e., particular individuals who do not occupy a position of authority may exert influence on the system because of their own personal abilities, because of their position in other systems, or because of any of a number of other variables.

In order to analyze a system, we can make use of two additional terms: *prestige* and *esteem*. The term "prestige" refers to the value that members of a system place on a given position within that system—regardless of the person who occupies the position. To the extent that system members value a position, feel that it is important, feel that it would be a desirable position to hold, feel that it contributes to the accomplishment of the system's goals, the position can be said to have a prestige value. We talk about a doctor as having high prestige, a corporation vice-president as having high prestige. A more commonly used term for "prestige" is "status"; however, the theorist reserves the term "status" to refer only to the position itself, not to the value placed upon it.

"Esteem" is to a person what prestige is to a position. The value that members of a system place on a position, regardless of who occupies it, determines the prestige of that position. The value that members of a system place on a given person, regardless of position, determines the esteem of that person. People we esteem are those whom we value. When we say that we hold a man in high esteem, we are saying that we respect him, approve of his behavior, etc. Both prestige and esteem are important factors within a social organization.

Roles and Norms

Within an existing social system, people are assigned to roles. A given individual performs a specified set of behaviors and occupies a specific position. To some extent, these behaviors are performed by any person occupying that position—regardless of who he is or what his personal characteristics are. In part, however, the individual also affects the behaviors he performs in a given role. We can divide role behaviors into two groups: the *must's* (independent of the person) and the *may's* (dependent on the individual).

For any given role, there is a set of behaviors that must be performed by anyone occupying that role position. There also is a set of behaviors that must not be performed. Both are included as must behaviors. We can call these "must-do" and "can't-do" behaviors.

For an example, we can use the Army as a social system. One role within that system is that of captain. The term "captain" describes a set of behaviors and a position within the system. Men who occupy this role must perform certain behaviors. A captain must follow the orders given to him by a major. Majors occupy a position of higher rank. The captain must take orders from a major within his organization—regardless of who the major is or who the captain is. Whether they are enemies or friends, whether they know each other or not, both the major and the captain perform the behaviors required of them.

A captain must salute officers of higher rank, and he must do it first. A captain must say "sir" to officers of higher rank, etc. These are examples of "must-do" behaviors. The captain also has a set of "can't-do" behaviors which he has to avoid. The captain cannot mix socially with enlisted men. The captain cannot make derogatory comments about his superiors. The captain cannot refuse to support the Constitution of the United States. These limitations on his behavior are determined by his role. They are specified as "can't-do" behaviors, and he is not allowed to deviate from them and continue to occupy that position.

The set of "must" behaviors goes with the role. It is independent of the person occupying that role: everyone who occupies the position of captain performs the same "must-do" behaviors, and avoids the same "can't-do" behaviors. *These behaviors are independent of people; they are fixed by the system.*

A third set of behaviors can be called "allowed" behaviors, the *may's*. These are not fixed by the role itself, but are a matter of choice and selection by the person occupying that role. A captain may or may not mix socially with other members of the same rank. He may or may not attend church on the base, he may or may not come to work before starting time, or stay after quitting time. These behaviors are left to individual choice; they are not determined by the role.

The behaviors of a person occupying any role can be analyzed in terms of *must's* and *may's*. We can describe an entire system of role-behaviors explicitly. They are contained in job descriptions, manuals of operation, standard operating procedures, etc. Other systems do not specify the role-behaviors explicitly, but rely on other members of the system to teach the appropriate behaviors to new members. For any system, some of the must behaviors probably are specified, and some are not. One of the first tasks for any new member of an organization is to learn what is expected of him, what role-behaviors he must perform.

Within any group, there is pressure exerted by the group to insure that group members conform to their roles, that they behave as they are supposed to. When members respond to these pressures, when they perform the *must* role-behaviors, they are rewarded. When they deviate from the prescribed role-behavior, they are punished. They may be demoted to a lower position, rejected by other group members, even expelled by the group.

Group members are under other pressures than those toward mere conformity to role. Within any group, there are what we call *group norms*. A group norm can be defined as a uniformity of behavior, among two or more members of the group, that is maintained by group pressures. Norms exist for subcategories of a system, and for the entire system as well. There may be a norm for all secretaries within an organization, regardless of the particular department in which they work; e.g., secretaries take fifteen minute coffee breaks, twice a day. This is a statement describing uniform behavior within the organization. Secretaries who take breaks longer than this may be punished by the group. Secretaries who take breaks shorter than this also may be punished by the group.

In either case, if the group exerts pressure on the individual to behave in a given way, the behavior under pressure is a norm. Within any organization, there may be norms concerning how many pieces of work will be turned out per day, how long people will take for lunch, what time they will arrive and leave the office, how they will dress. There are accepted ways of doing things that everyone is supposed to follow. Usually, norms are not made explicit in job descriptions or statements of role. They are learned by participation in the work of the organization. Other members teach new members what these norms are. They say, "This is the way we do things around here," or "We don't do that sort of thing," etc. If a new member does not learn and understand the group norms and behave in ways appropriate to them, he may be rejected by the group—and never know the reason why.

One final point about roles and norms. We have talked in terms of a single social system. None of us exists as a member of a single social system. We belong to many groups, we play several roles, we occupy many positions, we support large numbers of norms. The same man may occupy the position of father in one system, janitor in another, president in a third, elder statesman in another, pledge in another, etc. We play a role in each of the groups to which we belong, with both rank and specified behaviors. From system to system statuses may be congruent, they may be independent, or they may conflict. Our behaviors may be the same or different. What is appropriate for one system may be inappropriate for another. The interrelationships of social systems are some of the crucial variables in explaining communication behavior. We shall return to it when we talk about communication and social organization.

Dimensions of Group Goals[1]

The existence of a social system testifies to the insufficiency of man as a self-determiner of his own goals. By ourselves, we cannot achieve all our goals. We need to become interdependent with others. In order to accomplish the tasks we want accomplished, to produce the products we want produced, to earn our livelihood, we need to belong to social systems. One of the goals of a social system is the production of a product, the accomplishment of a task. *We can label productivity or task accomplishment as one dimension of the goals of a group.* Groups form and maintain themselves in order to increase the productivity of each of the members of that group, in order (a) to produce things that could not be produced alone, (b) to produce them more efficiently, or (c) to produce them more effectively. This is a strong personal goal. It also is one of the purposes of group existence.

With the development of social systems, a second kind of goal emerges. This goal is not pertinent to the individual, but only to groups. The group has a need to maintain itself, to continue its existence as a system. *Group maintenance is a second dimension of group goals.*

If members are not satisfied with group membership, are not willing to continue as members of a group, the group will disintegrate. If the group disintegrates, the productivity goal cannot be accomplished. The accomplishment of productivity goals assumes at least minimal success in accomplishing maintenance goals. *Group productivity is dependent on group maintenance.*

Group maintenance contributes to group productivity; however, maintenance of the social relationship may be the major or even the only goal of the group. In other words, some social organizations do not develop in the attempt to produce a product or accomplish task-goals. Their reason for existence is the mutual satisfaction that

[1] For a major source of this discussion, see Helen H. Jennings, *Leadership and Isolation: A Study of Personality in Interperonal Relations.* Longmans, 1943.

members derive from membership. Group maintenance, the continuity of satisfying interpersonal relationships, may be the sole purpose for existence of a social system.

Group productivity and group maintenance compose two dimensions of group goals; a third dimension is the form of interdependence among group members. Deutsch, in discussing goal interdependence, developed a continuum which is bounded on one end by what he called *promotive interdependence* and at the other by what he called *contrient interdependence*.[2] These are not intended as separate categories, but as two extreme values of interdependence. We can define promotive and contrient interdependence as follows. Given a social system, two or more group members are interdependent with respect to a goal to the degree that the attainment of the goal by one member is related to the attainment of that goal by other members. The interdependence of goal is promotive to the extent that one member cannot attain his goal unless the other members do too. The interdependence of goal is contrient to the extent that one member cannot attain his goal unless the other members cannot attain it.

It is easy to find illustrations at both extremes of the promotive-contrient continuum. For example, take the members of a football team. One of the goals of the team is to win the game. In order for any one member to win the game, all members of the team have to win—the group is highly promotively interdependent. On the other hand, we can take both teams in a football game as a social system. Both teams have the same goal. The two teams are interdependent. Neither can win the game without the participation of the other; however, the two teams are contriently interdependent. For one team to win, the other team must lose.

We can find similar examples within any social system. If the boss announces that one member of the organization is to be promoted soon, this tends to increase the contrient interdependence among members who desire to be promoted. They know that they cannot be promoted if anyone else is promoted. They want the

[2] Morton Deutsch, "A theory of cooperation and competition," *Human Relations*, 2:129–152, 1949.

same goal; their behavior is interdependent, but it is highly contrient.

It is not accurate to say that a given system *is* promotive or *is* contrient. They are merely emphasis points, extremes along a single dimension. The same group may be promotive in some ways and contrient in others, promotive at one moment and contrient at the next. The promotive-contrient goal dimension and the productivity-maintenance goal dimensions are themselves interrelated. There is some evidence that promotive interdependence produces higher member satisfactions (maintenance goal) than does contrient interdependence. There also is some evidence that contrient interdependence may, at least temporarily or under certain conditions, produce higher task productivity than does promotive interdependence. Unfortunately, there is not enough evidence to state clear relationships between promotive-contrient interdependence and productivity-maintenance goals. It clearly is an area for considerable further research and theory development.

The kind of goal and the kind of goal interdependence that groups emphasize determine in part the behaviors and success of the group. We need to know a great deal more about how these factors operate. For example, the promotive-contrient distinction can be viewed as a cooperation-competition distinction. The question often is raised, which is better—cooperation or competition? The answer seems to be, it depends. It depends on the *level* of promotiveness or contrience, the *goals* which the group has, the expectations which members have about how they ought to be interdependent, etc. We cannot make broad generalizations that cooperation is superior to competition or vice versa. It depends on what we have, what we want, and how we are accustomed to using what we have to get what we want.

Many labor-management disputes in industry can be analyzed from a productivity-maintenance point of view. Although it is an oversimplification, we can say that a labor union is more interested in worker satisfactions (maintenance) than it is in task productivity. On the other hand, management is more interested in productivity than it is in employee satisfactions. An understanding of the ways social systems operate clearly implies that both are necessary to the continued successful operation of the work group. Neither is adequate by itself. The two goals of productivity and maintenance have to be reconciled so that each contributes to the development of the other.

In summary, we have tried to define several of the key concepts of a social system. Social systems are collections of interdependent roles. A role includes a set of behaviors which are prescribed for a given position within a system. It includes the assignment of the position as well.

The collecting of behaviors under a given role is based on (a) the perceptions of the group as to what is a useful way of structuring behaviors, and on (b) the ways in which specialization of function has been developed. The assignment of position to a role within a system can be attributed to many factors, including the importance of the role-behaviors to the accomplishment of the group goal, the availability of people who can perform the required behaviors, the values placed by the group on a given set of behaviors, or any of a number of other factors, some of which are external to the system.

The group exerts pressure upon its members to adhere to the roles prescribed for them. It applies particular pressure (rewards and punishments) to insure conformity to group norms. Norms are uniformities of behavior among several group members, which are maintained by group pressures. Some norms are restricted to a sub-set of roles within the system: there may be executive norms, officer norms, etc. Other norms may cut across the entire system and apply to every member of the group.

The ranking of positions within the group produces differences in authority among group members. Members are given varying rights to control the behavior of other members, depending on the amount of authority attached to a given position. We attach values to positions, independently of person—we call this prestige. We attach values to people, independently of position—we call this esteem.

In talking about group goals, it is useful to distinguish between productivity or task accomplishment goals, and maintenance or member satisfaction goals. Both are essential to task-oriented groups. Maintenance-oriented groups may not have any task goals, but may merely exist to provide rewarding interpersonal relationships among the members.

A third kind of goal distinction relates to the kind of interdependence involved. At a given time, a group may emphasize contrient interdependence; at another time, it may emphasize promotive interdependence.

With this superficial background in the terminology and basic meanings of group structure, we can attempt to relate communication behavior to the working of a social system.

Communication and Social Systems

Communication is related to social organization in at least three ways. First, *social systems are produced through communication.* The development of a role system presumes prior communication among members of the system. Through role-taking, interaction, a group of people become interdependent. Uniformities of behavior, interdependence of goals, the commonalities that are involved in a system, pressures to conform to norms—all these are produced through communication among group members.

Communication increases the likelihood of similarities among people, increases the chances that people can work together to accomplish a goal. The allocation of position, the specification of role-behaviors, the teaching of normative modes of behavior are all accomplished through communication.

We certainly cannot say that the desire to communicate causes social organizations; however, we can say that the availability of communication increases the likelihood of social development. In light of this, we can predict that social organization will be more extensive, more complex, among peoples who have adequate opportunities to communicate. The first step in developing social groupings is to increase the opportunity for communication to occur.

Once a social system has developed, it determines the communi-

cation of its members. Social systems affect how, why, to and from whom, and with what effects communication occurs. For example, our social position within a system increases the probability that we will talk to people in equal or adjacent positions and lowers the probability that we will communicate with people whose positions are either much higher or much lower than ours.

Social organization limits the range of receivers for a given individual, limits the number of people with whom he transmits and receives messages. The system also determines in part what kinds of message content will be transmitted to whom by whom. We transmit the content that is appropriate to our own roles. We tend to avoid content that is not appropriate to our own roles—unless we are dissatisfied with our roles and are trying to change to another position.

The system determines the frequency of messages for any given person. Some people occupy positions that are communication-prone. These include receptionists, salesmen, barbers, elected politicians, waitresses: people whose role-behaviors increase their contact with others. Some roles inhibit communication by restricting the kinds and numbers of people with whom occupants of that position can communicate: accountants, security police, top management executives, and confidential assistants have restrictions placed on whom they can communicate with, what they can say, and whether they should play primarily the roles of receivers or sources.

Possibly most important of all are the ways in which the system affects how members treat their messages. The imposition of group norms often occurs in the area of message treatment. Given a particular source, receiver, and content, different systems have different ways of treating content. There is what can be called a "system style," a characteristic way in which members of a given system encode and decode messages. We are talking about a system's style when we make statements of the order "You can always tell a Marine," or "He must be a Procter and Gamble salesman the way he talks," or "He's a Harvard man." A given system develops ways of doing things, ways of talking about things. These normative behaviors are imposed on members of the system. Failure to comply with them, to conform to group standards, produces punishment and rejection.

Communication affects the social system: The social system affects communication. Neither can be analyzed separately without distorting the nature of the process. One of the significant ways in which the communication process and the social process are interdependent is in the area of uniformity of behavior. People who have communicated with each other for a period of time tend to have similar behavior patterns. The tendency toward similarity is a prerequisite to the development of a system. As the old proverb puts it, birds of a feather flock together.

The converse of the proverb also describes behavior. As people merge their own personalities into a system, as they are pressured into the kind of conformity that is necessary to the successful operation of a system, they become more similar to other members of the system. It is fair to say that birds of a feather flock together. It also is defensible to say that birds that flock together tend to become of a feather.

Social systems are related to communication in a third way. The operations of a system can be used to make predictions about how members of that system will behave. *Knowledge of a social system can help us make accurate predictions about people, without the necessity of empathizing, without the necessity of interaction, without knowing anything about the people other than the roles that they have in the system.*

For every role there is a set of behaviors and a position. If we know what the behaviors are that go with a role, we can predict that those behaviors will be performed by people who perform that role. Second, if we know what behaviors go with a given rank or position, we can make predictions about people who occupy that position.

There are certain behaviors that go with the role of nurse, student, union president, mother, oldest son, secretary, executive in top authority position, lawyer. Through experience, we learn which behaviors accompany which roles. When we meet a person who occupies a given role position, we can predict something about his behavior. We can hypothesize that he will do such and such a thing because he is a student, that he will perform certain behaviors because he is a doctor, etc.

Even if we do not know a person as an individual, even if we have had no prior communication with him to determine his attitudes, his knowledges, his communication skills, we still can make fairly accurate predictions from a knowledge of his position in one or more social systems.

We also can make predictions from a knowledge of group norms. There are certain characteristic behaviors of the members of a given organization. When we learn that a person is a member of that organization we can make predictions about his behavior—providing that we are aware of the norms of the group.

For example, in one industrial concern, all employees are expected to be friendly and helpful to visitors. A norm of the company is that visitors will be escorted round the plant and shown anything they want to see. Any questions that the visitor has will be answered to the best of the employee's ability. Knowing this, one can feel free to suggest to a visitor from a foreign country that he should become acquainted with the X company. One can predict how he will be received, because how they do things at that company is known.

Another company in the same industry does not have this kind of group norm. Employees are expected to concentrate on their own job and not stop to talk to anybody who is not directly related to their job, regardless of the position of the employee. We would not send foreign visitors to this company. We can predict that they will not be warmly received.

In both these companies, pressure is maintained to insure that the norms of the company are followed. Employees who deviate from the norms are reprimanded. Employees who follow them are accepted by other employees, etc. In one company, the group norm is just the opposite of what it is in the other company. Appropriate behavior in the one case is inappropriate in another. An employee who changed jobs would have to learn the norms of the second company or he would get in trouble.

Normative behaviors are not the only kinds of predictions we can make. An individual's beliefs, attitudes, knowledges are themselves shaped in part by the groups to which he belongs. If you learn that a man is a Southern Democrat, a Roman Catholic, a troop leader in the Boy Scouts, or an officer in the local Temperance Union, you can make certain predictions about his beliefs and attitudes on various subjects, without knowing the man personally. Of course, you cannot predict all his attitudes and beliefs—only those pertinent to a given role or system.

By the same token, if you know that a man is an engineer, a college professor, a plumber, a foreman in a chemical plant, you can make predictions about what he knows about certain topics. People with particular attitudes, beliefs, and knowledges gravitate to particular positions within different systems. At the same time, people who belong to a given system develop particular attitudes, beliefs, and knowledges.

Knowledge of the systems of which our receiver is a member helps us predict (a) what he believes, (b) what he knows, and (c) how he will behave in a given situation. Another use of knowledge of the system is that it helps us select receivers in the first place. If we have a specific purpose, we can analyze the positions within a system and determine which members of the system are in a position to do what we want done, and which are not. We would waste time and effort by going to the wrong person, that is, a person who does not occupy a role in which the behaviors we want can be performed.

Within any system, certain people can do some things and other people can do different things. Each position has a given amount of authority. When we analyze our own purposes, we often can determine what behaviors have to be performed by others if we are to reach our goal. We then can determine which roles within the organization have the authority to approve what we want done, and who would actually do it. We can use this information in selecting a receiver, predicting his purposes, predicting his responses, predicting his attitudes, his values, his knowledges, his ability, and the possibility that he can do what we want if he decides to be of help.

People who do not understand the working of a given system often complain about the system. They say that "they cannot get anything out of it," or that "this system is just inefficient." People who do understand how a system works can use their knowledge to improve the efficiency and effectiveness of their communication. A U. S. government agency, a large university, a local Chamber of Commerce, a women's club, a fraternity—all these are social systems; all have their own roles, their own ranking structures, their own norms, their own beliefs and attitudes. If we learn what these are, we can communicate within the system—we "know the ropes." If we do not learn what these are, we are lost when we try to get what we want. In either case, the systems of which the source and receiver are a part are relevant to the kind of communication that occurs.

Communication Breakdowns: Problems in Prediction

We have described the major factors in a social system and pointed out how knowledge of these factors can be used in improving communication, in making accurate predictions without emphasizing interaction or empathy. It is true that social organization provides useful tools of communication; however, there are problems in predicting behavior from a knowledge of social systems. Furthermore, communication within a group also has problems because of the complexities of group behavior. We can analyze a few of the major communication problems within the context of our prior discussion.

PREDICTING ROLE BEHAVIORS

Each role within a system has a set of behaviors that go with it: the *must* behaviors for that role. It is easy to say that we make predictions from a knowledge of the role behaviors that accompany a given position, and to let it go at that. In practice, it is not that easy. Roles are structures that are imposed on behavior. The structure we impose may not correspond to the structures that others impose. In other words, one can look at role behaviors from several points of view. All of them may be relevant to a given situation. In analyzing role behaviors, we need to use at least three approaches: role prescriptions, role descriptions, and role expectations.

1. *Role prescriptions:* the formal, explicit statement of what behaviors *should be* performed by persons in a given role.
2. *Role descriptions:* a report of the behaviors that *actually are* performed by persons in a given role.
3. *Role expectations:* the *images* that people have about the behaviors that are performed by persons in a given role.

In the ideal system, prescriptions, descriptions, and expectations about a given role are equivalent. In most groups, they are not equivalent. If they differ radically, communication breakdowns occur within the system.

We make communication predictions from the expectations that we have about role behaviors. If our expectations differ from those of the person performing the role, we get into trouble. For example, the sales manager of a television station may assume that the behaviors of the program director include attempts to sell program concepts to prospective clients. With this expectation, he may ask clients to talk to the program director, or ask the program director to talk to clients.

The program director may not have this expectation about the behaviors he should perform. If he does not expect to talk to clients, he may get irritated if someone approaches him or if he is asked to do this. In turn, the sales manager may get irritated because the program director refused to, or at any rate did not put forth what the sales manager considered an adequate effort. The expectations of these two people about the role behaviors of the program director caused a breakdown in communication between them and a consequent failure to accomplish a mutual goal—profits for the station and for themselves.

Different expectations on the part of an employee and his supervisor about how the supervisor should behave can cause frictions or labor grievances. Differences between the expectations of a retail clerk and a customer about the role behaviors of either can cause friction and loss of sales or prestige for the store.

Any of us can cite a number of illustrations of difficulties in communication that are attributable to ambiguities or conflicts in the expectations of the source and the receiver in a communication situation. We make predictions based on our expectations. So do other people. If we operate from conflicting expectations, we will make conflicting predictions. People will not behave as we predicted, and communication will break down.

Another kind of example, related to differences between expectations, prescriptions, and descriptions, can be drawn from an Air Force technical training situation during the Korean War. When new airmen took basic training they were given aptitude tests. The word was spread that the brighter airmen would go to technical training schools. The word was spread also that only the brightest airmen would go to weather school to study meteorology and forecasting. Airmen were told that they would study full time while they were in weather school, that they would be treated as students, and that the Air Force wanted them to learn their jobs quickly.

The role behaviors of a weather school student were prescribed and published for all to read. Airmen who passed the aptitude requirements for weather school were placed in school and shipped to a training base. Before arriving, they read the prescribed role behaviors, they read the publicity on the importance of weather school, they developed specific expectations about what they would do when they arrived at their training base. On arrival, many of them were placed on K.P. or mess duty, often for as long as a month or six weeks while they waited entrance into school. A near mutiny broke out among the troops.

The airmen felt cheated, felt they had been lied to, felt that the Air Force had tricked them. What had happened? They had been informed about the behaviors they would perform (role prescription). They had developed favorable expectations about this and were looking forward to performing these behaviors (role expectations). When they arrived they did not perform the behaviors prescribed for weather students. Instead, they performed kitchen police behaviors (role description).

The discrepancy between prescription, expectation, and description produced a highly negative response from them. The Air Force was surprised at the results. After doing an evaluation, officials decided that the conflict just described was causing the negative reaction. From then on, entering students were told while at their basic training base that they might have to serve as kitchen police for a period when they arrived at their training station. The administrative requirements of the base were explained to them. The complaints subsided, within limits.

A basic principle of communication in administration is that role-behavior prescriptions, descriptions, and expectations should be closely related to each other. People should (a) be told what they are to do, (b) be given an accurate prescription, and (c) be led to expect what will happen—before it happens. When prescriptions, descriptions, and expectations differ significantly, communication breaks down. One of the frequent complaints heard in a system is "I never know what's expected of me." People desire to reduce uncertainty. This carries over into their own role-behaviors. Most individuals who occupy a role want that role defined, want ambiguity reduced. Failure to do this increases tensions, increases uncertainty, and reduces accuracy of prediction.

PREDICTING ROLE POSITIONS

Every role has a position within the system, with a given amount of authority, power, prestige, rank. Occupants of a position are very *protective* of their authority and prestige—they do not want to lose it. Ignorance or dismissal of the importance of position causes serious communication breakdowns. Again, we can make the distinction among prescriptions, descriptions, and expectations. Everything that was said about role behaviors applies to role positions. There is no need for repetition. We can add several points.

1. When an individual feels that his position is under attack, he reacts negatively.
2. The *expectations,* not the prescriptions or descriptions, that people have about authority control their behavior.
3. Social systems are composed of interlocking roles with interlocking authority. By-passing certain positions that are perceived as relevant (not going through channels) attacks people who occupy the positions that are by-passed.
4. The power of an individual and the authority of his position do not necessarily coincide. When his power is less than his authority, he tends to become dissatisfied. When his power is greater than his authority, his colleagues tend to become dissatisfied.
5. It is not accurate to say that everyone wants more authority or power. It is accurate to say that everyone wants to be perceived as having the authority that he perceives himself to have.
6. People who are satisfied with their present position of authority behave differently from (a) those who want to achieve more authority, or (b) those who fear that their present authority might be reduced.

Many more points could be added. Entire books could be (and have been) written about the dynamics of position, authority, prestige, and power and how these are related to behavior. Whenever we initiate communication within a system, we have to take account of both our own purposes and the purposes of other people within the system. We may see a quick way to get what we want, to "cut red tape." In doing this, however, we may be damaging the self-perceptions of people whom we have by-passed. We may have threatened their position, communicated to them that we do not feel their role to be essential in the operation of the system. This is not tolerable to the individual who receives such a message. We may save time in the short run by going out of channels. In the long run, however, the time we "saved" may be lost many times over.

Ambiguity of authority interferes with communication fidelity. An effective system presumes that its members are aware of their positions, their responsibilities and authority. Another frequent complaint that is heard within task-oriented systems is "I never know who's boss around here," or "You're never sure whom you are supposed to take orders from and who is supposed to take orders from you." Ambiguities in authority structure increase the tensions within the organization and reduce the satisfactions that members get from belonging to the system.

Too much ambiguity of authority causes trouble but no ambiguity also may cause difficulties. A rigid authority-power structure within a system can produce stagnation of the system. As communication channels become increasingly complex, as more and more group members get involved in decision-making or approving and relaying messages that were sent to someone else, the efficiency of the organization is reduced. At times, we have to re-allocate authority and power, we have to increase ambiguity temporarily so that innovations can be made.

There are no hard and fast rules about the most desirable relationships among authority prescriptions, descriptions, and expectations. In a system that is relatively stable, the three should be congruent. The desired level of congruity at any given time is determined by our purposes and the existing state of the system. In understanding any system, we need to take into account the kinds of purposes that are being expressed, the kinds of goals that are being achieved, and the stability of authority patterns that exists, as related to purpose.

MULTIPLE ROLES: REFERENCE GROUPS

When we talked about roles, we assumed for the most part that a *given* person had a *given* role in a *given* social system. Although it was pointed out that we belong to more than one system at a time, the discussion was limited for purposes of clarity to a given system.

Obviously, we do operate simultaneously in a large number of systems. In a complex society such as the United States, an individual may have roles in twenty-five to fifty groups or even more. He occupies a position in each group, he performs behaviors in each group. In addition to the groups of which he is a member, there are groups to which he would like to belong or with which he identifies himself. All these groups serve as references for him at one time or another. *Reference groups are the social systems that serve as reference points for the individual, groups whose norms and role-behaviors are pertinent predictors of his own behavior and beliefs.*

When we attempt to predict behavior from our knowledge of a social system, it is important that we select the systems that are crucial to behavior. Individuals who belong to multiple groups perform multiple roles. For any given situation, some of these roles are useful in predicting behavior, and some are not. The key question is, which groups is he using as a reference for his behaviors; which role is he performing now, what norms are pertinent to him, what position does he perceive himself as occupying? No answer can be given to this question without a consideration of the specific situation in which behavior occurs. All we can do is develop a caution about the predictions we make and check our predictions against as many groups as possible.

ROLE AND NORM CONFLICTS

The problem of conflicting role behaviors, positions, and norms is related to the previous discussion. As an individual moves from system to system, he may find himself in conflict. The role position he occupies in one group may be antagonistic to the position he occupies in another group. The norms subscribed to by one system may be antagonistic to the norms subscribed to by another. The beliefs that are held by one group may be antagonistic to the beliefs of another. All these inconsistencies can and do occur. When role, or norm, or belief conflicts occur, they cause two kinds of communication difficulties: (1) the accuracy of our prediction of a man's behavior goes down, beause we cannot be sure how the individual will resolve the conflict, which set of behaviors, positions, norms, or beliefs will be dominant for him, and (2) there is a decrease in the individual's own ability to make responses that are consistent over time—he may see himself in conflict and react confusedly or erratically to the ambiguity that is produced.

Let us take an example of role conflict. Since World War II, many veterans serve in the military reserves, retaining the rank that they held when they were discharged from service. At the same time these individuals have entered or re-entered a task-oriented system, their job or profession. Let us suppose that one individual was discharged as a captain from the service and went into a large company for his working career. He was successful in the company and rose to become a vice-president in charge of production.

At the same time, let us suppose another man was discharged as a colonel and returned to the same company as a foreman. He was not successful in increasing his position in the company and remained a foreman, under the supervision of the vice-president for production. Both men remained in the active reserves.

In one social system, the company, one man (vice-president and captain) was the superior officer of the other (foreman and colonel). In the other social system, the military, the rankings were reversed. This is role conflict.

The behavioral relationships between these two men differ from system to system. So do the authority relationships. This kind of difference is difficult to handle. We could predict that problems would arise in the expectations that each would have about how he should be treated by the other. The factors that determine allocation of position in the military are not the same as the factors that determine position in the company; therefore, one man may have a high position in one and only a medium position in the other.

Conflicts in norms also affect communication. There has been a considerable amount of research on the effect of conflicting norms. We can use one study as an example of norm conflict.[3] This study used students who were working for a school as proctors: they supervised the taking of examinations to see that everything went properly. Proctors were assigned so that some of them supervised examinations taken by their own roommates and best friends. The roommates were asked to cheat on the examination in such a way that the proctor would observe them. The experimental question was concerned with predicting the proctor's behavior.

The proctor belonged to two systems: the school faculty and a friendship group with his fellow students. A norm of the faculty is that students should be reported for cheating. A norm of the friendship group is that all members should protect all other members from harm from outsiders. The proctor was faced with conflicting norms: if he conformed to the faculty norm, he would be violating the student norm and vice versa. We all can find examples of this kind of norm conflict in behavior. In fact, norm conflicts are used as basic plots in the theatre because they provide vivid vehicles for the expression of emotion.

Communication behavior involving role or norm conflicts increases the tensions of the persons involved and makes it difficult for them to produce a response. The possibility of role or norm conflict needs to be taken into account when we make predictions about communication behavior. To the extent that there is conflict, our confidence in our predictions goes down.

COMMUNICATION ACROSS SOCIAL SYSTEMS

Most of our discussion has been limited to a given social system. Communication behaviors are considerably broader than this. Members of one system often communicate with members of another. Representatives of an entire system, or of a collectivity of systems, communicate with representatives of a different system. Everything

[3] Sam Stouffer, "An analysis of conflicting social norms," *American Sociological Review*, 14:707–717, 1949.

that we have said about problems within a system applies to cross-system communication.

METHODS OF STRUCTURING ROLE BEHAVIORS. The development of a role requires the assembling of behaviors into a set, plus the naming of the set. There is no "right" or "true" way to collect behaviors. One system may use one method. A second system may use quite different methods. When we are communicating across systems, we cannot assume that the behaviors which go with a given role are the same as they would be in our own system.

For any of a number of reasons, a system may have grouped behaviors differently. If we do not recognize this, we can make predictions about behavior that are seriously in error. For example, the behaviors that are prescribed for students in an American secondary school are quite different from the behaviors prescribed for students in a university. If a student changes from high school to college and is not aware that his behaviors should change, he can meet with failure and never realize why.

High-school students are not expected to set their own study plans, to pace their own work. The teacher tends to do this for them. In college, the teacher does not exercise this kind of supervision. The student is expected to handle more of his work on his own. If the student does not do this and waits to be told, he may fail a course—even though he could have passed it.

METHODS OF ALLOCATING AUTHORITY. All social systems allocate positions to roles. The concept of ranking is pertinent to any system; however, the methods of ranking may differ significantly. If we assume that one system ranks on the same basis as another, we can make erroneous predictions about communication behavior.

Take professional sports as an example. Professional football is a social system, headed by a commissioner. The commissioner of football has a position within the system. He exercises great authority. Other professional sports also have commissioners; however, in most of those systems they do not have the authority that the football commissioner has. The roles are the same, the authority levels are not.

We could draw other examples by comparing the authority of the chief of state or the foreign minister from country to country, the authority of the university professor in European and American countries, etc. A given role may have one authority position in one system, and a quite different position in a second system. Failure to realize this produces errors in prediction.

KINDS OF GOAL INTERDEPENDENCE. Systems may differ in the ways in which they group behaviors among roles, and in the ways that they assign positions to roles. They also may differ, and often do, in their concepts of goal interdependence. One kind of system may emphasize contrient interdependence. Each member of the system may compete against other members of the same system in achieving a goal. Another system may emphasize promotive interdependence, in which all the group members work together to reach a common goal.

Foreign visitors to the U. S. have great difficulty in understanding the way in which a company such as General Motors or Chrysler is organized. General Motors has several automobile divisions: Pontiac, Chevrolet, Buick, etc. Each of these divisions is part of the same system, General Motors; however, each perceives itself as contriently interdependent with the other divisions. In other words, Chevrolet dealers compete with Pontiac dealers, etc. All group together in competing against Chrysler, Plymouth, Dodge dealers, or Ford dealers.

This kind of goal relationship differs from those found in other countries, or even in other companies within this country. If we forget that the interdependence relationships differ from system to system, we have trouble in understanding how a particular system operates.

A second example can be taken from education. In the United States, teachers often try to motivate their students by getting them to compete with each other for grades, to compete for quicker accomplishment of tasks, and so forth. Suppose a teacher from this kind of system began to teach a group of Navaho Indian children. Their perceptions of interdependence are different. If you send a group of Navaho children to the board to work on an arithmetic problem, no one will "finish" first. If one child completes his work, he carefully checks to see how all of the other children are coming. He does not turn away from the board until the last child is through—then all of the children turn together. They do not want to finish "first" or to "beat" another student in the same class. If an outside teacher tried to motivate the class by providing a kind of contrient stimulation, he would meet with failure.

DIFFERENCES IN NORMS, VALUES, BELIEFS. Much of the prior discussion has been related to beliefs and values that are held by members of a given system. We can talk specifically, however, about such differences as they affect communication. Each social system develops its own norms. They may differ radically from system to system. As we communicate across systems, we need to take these differences into account or we will not be effective in our predictions.

Some systems have norms about "pride of workmanship" or "punctuality." Members of that system may pride themselves on turning out flawless products or on being at a particular place at exactly the time when they said they would be there. Other systems may not operate under these norms. They have different norms of their own.

An American's concept of punctuality is quite different from a Tunisian's or an Indonesian's. In the American system, if you arrive at a man's office fifteen minutes after you said you would be there, you have violated a norm. In a Tunisian system, you might arrive at a man's office an hour late, sometimes a half a day late and not violate a norm at all. An American who works in a Tunisian system has to alter his concepts of group norms. If he does not, he will be insulted, hurt, and critical of the Tunisian's behavior— because he is bound by the norms of his own system, and does not realize that they are neither "right" nor "true" for another system.

One system may hold "getting the job done" as a more important value than "making people feel comfortable"; that is to say, the system places more emphasis on productivity goals than on maintenance goals. Another system may place more emphasis on maintenance goals, may prefer to forget about getting the job done if it requires hurting a particular individual's dignity or respect, or losing a friend. If members from these two systems communicate with each other about task-accomplishments, they will have real trouble in understanding the point of view of the other person until they realize that values differ from system to system.

LANGUAGE AND THOUGHT. We have suggested that languages affect thought, that language units are thought units. If this is so, systems that employ different codes may well employ different methods of thought. A German's language is different from an American's language. It may follow that his methods of thinking are also different. His basic approaches to problem solution may be different. There is little evidence as yet to substantiate this thesis; however, it is a possibility that needs to be taken into account when we communicate across language boundaries, across systems that employ different codes. Problems of international negotiation, either political or commercial, are related in part to language differences.

The Concept of Cultural Context

In Chapter 2, we talked about membership in social systems as a determinant of communication. This chapter has been devoted to specifying some of the ways in which social organization affects communication behavior. We also said that all communication occurs within a cultural context. How is the concept of culture related to our discussion?

Culture is all man's shared beliefs, values, ways of making things, ways of behaving. Culture includes games, songs, and dances; the ways of building a shelter, growing maize, and navigating a boat; the structure and operation of families, governments, and educational systems; the division of authority, assignment of roles, and establishment of norms within such systems; language, and all other codes, and the shared concepts which are encoded; and a complex of ways to pass itself along, to adapt itself to changed environment, and to ensure through social pressure and rewards the carrying out of its imperatives. These shared behaviors and predispositions, part of us and of the people who surround us, we call the cultural context.

Groups and Individuals: The Basis for Prediction

Chapters 2, 3, and 4 emphasized ways in which we can predict communication behavior from our knowledge of a particular individual; his personality, his way of learning, the rewards he receives. Chapters 5 and 6 have emphasized social or group bases for prediction. At no time have we discussed physiological bases for prediction, although they too are relevant to behavior.

The question is asked, which of these points of view is most useful in understanding behavior, in predicting about communication? I hope it has been implied throughout that there is no adequate answer to that kind of question other than "yes." All of these points of view are relevant to behavior.

Man is a biological animal. Man is an individual. Man is a social agent. The point of view of the observer determines which of these man "really" is.

When we communicate, we intend to affect—to have influence on—our environment and ourselves. In doing this, we can profit from predictions about how others behave, how we behave. We can gain greater understanding, we can gain greater effectiveness. In making predictions, we have to take into account all the factors that affect behavior. Some are social, some are personal. Even when we make that statement we need to realize that all are both— separations of personal and social characteristics are merely for convenience. They cannot be separated.

Culture affects personality. Biological needs affect social organization. Knowledge affects attitudes. Language affects thought. Thought affects belief. Beliefs affect social systems. Social systems affect biological states. None is primary, none is basic. All the factors discussed are related to all the others.

Human life is a process, as is communication, learning, social organization. The point of view of a communication theorist is that no single aspect of human behavior can be analyzed adequately in ignorance of any of the other aspects of human behavior. We cannot gain a maximum understanding of the process of communication unless we attempt to relate all the variables to each other, unless we are willing to use whatever knowledge we have, however we gained it, from wherever it came, to help us explain and predict how people are what they are, and what they are becoming.

When we communicate, we should base our predictions on everything we know. Everything we know is only a part of what is known. Everything that is known is only a part of what is knowable. Probably, everything that is knowable is only a part of what determines behavior. It seems plausible to argue that human behavior can never be predicted with complete accuracy. That is what makes it fun.

Suggestions for Thought and Discussion

1. Compare the relative value of empathy and knowledge of a social system as a basis for predicting behavior. What are the advantages and disadvantages of each? Discuss both in terms of accuracy and energy. Is it possible to use one but not the other; that is to say, are they independent? Defend your answer.

2. Analyze a social system of which you are a member. Draw a picture of the positions of roles within the system—rank each role. Speculate on the basis for stratifying the roles within this system. Why is it that the top-ranking role is top-ranking, etc? Can you defend the present ranking system of the organization on the basis of group productivity and maintenance, or would there be a more efficient and effective method of organization?

3. Find examples of people you know who have more esteem than prestige. How does this affect their behavior within the system and how others behave toward them? On what basis did the esteem for them develop?

4. Suppose a friend of yours had just married the boss's daughter of a large company. As a result of his new position in his wife's family system, his father-in-law was taking him into his company as a vice-president. What advice would you give your friend about how he

should behave at work? What problems might he have on the job? How could he solve these problems for himself?

5. Analyze a social system of which you are a member. Try to specify the norms that operate within the system. Observe carefully the behaviors of other members of the system. Which of them conform to the norms, and which do not? Which are more popular within the group, the conformists or the deviates? How is conformity to group norms related to leadership within the group?

6. Find examples of communication breakdowns that occur in your own experience. Analyze them in terms of the problems in prediction discussed in this chapter.

7. Suppose you decided to enter the foreign service of the U.S., and were assigned to duty in a foreign country. What things would you want to know about the country in order to improve your communication effectiveness?

8. Discuss the relative merits of promotive and contrient interdependence. Which kind of goal interdependence do you prefer? Which is closer to the "democratic ideal?"

Meaning and Communication

IN PRECEDING chapters, we have tried to analyze the ingredients of the process of communication. In doing this, we have approached communication behaviors from various points of view, attempting to incorporate each into our general model. We have not concentrated on the actual behaviors involved in communication—the messages that we transmit back and forth. In this and following chapters, we will focus our attention on several aspects of the *message* as a communication ingredient. It is only through the production, transmission, and reception of messages that any kind of communication effects occur.

In communicating, we attempt to accomplish goals relating to our basic intention to affect our environment and ourselves. Often, we say that we want our receivers to make certain responses, to know certain things, to believe in one way or another, to be able to do various things. In accomplishing these purposes, we are limited to the production of messages. True, we can think about these messages in various ways, we can analyze ourselves and the receiver with varying amounts of skill. Nevertheless, communication can invariably be reduced to the performance of a set of behaviors, the transmission or reception of messages.

What are messages? They are behavioral events that are related to the internal states of people. They are scratches on paper, sounds in the air, markings on stone, movements of the body. They are the products of man, the results of his efforts to encode his ideas. They often exist long after their sources and intended receivers are gone; nevertheless, they are human products intended to produce effects on humans.

In producing or receiving messages, we require the use of a *code*. In producing a message, we encode it: we choose symbols and arrange them in a systematic way. In receiving a message, we decode it. We try to translate this code into our own nervous systems, in a way that is meaningful.

The concept of meaning is central to communication. It can be argued that the major concern of communication is meaning. We use the word "meaning" frequently when we talk about communication, or when we communicate. We search for words to express our meaning, we ask others to tell us what they mean, we criticize beginning writers for not expressing their meaning clearly, we worry about "hidden meanings" in the messages we send and receive. We look for the meaning in art, for the meaning of musical forms, for the meanings in people's behavior. We ask, what does this mean to me, does this have meaning for you, can you figure out what was meant?

What do we mean by meaning? Where do we find it? How do we know it when we see it? If the only communication ingredient common to both the source and the receiver is the message, it would seem that our search for a meaning for "meaning" might profitably begin with an analysis of the message itself.

Messages are the expressions of ideas (content), expressed in a particular way (treatment), through the use of a code. There are many codes in communication: visual symbols, gestures, hand signals, speech, writing, etc. We must choose one or another code whenever we communicate. The most common code we use is verbal, a language such as English.

For the present, we shall restrict our discussion of a code to a discussion of language. Much of what we say is applicable to other codes as well. Most of it is applicable to other linguistic codes, though the applicability of some of our discussion will be restricted to English.

The Origin of Language

In analyzing the role of language, we could profit from a thorough explanation of the origins of language, the basis for man's development of verbal codes. Unfortunately, we cannot provide such an explanation. No one who was around when languages began to develop wrote a book about it. All we have to go on is speculation about language origins. These speculations are useful, however, in indicating the ways in which we can analyze our meaning of meaning.

Thorndike summarized most of the speculations which have been made about language origins and added his own thinking to them. In his article on "The Origins of Language,"[1] he listed four sets of hypotheses about the basis of man's use of sounds to express his meaning. Somewhat picturesquely, he labeled the four groups as the "ding-dong," the "bow-wow," the "pooh-pooh," and the "yum-yum" theories of language origin.

THE DING-DONG THEORY. This is the notion that each thing in the physical world has some sound associated with it (bells go "ding-dong."). These sounds *mean* the thing—all men react the same way toward them. This is a rather ridiculous notion, although it was honored for a long time. We can think of many things for which we have no sounds and of many sounds for which we have no things.

THE BOW-WOW THEORY. According to this view, man copied sounds made by other animals. This is rather implausible too, but it also was highly thought of for a long time. There is considerable doubt that a dog really barks "bow-wow"; sounds for dogs' barks differ from language to language, although the dogs do not. It is probable that certain words might have been created this way, but not much of any natural language.

[1] E. L. Thorndike, "The origins of language," *Science*, 98:1–6, 1943.

THE POOH-POOH THEORY. This notion argues that man makes certain *instinctive* sounds, and that we have meaning for these sounds because we all make them. Modern linguistic research has denied the truth of this position rather consistently.

THE YUM-YUM THEORY. A physicist by the name of Paget argued that man responds gesturally to any stimulus. Part of this response is made by the mouth. According to Paget, sounds are produced as a result of the positioning of the tongue in the mouth cavity. They are a reduction of the original gestures of man. This is possible— but again, extremely unlikely. As Thorndike comments, "I do not believe that any human being before Sir Richard Paget ever made any considerable number of gestures with his mouth parts in sympathetic pantomime with gestures of his hands, arms and legs."

None of these views of language are highly plausible. All of them are interesting in that they make certain assumptions. They assume that:

1. Man created sounds to *mean* something for him.
2. He created these sounds in such a way that they were related to meanings which he already had.
3. The creation was an act of man, not of God.

Thorndike's own position is based on the model of human learning that we talked about in Chapter 4. It is somewhat more acceptable as a theory of language origin. We can agree that some words in English might have been created under the conditions of the "ding-dong," "bow-wow," "pooh-pooh," and "yum-yum" theories of language origin. Most words cannot be traced to these kinds of sources. Most words seem to have had arbitrary origins. By arbitrary, I mean that there was no necessary reason why a particular word was developed to mean a particular thing for people. It just happened that way. This suggests a fourth assumption about the origin of language: *language symbols are arbitrary.* This view of language origin is more general and includes all of the others. Thorndike referred to this view as a "babble-luck" theory of language origin.

THE BABBLE-LUCK THEORY. Research indicates that all infants

make sounds, they babble. This production of sounds appears to be rewarding in itself. Certainly the parent rewards the production of sounds in the infant. Gradually, the infant learns a language. Thorndike argues that the development of babbling, sound-production, in the infant is analogous to the development of language itself in the history of man.

Let us assume that pre-language man babbled frequently. He did this while he worked with the physical objects of his existence. Over time, certain sounds (babbling) were made by chance (luck) when certain objects were touched or handled. Again, over time, by chance, men heard each other make certain sounds when they both were handling certain objects.

After a long, long time, these sounds became relatively fixed or permanent. How so? Man might have found that he could use these sounds as substitutes for the objects. He got a response from other men when he used certain sounds. This response was *rewarding* to him—the response increased his ability to affect his environment and his fellow men. Gradually, men began to respond to a certain set of sounds in a similar way, they began to make similar responses to these oral symbols. This is what we meant earlier when we talked about significant symbols. *Significant symbols are symbols that produce similar responses in more than one person.*

Language includes a set of *significant symbols,* but it includes more than that. We *sequence* these symbols. We put one first, another second, another last. We impose a *structure* on the arrangement of the symbols.

Language is a system, involving both elements and structures. As in any system, we can define elemental and structural units at many levels depending on purpose. At any level, however, language includes a set of symbols (vocabulary) and the meaningful methods of combining those units (a syntax). A *grammar* is the description of the structural characteristics of the language.

Both the symbols and the structural relationships must produce similar responses from a group of people (language-users). When a group of people encode and decode a set of symbols that are mutually significant to them, and when they combine them similarly, then this group of people can be said to have a language.

In summary, the best assumptions about the origins of language imply the following statements:

1. Language consists of a set of significant symbols (vocabulary) plus meaningful methods for their combination (syntax).
2. The symbols of a language were chosen by chance. They are not fixed or God-given.
3. Man constructed his own language under the same principles of interpretation, response, and reward that govern all learning.
4. Man gradually created language in order to express his meanings to himself and others, to get other people to have the same meanings, and to make responses that increased his ability to affect.

The Meaning of Meaning

One of the values of remembering the babble-luck theory of language origin is that it prevents us from believing that there is some "correct" or "necessary" relationship between symbols and objects, between maps and territories. We all know the story of the person who, when asked why he called a pig a "pig," replied, "because it is so dirty." This is far-fetched, but you have probably heard discussions about "proper" language, or the "correct" way of using language, or of the "real" meaning of certain words that might remind you of the man with his pig.

We use language to express and elicit meanings. This is the function of language. *Meaning is inherent in the very definition of language.* In teaching others about communication, in communicating ourselves, in criticizing the communication of other people, meaning is and should be our chief concern.

Clearly, meaning is related to the codes we choose in communicating, the languages we use in encoding our intentions into messages and in responding to a decoded message. In trying to arrive at a meaning for meaning, let us analyze several English sentences in which the word "meaning" (or a derivative of it) occurs, and see if we can abstract some commonality from them. Here are six sample English sentences:

1. To use words properly, you must know what they mean.
2. The purpose of some writing is to communicate meanings.
3. I hear thunder. That means rain soon.
4. In English, the letter "s" at the end of the noun usually means "more than one" or "plural."
5. My family means much to me.
6. Words do not have meaning—only people do.

Most of us have encoded or decoded sentences like the six listed. Clearly, the word "meaning" in these six sentences does not seem to be used in the same way. The first sentence implies that meanings are the properties of words, to be memorized when the word is learned. In the third sentence, the word "meaning" seems to indicate that one thing leads to another—in this case, thunder leads to rain. In sentence five, the writer apparently is telling us the state of his feelings when he thinks of his family. Finally, sentence six says that meanings are not found in words at all, that they are found only in people.

These uses of the word "meaning" are not the same. Some of them even seem inconsistent with the others. Apparently, we cannot determine what is meant by "meaning" by analyzing it in sentences such as these. We *can* agree that the word "meaning" seems to have many meanings for us. We are left with the question, what are meanings? What do words *really* mean? Or, as the sixth sentence implies, do words *really* mean at all?

Can a word have a meaning? Words are only scratches of ink on paper, speech is only a set of sounds that are transmitted through the air. Is meaning a physical thing such that it can be found on paper or in the air? Is meaning something found in the message, something external to people?

There is evidence to indicate that many people would answer these questions affirmatively. Some people tell us to look in the dictionary to find the meaning for a word, that a given passage in literature means "exactly what it says," that meaning is present in messages, available to any person who cares to look for it.

It is the thesis of this chapter that meanings are not in messages, that meaning is not something which is discoverable, that words do not really mean anything at all, that dictionaries do not and cannot provide us with meanings. It will be argued that *meanings are in people,* that meanings are covert responses, contained within the human organism. Meanings are learned. They are personal, our own property. We learn meanings, we add to them, we distort them, forget them, change them. We cannot *find* them. They are in *us,* not in messages. Fortunately, we usually find other people who have meanings that are similar to ours. To the extent that people have similar meanings, they can communicate. If they have no similarities in meaning between them, they cannot communicate.

If meanings are found in words, it would follow that any person could understand any language, any code. If the meaning is in the word, we should be able to analyze the word and find the meaning. Yet obviously we cannot. Some people have meanings for some codes, others do not.

The elements and structure of a language do not themselves have meaning. They are only symbols, sets of symbols, cues that cause us to bring our own meanings into play, to think about them, to rearrange them, etc. *Communication does not consist of the transmission of meaning.* Meanings are not transmittable, not transferable. Only messages are transmittable, and meanings are not in the message, they are in the message-users.

This point seems apparent; however, all of us forget it now and then. Serious breakdowns in communication can be attributed to the false assumption that there is meaning in the message, rather than only in the source and receiver. The methods of teaching a foreign language will differ radically, depending on whether the teacher assumes that meanings are in words or in people.

The ways in which people argue, and the things they choose to argue about, depend in part on which point of view they accept. Many of our arguments are based on the assumptions that a given word has a specific meaning and that any one who uses that word intends to express that meaning.

It often requires several hours, or even decades, for people to realize that they were agreeing, but merely using different words to say the same thing. People are often shocked to find others "going back on their word," when the facts of the matter are that each party to the agreement meant something quite different by the same words, the same contract. "Democracy" to an American is not "democracy" to a Russian. Both have meanings for the term—the term has no meaning of its own.

All of us tend to be egocentric. We tend to interpret the world from our own vantage point. This makes it very difficult to interact, to empathize. It makes it difficult to communicate at all. It often has been said that words do not mean the same to all people. It is more accurate to say that *words do not mean at all.* Only people mean, and people do not mean the same by all words.

We violate this belief often in our own behavior, because of our self-centered perceptions. Even the Golden Rule might well be amended. The Golden Rule tells us to "treat others as you would have them treat you." This is an egocentric admonition. In our dealings with people, particularly those from a different culture, it is more useful to say "treat others as they would like to be treated—which may be quite different from the way you would like to be treated."

If you asked a visitor from Latin America to tell you about his work, you would be shocked if he were to begin to talk to you in Spanish. You probably would say, just because he understands (i.e., has meanings for) Spanish, he should not expect me to. Yet, Americans abroad, or even at home talking to visitors from abroad, expect a foreigner to talk and write to them in English. Americans often cannot understand why foreigners talk so "funny," why they do not use the *right* words to talk about things, instead of those silly foreign words. Though possibly somewhat overstated, this kind of feeling exists—and is attributable in part to the false belief that there are meanings in words.

One communication problem can usefully be labeled the *"I told them"* fallacy. This fallacy is attributable to the false beliefs that there are meanings in words and that the use of words will insure understanding on the part of the receiver—unless he is too stupid to know the meanings that the words have.

In an industrial organization, the supervisor continually writes memos to his subordinates, but his employees do not do what he wants them to do. He cannot understand why they did not get the meaning. If you ask him what the problem is, the typical reply is, "I can't understand what's wrong with those people—I TOLD THEM. You just can't get decent help these days."

The "I told them" fallacy also occurs in technical writing situations. Suppose a reporter interviews a scientist for a story on what the scientist has been doing. The scientist explains a new process he is working on or some new technique he has discovered. The next day, the scientist reads the story that the reporter wrote. It is all wrong; it does not say what the scientist wanted said. The result: he is angry with the reporter, refuses to grant any more interviews, and justifies his position on the grounds that, "You tell these people what they need to know—and they don't print it."

In agricultural extension work, the extension agent often is asked a question by a farmer, such as, "How can I keep my pigs from dying?" Often, the agent "helps" the farmer by giving him a scientific bulletin prepared by government scientists on the "proper care and feeding of swine." The farmer reads it, until his energy gives out, and then gives up because he cannot find the answer to his question. If he complains, the extension agent's defense often is, "But I TOLD HIM what he needed to know."

Whenever you hear someone say "I TOLD HIM" you can assume that he believes that meanings are in words and that communication consists of finding the "right" words—and sending them to the receiver. If the receiver does not understand the words, the source says something of the order "I can't give him understanding, I can only give him information." Communication breaks down, because the source believes that meanings are in words, rather than in people.

We have said that meanings are in people, that words do not

have meaning. Meanings are personal, they differ from person to person. In order to demonstrate the basis for this position, we need to take a look at how people learn meanings and at what we mean by "meaning" when we say that it is the property of people.

How We Learn Meanings

When you were born, you had no meanings. No object or symbol in the world meant anything to you. As William James put it, the world was a "blooming, buzzing confusion."

This confusion is soon reduced. Before long, a normal infant learns to organize the world; he structures it. He sees things and organizes them into shapes and objects. He hears things and organizes them into sounds.

Soon he begins to move—randomly at first, but soon with purpose. He produces sounds of his own, soon selectively. The sounds of a three- or four-month-old baby are about the same from country to country, but by the time the infant is seven or eight months old his sounds are more like the sounds that his parents make than they are like the sounds of other infants whose parents speak different languages. Clearly, an infant learns. He learns to structure his perceptions, to produce sounds in combination, and to *mean* something by his sounds.

We will concentrate on oral, rather than written, communication in discussing how we learn meanings because oral language is learned first. Only much later do children begin to learn the relationship between sounds and letters, or writing. In fact, 80 per cent of the world's adults have never learned these relationships.

How do we learn these things? How do we get meanings from the world? Let us look at this process, and see if it can give us some leads about the nature of meaning and communication.

Let us look first at a general kind of learning—conditioning. Most of you have studied Pavlov's dog at one time or another. Let us review how Pavlov's dog "learned." Pavlov presented a stimulus to his dog, such as food. The dog made a response, such as salivating.

The dog did not have to "learn" to salivate. When food was

placed in his mouth, he salivated automatically. We call this a reflexive response. Sometimes we say that such a response is "wired-in."

Pavlov also presented another stimulus, just before he gave the
dog food. He rang a bell, and then gave the food. The dog responded to the bell in the way that you would expect a dog to
respond to a bell. Time after time, Pavlov repeated this procedure.
He rang the bell, then gave the dog food. Each time, the dog salivated. After many trials, Pavlov observed that when the dog heard
the bell, he salivated—before Pavlov gave him the food. In other
words, he began to respond to the bell in a new way. He began
to make responses to the bell that earlier he had made to the food.

Pavlov and others have called a stimulus such as the food an
"unconditioned stimulus"; that is to say, a stimulus that produces
a certain response under any conditions. We call a stimulus such
as the bell a "conditioned stimulus"; that is to say, a stimulus that
does not elicit a certain response (such as salivating) in the first
place, but that began to after it was paired with the unconditioned
stimulus. We say that the dog became conditioned to the bell. We
call this "learning by conditioning."

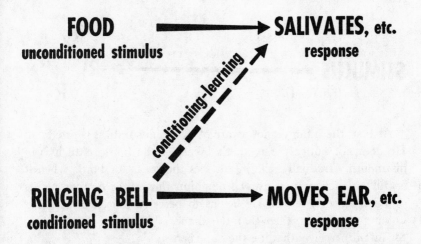

For many years we thought that people learned meanings for
language in the same way. In fact, some psychologists defined the

meaning of a stimulus as the overt response that a person made to it. In the last ten or fifteen years, we have modified our views about learning—especially human learning. Yet our present views about language learning and meaning are still similar to this classical model of conditioning.

Let us look at the process of human learning. Specifically, how do we learn meanings;—meanings for things, and for words? As mentioned earlier, the newborn infant has no meanings for objects or events in the physical world. He acquires meanings through experience. What are some of his early experiences?

Shortly after birth, he eats. A stimulus, food, is presented to him. This may be the breast of the mother or the nipple of a bottle. He makes several responses to this stimulus. He salivates; he burps; he gets "full"; etc. We can see some of these responses. Others are hard to observe.

We call things like food in mouth or hand on a hot stove "proximal" stimuli; the stimulus is in contact with the person. A proximal stimulus elicits several responses: R_1, R_2, R_3, etc. Some of these responses are easy to see; others are not. Many of them are reflexive or wired-in.

$$\textbf{STIMULUS} \xrightarrow{\hspace{4cm}} \quad \begin{array}{c} R_2 \\ R_1 \quad R_N \\ R_3 \end{array}$$

(PROXIMAL)

At first, the infant is not aware of a stimulus until it is proximal. He does not notice the mother's breast or the bottle until it is in his mouth. Gradually, the infant sees the breast or bottle when it is still an inch or two away from him, then three or four inches away, then several feet. He begins to perceive that some shape is holding the bottle, then that the shape is a person. Much later, the infant perceives that it is the same person.

We call things like the bottle approaching the mouth, the mother holding the bottle, etc., "distal" stimuli. They are not in contact with the infant. They do not elicit wired-in responses. They are paired with a proximal stimulus.

These distal stimuli become related to the original proximal stimulus. Eventually, the infant responds to these stimuli in some of the same ways that he originally responded to the proximal stimulus.

We can see many parallels between this discussion and our earlier discussion of Pavlov's dog. The proximal stimulus looks like Pavlov's "unconditioned stimulus." It is. The distal stimulus looks like Pavlov's "conditioned stimulus." It is not quite the same, although similar.

The dog responds to the bell in about the same way that it responded to the food. The infant does not respond to the distal stimulus in exactly the same way that he responds to the proximal stimulus. What does he do? We are not exactly sure what he does. We do have some hunches. In fact, we have more than hunches. We have a hypothesis, a theory, developed by Osgood and labeled the "mediation hypothesis."[2]

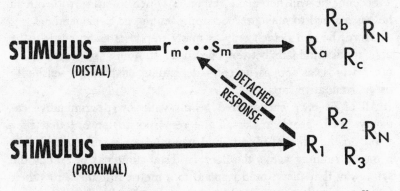

Osgood suggests that the infant begins to respond *internally* to the distal stimulus. Clearly, the infant does not make all of the responses to his mother that he made to the bottle or breast. He does make some of them. Osgood hypothesizes that the infant's

[2] Charles E. Osgood, *Method and Theory in Experimental Psychology,* Oxford University Press, 1953, pp. 392–412.

internal responses, which become fixed over time, stimulate the infant to make certain overt responses. Some of these are the same ones he made to the proximal stimulus; some are not.

What responses are internalized? Osgood suggests that they are parts of the response to the proximal stimulus that are separable from the rest; that is to say, responses that the individual can make when the proximal stimulus has not been presented.

According to the mediation hypothesis, three principles determine which responses are separated from the rest and internalized. We are likely to separate (a) responses which do not require much effort to make, (b) responses which do not interfere with the responses we made to the distal stimulus in the first place, and (c) the fewest responses necessary to discriminate between this and other stimuli. In our example, we would say that the infant will classify the responses he makes to food in his mouth. Some of these he will make to food approaching, or to his mother.

First, he makes the easy ones. He probably will not salivate, but he will move his mouth. He will not burp, but he will gurgle.

Second, he will not make responses which interfere with others he has learned to make to food approaching, or to his mother.

Third, he will detach only as many responses as he needs to be able to discriminate betwen one distal stimulus and another. In other words, as few as he can—depending on his own sensitivity or discriminative capacity.

All of us have encountered people with low discriminative capacity. Such people make all the responses to a word that they made to the original object. For example, some ladies respond to a mouse running across the floor (a distal stimulus) in exactly the same way that they would respond to a mouse running across their feet (proximal stimulus). Most of us laugh when women make such responses; however, if people behave like this all of the time, we commit them to an institution.

Let us take another example: If someone were to throw a ball at your face, what would you do? As it approaches, you probably would blink your eyes, or even duck your head. You have not always responded this way. A small child does not blink or duck his head as the ball approaches (a distal stimulus). He only blinks or ducks when the ball actually touches him (a proximal stimulus). Only after repeated trials does the child respond to the approach of the ball in some of the ways that he originally responded to the actual contact.

Most of us can recall a childhood game, "flinch," which is based on the reversal of this process. In "flinch" someone throws an object toward you or brings his doubled fist toward you. If you move, or blink, you "flinched," and have to take your punishment.

How can we analyze "flinch"? As an infant, it took many trials for you to learn to respond to the approach of a ball or a fist (distal stimulus) in some of the ways that you originally responded to the touch of a ball or fist (proximal stimulus). Finally, you learned. "Flinch" tries to reverse this. In "flinch," you learn *not* to respond in the same way to both the distal and proximal stimuli. The approaching ball or fist comes to elicit a new overt response, and a new conditioning relationship is established.

We can summarize what has been said about how people react to proximal and distal stimuli, how people learn, as follows:

1. A proximal stimulus elicits in part a wired-in or reflexive response.
2. Distal stimuli are paired with the proximal stimulus.
3. People begin to respond (internally) to the distal stimulus, by detaching and internalizing some of their original responses to the proximal stimulus. Specifically, people detach the responses which:

   a. require the least effort;
   b. do not interfere with the response they used to make to the distal stimulus;
   c. enable them to discriminate between this stimulus and other stimuli.

4. These internal responses become relatively fixed over time.
5. The internal responses serve as a stimulus to the individual to make some sort of overt response.

6. The individual may or may not make overt responses to the distal stimulus.

What has all this to do with communication, with meaning? One more point needs to be made. This is the crucial one:

7. The internal response—and the internal stimulus that comes from it—can be defined as the "meaning" of the external stimulus, for the person who is responding.

What I have suggested is that meaning is not something that we find in objects or things. Meaning is found in people. *Your meanings for things consist of the ways that you respond to them, internally, and the predispositions which you have to respond to them, externally.*

There are several implications of this definition of meaning:

1. Meanings are in people. They are the internal responses that people make to stimuli, and the internal stimulations that these responses elicit.
2. Meanings result from (a) factors in the individual, as related to (b) factors in the physical world around him.
3. People can have similar meanings only to the extent that they have had similar experiences, or can anticipate similar experiences.
4. Meanings are never fixed. As experience changes, meanings change.
5. No two people can ever have *exactly* the same meaning for anything. Many times two people do not have even similar meanings.
6. People will always respond to a stimulus in light of their own experiences.
7. To give people a meaning, or to change their meanings for a stimulus, you must pair the stimulus with other stimuli for which they already have meanings.
8. In learning meanings, people operate on the principles of (a) least effort, (b) noninterference, and (c) discriminative capacity.

We have not yet talked about meanings for linguistic stimuli; that is to say, sounds and written symbols that we call "words" and "sentences." How are these learned? The same process occurs. Everything we have said about how people learn applies to the learning of language, of meanings for language symbols. Our original discussion can illustrate how this occurs.

By the time the infant is about a year old, he has acquired many meanings. The "blooming, buzzing confusion" that James referred to has been eliminated. The child has structured his environment—has acquired meanings. The child has learned and retained internal response-stimulus patterns for many of the stimuli to which he has been exposed. He now is ready to transfer these meanings to language stimuli.

First, the child learns combinations of sounds. We might call these "oral words." We can look on these as linguistic stimuli. We teach the child a meaning for these sounds by capitalizing on the proximal-distal pairings for which he already has meanings. We present an oral stimulus, such as "ball" or "mother." We pair it with the actual object, the infant's ball or his mother.

Over time, some of the original meaning for the nonlinguistic, distal stimulus is detached and becomes attached to the word "ball" or the word "mother." The same process has occurred again. A new stimulus is paired with another, for which we already had meaning. Some of this meaning rubs off onto the new stimulus. Coupled with the results of other such pairings, this meaning becomes our meaning for the new stimulus—the word.

Again, let us think about how we teach meanings to a child. When we consciously attempt to teach him meanings, we usually say the word, in the presence of the object. We point to the mother, and repeat, endlessly, the word "mother." We pick up the ball, and repeat, over and over, the word "ball." Even when we are not trying to teach him, we still help him by saying sentences and accompanying these with the appropriate behaviors.

With patience and time, we can teach the child to respond to the word or the sentence, instead of the thing. By the time the child is four or five, he has many meanings for the sound combinations

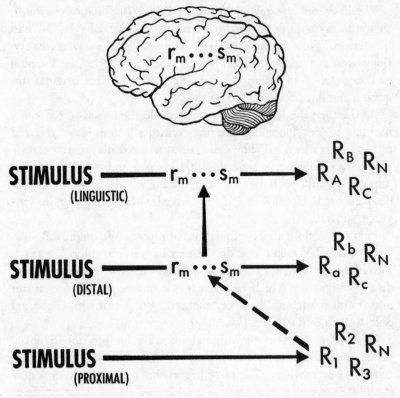

in his native language. He also has learned, through the same process, to put these words together in some sort of sequence acceptable to his parents and others.

How does the child learn meanings for the written word? By the same process. The written word is paired with the oral word, or possibly with the original object again. The job of the first- and second-grade teacher is not so much to give the child meanings, as to teach him to transfer his meanings to written symbols.

Man may be defined as a communicating animal. The essence of being human is contained in our facility to encode and decode linguistic stimuli; to interpret them, to give them meaning. This ability sets us off from other animals; however, it can lead us into pitfalls if we are not careful. Many of our communication problems develop because we forget the following cautions:

1. We must not forget that the word-symbol is not the thing; it merely represents the thing. There is no "right" or "God-given" meaning for words. Meanings are not in things, they are in people. Everyone does not have the same meaning for a word. We should not react to a word until we are sure of the meaning intended by its user.

2. Words are shorthand. We use them as convenient, portable substitutes for things. When we combine them, we can learn more from them than we might learn from the things they represent. Yet we must not forget that our meaning for any given word is merely a part of our original response to the thing that it represents—a part which has been detached through learning.

All that we have said about the learning of meanings is analogous to what we said earlier about learning and the communication process. *We learn language, or through language, in the same way that we learn many other things*. A person's responses must be rewarded, if they are to be retained. Stimuli must be presented in terms of the receiver's own experience and interest.

When we talked about the communication process and learning, we said that all messages have to be decoded and interpreted, and that some new message is encoded. We are saying the same thing when we say that a stimulus is perceived (decoding), some internal response-stimulus pattern is set up (interpretation), which we will call meanings, and some overt response (encoding) is made. In other words, *the process of learning language is the same as the process of learning anything*. Language behavior is learned behavior; language learning is inherently related to communication. *Meanings are our interpretations, the receiver-and-source behaviors that we perform internally.*

We learn many meanings when we are very young; however, we learn additional meanings, we change our meanings, lose them, distort them, every time we communicate. Communication is a process.

It involves a source, with certain meanings, who selects words and sentences to present to a receiver, who also has certain meanings. Communication is successful if and only if the receiver has meaning for the message, and if his meanings are similar to those intended by the source.

Meaning itself is a process. Sources can be gauged by their ability to select and arrange words that elicit the intended meanings from their receiver, that change the receiver's meanings, his way of looking at the world, that provide the receiver with insight he did not have before. To understand the nature of meaning and how meanings are learned, is to be prepared in part for effective communication. We cannot transfer or transmit meanings. All we can do is encode messages intended to elicit the meanings we desire.

In summary:

1. Meanings are found in people, not in messages.
2. Meanings are learned. They are a function of personal experience.
3. We learn words and acquire meanings for them by perceiving a word as related to other words, or objects, or perceptions—for which we already have meanings.
4. We learn meanings for oral sound combinations first, and only much later for written words.

Suggestions for Thought and Discussion

1. How did language originate? Why did it originate?
2. Are significant symbols and the structural relationships among them both indispensable to communication? Is one of these factors more important than the other? Are both the symbols of a language and the structural system of a language subject to change? What produces change?
3. Choose any word. Use the word in four sentences, illustrating a different meaning with each sentence. Think carefully, and write another sentence: your answer to the question "What does this word that you have chosen *really* mean?"
4. Review your answer to Question 3. Does your answer seem to indi-

cate that meaning is in the word itself, rather than in the people who use the words? If so, revise your answer to incorporate your understanding of the nature of meaning.

5. Describe at least three examples of the *I told them* fallacy from your own experience or from the experience of others with whom you have been associated. In each case, how could the communication breakdown have been prevented?

6. What is the difference between an unconditioned stimulus and a conditioned stimulus? What is a wired-in response? Discuss the mediation hypothesis. Illustrate the mediation hypothesis by an example. Summarize the learning process, and define meaning in terms of your summary.

7. "Your meanings for things consist of the ways that you respond to them, internally, and the predispositions which you have to respond to them, externally." Discuss each part of this statement. Supply an example of a meaning you have for something and discuss how each part of the statement applies to the example.

8. Make a careful analysis of the eight implications derived from the definition of meaning quoted in Question 7. There are, of course, additional implications, both general and specific; there are implications for teachers, implications for students, implications for dictionary-writers, etc. Supply several more implications, including at least one for teachers, one for students, and one for dictionary-writers.

9. Define and discuss "words" in terms of the definition of meaning quoted in Question 7.

CHAPTER 8

Dimensions of Meaning

WE have looked at the ways in which meanings are learned and how words come to have meanings for us. What we have said has implied that meanings are very personal and that they are determined by each individual for himself. Yet in our introductory discussion of language, we concluded that a language implies some *regularity* among a group of people who use it; in other words, that people have common or public meanings for words and word-sequences. Cursory analysis might indicate that these two statements are contradictory. They are not so intended.

It is correct to say that all meanings are found in people, that they are learned, and that they are personal. However, if we could not abstract some uniformity in meaning, some public dimensions of meaning, and if we could not code these into some system, we could not communicate. We cannot communicate very well if we just run around using words for our own private purposes and completely disregard any consistency or uniformity in their meaning. Lewis Carroll points out an example of such behavior, in his delightfully insightful discussion between Alice and Humpty Dumpty:

"I don't know what you mean by 'glory'," Alice said.

Humpty Dumpty smiled contemptuously. "Of course you don't —till I tell you. I meant 'there's a nice knockdown argument for you!' "

"But 'glory' doesn't mean 'a nice knock-down argument,' " Alice objected.

"When I use a word," Humpty Dumpty said, in rather a scornful tone, "it means just what I choose it to mean—neither more nor less."

"The question is," said Alice, "whether you *can* make words mean so many different things."

"The question is," said Humpty Dumpty, "which is to be master —that's all."[1]

Though we might admire Humpty's courage and individualism, and though we may know people like him, we would agree that communication would be somewhat impaired if we were to follow his rules.

We should never forget that meanings are found in people; nevertheless, it is suggested that we can separate certain dimensions of meaning and talk about them as if they were not the property of people. We are seeking a higher degree of predictability among language-users. We must have this if we are to communicate our own ideas and understand the ideas of others. Let us return to our earlier discussion of language-learning and see if we can abstract more than one kind of meaning from it.

Denotative Meaning

The first words we learn are words such as "mommy," "daddy," "ball," "doggie," etc. Traditionally, we refer to these as names for persons, places, or things. We also learn words that we refer to as names for processes or actions. These include words such as "talk," "walk," "sleep," and "go."

In trying to teach the child a meaning for these words, we usually say the word when the thing itself is present. We help the child learn, using techniques of conditioning. We say "mommy" and point to the child's mother. We say "ball" and point to the ball. We say "walk" when someone is walking, and point to the walking

[1] Lewis Carroll (Charles Dodgson), *Alice's Adventures in Wonderland, Through the Looking Glass, and the Hunting of the Snark*. The Modern Library, 1925, pp. 246–247.

process. In short, we draw for the child a relationship between these names and the objects they are naming.

Over time, the relations between these names and the corresponding objects become meaningful. To tell someone what a word means, we point to the object that it represents. If language is to develop, if we are to communicate, all people who use the language must be in agreement about these word-object relationships.

This is one dimension of meaning. It actually exists in people, but we can abstract it and make generalizations about it for all users of a given language. We call this kind of meaning "denotative" or "referential." We say that the word "ball" *denotes* or *refers* to the object ball; the word "run" denotes or refers to the process of running, etc.

Denotative meaning is a kind of shorthand. We cannot afford to carry the physical world around with us wherever we go. We cannot take the time to point to objects in the physical world every time we communicate. So we create words that we use to represent the objects. Denotative meaning consists of a relationship between a word-sign and an object. In fact, *we define denotative meaning as a sign-object relationship*.

We err when we forget that denotative meaning is a relationship. We use words that have clear references for us—but not necessarily for our receiver. If we will remember that the receiver must be aware of the relationship, and that the word itself cannot give it to him, we will increase the clarity of our messages.

How do we clarify denotative meanings in communication? In face-to-face speaking, we often go back to the original learning process. If someone has difficulty understanding us when we refer to things, we often point to the object that our word names or refers to. When we write, we cannot point directly; however, we approximate pointing by putting in scale models of the objects we are talking about. When we give instructions, we might draw a picture of the completed object or process. We might use illustrations: pictures, charts, drawings, etc. When we choose these visual aids, we use the denotative difficulty of our words as a criterion: hard words need illustration, easy words do not.

From our discussion, it should be clear that a complete denotative definition requires the presence of both the word-sign and the object. We can define a word denotatively by pointing to the object that it denotes. Any large-scale attempt to do this would be impossible; yet we need a collection of such definitions if we are to use words to mean the same objects, or if we are to teach meanings to people who do not have them.

The difficulty of providing denotative definitions is one of the problems we face in communication. It is easy to observe this difficulty in the work of the technical writer. He often tries to define technical words for the nontechnical reader. In doing this, he often turns to the dictionary in the hope that it can provide such a definition. This is not very helpful either. For example, here is the "definition" of brucellosis given by the American College Dictionary:[2]

brucellosis: infection with bacteria of the *Brucella* group

It might be argued that if you do not already have a meaning for the terms "bacteria of the *Brucella* group," this definition of brucellosis will not help. Furthermore, if you do have a meaning for the "bacteria of the *Brucella* group," you probably have a meaning for brucellosis, and do not need a definition.

DICTIONARIES AND DENOTATIVE MEANING

We often use dictionaries, or similar kinds of verbal statements, in "defining" our terms. This approach to definition has been labeled by Dale as the "clear only if known" fallacy.[3] When we communicate, we often use words that are unfamiliar to our receivers. In doing so, we try to define these words so that our receivers will have meanings for them. We are forced many times to do this by using other words. When these words are equally un-

[2] *American College Dictionary* (text edition). Harper & Brothers, 1953, p. 153.
[3] Edgar Dale, "Clear only if known," *The News Letter,* Bureau of Educational Research, Ohio State University, Vol. XXVII, No. 6, 1957.

familiar, we have gained nothing—and we probably have lost the receiver in the process.

We have introduced the dictionary into the discussion. In a later chapter on the concept of definition, we shall talk about the dictionary at some length. For the moment, however, there are one or two points involving dictionaries that we should consider. First, where do denotative meanings come from, how are they derived?

Many people mistakenly believe that the dictionaries decide meanings. We often assume that the dictionary is a final authority —a Supreme Court of the "correctness of meaning." A good dictionary is not such an authority and does not pretend to be. *A dictionary can only serve as a reporter: a collector and reproducer of usage.*

Some standard dictionaries attempt to approximate denotative definitions, by describing words in such a way as to serve the "pointing function." Often, pictures are used in an attempt to point to the object referred to by a word. The dictionary has severe limitations here. For the most part, it can only "define" a word by using other words. It is difficult to point with words. Without some prior knowledge of words and of the meanings people have for them, a dictionary is useless.

For example, if you know no words in Spanish, I can teach you some by using the words and pointing to their referents at the same time. This is relatively easy. Suppose I did not point, but merely defined words in terms of other words. This is not so easy. If you know no words in Spanish, you cannot learn many from a Spanish dictionary. The same is true in English. If I know no words in English, I cannot learn many from a dictionary.

The dictionary is a closed system. All that it can do is suggest that a group of words can be substituted, under some conditions, for another word. Use of a dictionary presumes some familiarity with the language and the ways in which people use it.

A dictionary is a necessary and very useful reference book on language; however, it is neither a final authority nor (I hope) a book on etiquette. Dictionaries report usage. The dictionary editors observe how people use words, what people mean by words. They collect words or phrases that people use as substitutes for other words. They group these and print them beside the word. For the most part, dictionaries do not provide definitions or denotative meanings. What do we, as communicators, need to keep in mind about a dictionary?

1. Dictionaries are great time-savers. They tell us a great deal about how people use this word or that one.
2. Dictionaries are reporters. We can often provide a better primary source: our own personal experiences and those of our receivers.
3. Dictionaries are fixed over time. Meanings are not. Many usages, or changes in usage, are not included in a dictionary.
4. Meanings are legislated by usage, not by dictionaries. People use certain words in certain ways—others, they do not. The dictionary *describes* usage. It does not—it should not—*prescribe* usage.

We have talked a good deal about denotative meaning: a relationship between a word-sign and the object to which it refers. We have reviewed how such meanings are learned, and some of the problems that are involved in using them. We have suggested that dictionaries cannot give us denotative meanings. We can learn these only by using the language, observing others as they use it, and determining which objects seem to be denoted by which words.

One further point can be made about our uses of denotative meaning. What is the domain of denotative meaning? What kind of reality does it refer to? In short, what are we doing when we use words with denotative meaning?

Denotative meanings are relationships between word-signs and objects that exist in the physical world. *When we use words denotatively, we are trying to name something in the physical world*. We are saying that (a) something exists, and (b) we are going to talk about it, or at least refer to it. We can say, therefore, that denotative meaning is concerned with physical reality—the existence of objects in the physical world. The domain of denotation is physical reality.

Whenever we attempt to conceptualize or structure events that exist in the physical world, we need words that name those events. As we structure our perceptions and name them, a relationship develops between the name and the event. We label this relationship the denotative meaning for the word. At times, we use words for which we have no denotative meanings. There is no problem here, unless we believe that we are talking about the physical world when we use such words, or unless we believe that we are naming things that do have physical existence.

Unfortunately, as words remain in the language, people forget that they do not have meanings in and of themselves. We often use such words to talk about the physical world—and may not have any referential or denotative meaning for the words. This is a form of linguistic illness, leading to unrealistic and meaningless communication. The illness is contagious and often reaches epidemic proportions. Its cause is the belief that words have meaning. Its only cure is a careful check to determine if we have in mind any actual physical events that correspond to the words we are using to talk about physical events. If we find we do not have such meanings, we are talking nonsense.

Structural Meaning

Let us turn our attention to another aspect or dimension of meaning. As we progress in our language usage, we find that we want to do more than merely name things. We tire of going around saying "mommy," "daddy," "go," "ball," "run," etc. We want to talk *about* objects and processes, not merely refer to them. We want to put names together, to point out relationships. Instead of saying "John" and "run," we want to relate the object John to the process of running. In other words, we want to talk in sentences, not in words. We want to say "John is running."

To construct sentences, we need some procedures for arranging words in sequences. We want to know which word comes first. which last, and so on. We want to know how we let people know whether we are talking about today, tomorrow, or yesterday. There are many similar things that we want to communicate.

For many of us the term "grammar" refers to the methods for sequencing words. Not rules, merely methods. Grammar does not prescribe a set of "rules," it describes a set of procedures for arranging language elements in ways that are meaningful for users of that language.

Of course, grammar has many meanings for us. A large number of people mean "the unpleasant concentration of the freshman student on an infinite and unworkable set of laws of language usage." Another group of people mean a manual of language etiquette: in certain situations, the good man writes or speaks this way, and does not write or speak that way. I have heard both parents and teachers say, "Nice girls say 'It is I,' not 'It is me' "; "good boys don't say 'John comed,' they say 'John came,' " and so on.

It is true that some girls say "It is I" and most adults say "John came"; however, they do not do this because it is *proper* or for moralistic reasons. We learn to use certain words and syntactic forms because (a) people with whom we associate use those words and forms, and (b) we want to be perceived as members of an "educated" group. The objection is to the moralistic, authoritarian defense often made of usage. It tends to mislead the child about the exciting process of language behavior.

We are not concerned explicitly here with the nature or development of grammar. We are concerned with an analysis of meaning. There is a dimension of meaning in form, and grammar describes the forms of a language, the language's syntax. Before we can discuss this meaning, however, we need to clarify what is meant by grammar.

We can dichotomize various points of view about grammar into two extremes: "prescriptive" grammar and descriptive grammar (actually, most of us can place our beliefs between these two extremes). The prescriptive grammarian looks on grammar as a set of rules or laws of sentence formation, passed by the Parliament on

Correct Grammar or some such body. These laws are not to be broken. A prescriptive grammar is analogous to a prescriptive dictionary. A prescriptive grammar tells you how you *must* arrange words, and a prescriptive dictionary tells you what you *must* mean by words.

Much of the justification for this position is historical. Until the 20th century, people were very concerned with social classes, and wanted to distinguish members of one class from members of others. Particularly, members of the aristocratic elite wanted to be able to recognize other members of the "club," and to exclude nonmembers. Language behavior was a good way to accomplish this. Grammar *meant* a guide to the rules of language behavior acceptable to the aristocratic elite, which could be used to distinguish "intellectuals" from "peasants."

Prescriptive grammar has another historical foundation. Until fairly recently, there was no science of the description of language structure—which we call descriptive linguistics. Many educators looked on language as something that was God-given and logical. They looked at the rules of sentence formation in early languages, such as Latin, and imposed these rules in other languages as well, such as English.

On the other hand, a descriptive grammar is derived from observation of the ways that people who speak a language put their words together. Descriptive grammar tries to make generalizations from usage, to list the generally acceptable and nonacceptable (i.e., used and nonused) sequencing of words.

Descriptive grammar looks on language from a communication point of view. Writers and speakers concerned with effective communication cannot look on dictionaries as ultimate authorities on word meaning. We also cannot look on prescriptive grammar as the final authority in word sequencing. Words mean what people use them to mean. Words are put together grammatically when they are put together the way language-users actually put them together. It is safe to say that a "grammar" which does not do this is not a *grammar* at all. It is a handbook, a guide. A "prescriptive" grammar is a book of rules, not a grammar, just as Blackstone's Commentaries are statements *about* law, not laws.

I do not intend to imply that "usage" and "descriptive grammar" are words we can use to sweep careful and effective composition of messages under the rug. Some words elicit less ambiguity than others. Some sentence constructions are more effective than others. Students occasionally interpret an emphasis on descriptive grammar as an "anything goes" philosophy. This is not intended. Effective and efficient encoding requires *care* in watching for misinterpretations, *precision* in wording and structuring the message, and *knowledge* of current usage on the language level at which you are communicating. Communication is hard work; it implies rigor. All that is suggested is that prescriptions on the selection and arrangement of message units should be based on (a) evidence as to the clearest and most effective methods of selecting and arranging these units, and (b) general usage by the people for whom the message is intended. Prescriptions should not be based on a moralistic or authoritarian dogma as to what is "proper" or "good."

From a communication point of view, questions such as (a) is "contact" a verb or a noun, or (b) can you end a sentence with a preposition, or (c) can you split an infinitive, are not questions for debate, or decisions by the Court. As communicators, we should ask three questions:

1. How do people actually construct sentences?
2. Why do they construct them that way?
3. Is one method of construction more or less effective than another, in accomplishing a given purpose?

We shall define grammar as a study of the formal relationships between language units; how they are put together, what inflections are used, etc. It can be argued that *we communicate through form*. We can abstract *structural meaning*, just as we abstracted denotative meaning.

If we have meanings for form, we have meaning for language syntax. We can accept the notion that the final authority on form is usage, that syntax changes with experience. What may be an unacceptable form of sentence structure today may be quite acceptable tomorrow, or next year. Our concern now is to look briefly at the structure of English, to see if we can isolate a dimension of meaning in the structure itself.

Let us look at the following expression, assuming that it is an English sentence:

"Most smoogles have comcom."

What does the word "smoogles" refer to? What does "comcom" refer to? Do you have any denotative meanings for either of these two words? Probably not. Does it follow that there is no meaning in this sentence for you? I do not think so.

Let's take another sentence:

"One smoogles have comcom."

Let's take another:

"Most smoogle has comcom."

Does either of these two sentences make you uncomfortable? Why? We *know,* do we not, that, in English, when we say "one" we do not say "have" but we do say "has." We *know* that when we say "most," we usually say "have." In general, certain kinds of words (nouns) are accompanied by certain kinds of other words (verbs), and not by other kinds.

What else might bother us about these two sentences? Usually (though not always), the adjective "most" is followed by a noun which has an "s" on the end of it; the adjective "one" is followed by a noun which does not have an "s" on the end of it. Also, nouns that have an "s" on the end of them usually are followed by certain forms of verbs; nouns which do not have an "s" on the end of them are followed by other verb forms. In general, we talk about adjective-noun-verb "agreement" for number.

What has this to do with meaning? It is consistent with our meaning for "meaning" to say that when we see the word "most," this *means* that the noun that follows will refer to more than one object. It also is consistent to say that when we see an "s" on the end of a noun, this *means* that the noun denotes more than one object. An "s" on the end of a noun also *means* (usually) that the verb which follows will also be in a form which denotes more than one, or plural.

In general, there is meaning in the form of language sequences. This kind of meaning does not refer to anything, it does not denote anything, but it does aid us in sorting out meanings, in communicating our ideas, and in understanding other people. We can label this second dimension of meaning "structural." *We get meaning from structure when one word-sign helps us predict another word-sign, or when the sequence of two word-signs tells us something about their relationship that we could not get from either word by itself.*

Structural meanings increase our predictive ability. They enable us to predict what is coming, on the basis of what has occurred. They reduce uncertainty. We continually make predictions about what is going to occur. Structural meanings increase our ability to do this. As we learn that the probability of one event occurring is conditioned by something else, we can predict more effectively whether the event will occur or not.

The development of structural meanings is analogous to the development of conditional probabilities. In our early stages of understanding, we must assume that all events are random, that there are no relationships between events, that the world is completely uncertain or shuffled. The physicist has a term for this uncertainty. He calls it *entropy*. As we begin to relate events, to impose a structure on them, we reduce our uncertainty, we reduce entropy.

Attempts to reduce entropy are one of the basic purposes of man in his desire to affect his environment. We carry these attempts into our language behavior, and impose structures that increase our predictive ability.

In summary, *structural meaning is found in a relationship between signs and other signs*. We said that denotative meaning was a sign-object relationship. Structural meaning is a sign-sign relationship. In order to analyze structural meaning, we do not have to go into the physical world and find objects that words refer to. We do have to analyze the formal relationships among words. For this reason, we can say that *the domain of structural meaning is formal reality,* not physical reality.

What are some of these structural meanings? We have mentioned or implied those of (a) number—singular or plural, (b) person—first, second, or third. In the sentence: "most smoogles have comcom," the formal meaning for the "s" in the word "smoogle(s)" is "more than one." The formal meaning for the word "have" is "more than one." If we were to use words to say what these formal meanings say, the sentence might read something like this: *Most* (there are more than one) *smoogles* (of course, there are more than one) *have* (remember there are more than one) *comcom.* Why do we say "more than one" at least three times in this sentence?

There are at least two reasons. First, that is the way that native speakers of English construct their sentences. Second, it improves the effectiveness of our communication. All of us are familiar with the concepts of repetition and reiteration in writing. We repeat important points, we use the same words twice. Sometimes we use different words to emphasize our meanings—we reiterate.

Reiteration and repetition also are built into language itself. For example, the structural meaning of adjective-noun-verb agreement is a form of repetition and reiteration. It is built in. The language contains many such simple little devices that we use, unconsciously, to structure our words so that clarity and understanding are improved.

For example, in English the letter *q* is always followed by the letter *u.* There are no words, other than personal names, which contain the letter *q* without it being followed by the letter *u.* When we see a *q,* we can predict that the next letter will be *u,* and be right every time. The probability of a *q* occurring without a *u* is zero —there is no uncertainty, no entropy.

We can look at this as a form of repetition or reiteration. The technical term for this relationship is *redundancy.* We define redundancy as the complement of entropy. As entropy rises, redundancy decreases. As redundancy rises, entropy or uncertainty decreases. This is mentioned to illustrate the point that redundancy in communication cannot be looked on as undesirable.

We need not be criticizing a message when we say it is redundant. All messages are redundant to varying degrees. Language has redundancy built into it. The question is not whether a message is redundant or not, but whether the redundancy is useful in increasing the effect of the message on the receiver.

Redundancy that is needed to increase understanding or acceptance is desirable. Redundancy that is not needed by the receiver is wasted. In both cases, redundancy is derived from sign-to-sign relationships within language, the extent to which we can predict one sign from another because of the structural relationships between them, and the meanings we have for those relationships.

This kind of sign-to-sign predictability is one kind of structural meaning. Let us look at another, by returning to our sample sentence: Most smoogles have comcom. Suppose we said: Most comcoms have smoogle. Would you get a different meaning from this sentence? Compare the sentences: "John saw Jim," and "Jim saw John." Is there a difference in meaning?

Clearly, the place of a word in a sentence helps us infer the possible meanings of the writer. In the sentence, "Most smoogles have comcom," we *know* that there are things called "smoogles," and that "comcom" is a property of some of the smoogles. If we turn the sentence around, we *know* that there is something called "comcom," and that "smoogle" is a property of some of the comcoms.

Similarly, when we say that John saw Jim, we are saying:

1. There is a person named John.
2. There is a person named Jim.
3. There is a process named seeing.

We are also saying something else. We are saying that John was engaged in the process of seeing, and that Jim was the consequence of John's engagement in the process.

Word order is, of course, important. What is "proper" word

order? We know that, in English, words that we call nouns occupy certain positions in sentences, namely (a) before verbs and (b) after adjectives. Is this proper? We cannot say. "Proper" is a prescriptive word, which we are using to evaluate a descriptive process. What we should ask for any given language is, how do people who use that language arrange their words to mean one thing or another?

For instance, in Spanish, many adjectives follow the noun. In German, the verb usually is not found immediately after the noun, but much later in the sentence. We are trying to make two points: (1) there is no universal rightness about word order—it changes from language to language, and (2) there is a particular set of word orders in a given language, and these orders help us get meaning—structural meaning.

Let us take a third and final example of structural meaning: the meanings in punctuation. Punctuation consists of a set of symbols that do not have denotative meaning, but that tell us the relationship between other words. Let us look at the following sentence:

The teacher said: "The student is an idiot."

What is the meaning of this sentence? We have denotative meanings for the words "teacher," "said," "student," and "idiot." The sentence is so structured that we mean by it that one person (named teacher) commented about another person (named student). His comment was a conclusion that the student was somewhat dull.

Let us repunctuate the sentence, and see if meaning is changed.

"The teacher," said the student, "is an idiot."

We have not changed any of the words or any of the denotative meanings. We have altered the structure of the sentence by using commas and quotation marks. Do you see any differences of meaning? What have we done? We have not altered any word-to-object relationships. We have altered the word-to-word relationships. We have changed meaning by changing structure. This is what we mean by structural meaning. It is a relationship between one sign-word and another. It is concerned with formal reality. It is not concerned with the reality of physical objects. It is concerned with the reality of relationships among symbols.

Confusions between denotative and structural meanings can get us into trouble. Let us just look at one example. When asked to define the words "noun" and "verb," many people say that a noun is the name of a person, place, or thing and a verb is the name of a process.

Our discussion of structural meanings implies that the terms "noun" and "verb" are *formal* concepts; their meanings should therefore be given in terms of sign-to-sign relationships. However, most of us learned that a noun is the name of (denotes) a person, place, or thing. We also learned that a verb denotes or names a process or action. Two things are wrong with these definitions.

First, from our earlier discussion we concluded that the distinction between objects and processes is based on a naive view of physics. Many times we make a process static: e.g., when we take a still picture. On the other hand, we make an event dynamic: e.g., when we describe a table as a set of molecules or atoms in motion. We do the same thing in writing. For example, we look on a "process" as an "object" when we say "Running is great fun." On the other hand, we make an event dynamic when we say "I will contact you."

In the first example, "Running is great fun," the prescriptive grammarian has devised a new concept to keep him out of trouble. He calls this a gerund. What is a gerund? Well, we are told that it *really* is a verb, but that it *behaves* like a noun. This becomes ridiculous. In the second case, "I will contact you," we have no new concept. We merely argue. Have you heard, or engaged in, arguments about whether "contact" is *really* a verb, or whether it is *really* a noun? This, too, becomes ridiculous. The arguments of the prescriptive grammarian fall of their own weight, and the intelligent student begins to reject as useless the study of language structure.

We can avoid this kind of impasse by remembering two things. First, the distinction between objects and processes needs to be revised to take into account the developments of twentieth-century physics. Where this distinction has infiltrated our language concepts, we need to eliminate it.

Secondly, we need to distinguish between dimensions of meaning. Concepts such as "noun," "verb," "tense," "person," etc., are used in an analysis of language form. Our meanings for them should be structural, relationships between signs and signs. Instead, we have developed denotative meanings for these terms. We have tried to define a structural concept such as "noun" by pointing to its referent: persons, places, or things.

"Noun" does not have a referent in the physical world. *Language concepts, like mathematical concepts, are structural in nature. They are concerned with formal reality and need to be defined formally.* Many of the confusions in a prescriptive grammar are derived through failure to make the basic distinction between denotative meaning and structural meaning. We have confused these two dimensions of meaning in developing our theories of language.

To increase our understanding of vocabulary and syntax, we must look for a description of words that *is consistent with how people actually use them* and that does not get us into a confusing situation. *Usage determines denotative meaning. Usage determines structural meaning.* What is meaningful today may not be tomorrow. What is meaningful for one group of people may not be for another. The effective source must continually analyze his receiver, must search for the kinds of meanings he has. In doing so, he needs to be culturally consistent, to fit into the language norms of the groups to which his receiver belongs.

Again, it should be emphasized that "usage" is not an escape hatch for sloppy composition. As language norms develop, alternative usages develop. We can choose one or another way of expressing our meanings. A scientific analysis of language can point to ambiguity or precision implied by certain word choices, certain syntactic constructions. The development of an individual's "usage" norms should be based on evidence of the maximum effectiveness of language in eliciting desired meanings.

We have talked about two dimensions of meaning which can be abstracted from our original model of how people learn meanings. We talked about denotative meaning. We said that it is a relationship between a sign and an object. It is concerned with the physical world and with naming what is in it.

We have talked about structural meaning. We said that it is a relationship between one sign and another sign. It is not concerned with the physical world. It is concerned with formal relationships, formal reality.

Contextual Meaning

We have a third dimension of meaning to discuss. Before we turn to it, we should mention a hybrid kind of meaning. It is denotative in the sense that we try to get denotative meanings for terms when we do not already have meanings for them. It is structural in the sense that we predict denotative meanings from the formal relationships between these terms and other terms for which we already have meanings. We usually refer to this hybrid kind of meaning as *contextual*. Let us look at an example or two of how we get meaning from context. Suppose we read the following paragraph:

All smoogles have comcom. In the spring, when the smoogle emerges from hibernation, his comcom is quite inferior in quantity and quality, and not of much use to man. If smoogles are given a high protein diet during the spring months, the comcom can be sheared by late May or early June. After shearing, the smoogle can be turned loose until the next spring. The comcom of about 50 smoogles is needed to make a lady's sweater.

Do you have any more meanings for "smoogle" and "comcom" than before? How did you get these meanings? Generally, the procedure is this. Someone puts a word for which you have no denotative meaning in a formal context (in this case, a paragraph), and surrounds it by words for which you do have denotative meanings. These meanings generate other meanings, because of the formal relations between them and the unknown words. This gives you hunches for a denotative meaning for the unknown words.

This is a very important aspect of the way we get meaning from messages, but few people have studied it carefully as yet, except in the course of decoding intelligence reports and translating ancient languages. One must always consider meaning from context. It is a highly useful device in introducing new or "hard" words. It might even be the best way to help define words that are new to the receiver, but that the source feels he must use in communicating about a given subject matter.

Let us try another example. Here is a word, "case." What meanings do you have for "case"? Your answers will not tell us a lot about the word "case," but they will say a lot about you—and your frame of reference. Let us put the word "case" in context, and see if there is more agreement as to our meanings.

1. "The lawyer asked for a postponement of the trial because he had not had time to prepare his case."
2. "To help students understand what you mean, you should use case studies often."
3. "This party is lasting longer than I thought it would; I'd better send out for another case."

Again, context contributes much to our meaning for a particular word. This is another reason why we insist on quoting people in "context," why we introduce a speaker to his audience so that the audience can interpret what the speaker says in the context of his background.

Connotative Meaning

Let us turn now to a third approach to a meaning of "meaning." We have said that all meanings are learned. We also said that people who use a language have common meanings for a large number of the terms in the language. These common meanings can refer to either (a) the object that a word denotes, or (b) the formal relationship that a word tells us exists between two or more words. This is true. Yet a good many of our meanings never become very public. They remain highly personal. Meanings for some words vary a lot among people. When we use words for which we have meanings, but our meanings are either (a) vague or (b) extremely personal, we call our meanings "connotative." Connotative meaning is primitive meaning—it is meaning which has never gone beyond the personal learning stage. Of course, these meanings are shaped by our culture and the social systems in which we live, but they are highly personal.

Connotative meaning is, of course, often a relationship between a sign and an object, but it involves *people* more than other meanings do. *We define connotative meaning as a relationship between a sign, an object, and a person.* Connotative meaning is person-oriented. When we use words that are highly connotative, we must take extra care to be sure that our receiver will mean something by them, preferably what we intended him to mean.

Connotative meaning is most closely related to personal experience. In fact, we say that connotative meaning is not concerned with physical or formal reality, but with *social reality.* Connotative meaning comes from the personal experiences of the person who uses the word and is closely related to who and what he is as a person.

One kind of example of connotative meaning can be drawn from words that we use as vague approximations to other words for which we have precise denotative meanings. Take words such as "tall," "short," and "large." We can always substitute other words for these—words that have specific referents; however, substitute words often differ drastically from person to person. For example, our meanings for "tall" vary according to our own height. When a man who is 5'8" tells another person who is 6'4" that a third person is tall, the image of this third person that is created for the

6'4" man will differ radically from the image intended by the 5'8" man. Words such as "tall" are terms whose primary meanings are connotative. They tell us something about the physical world of objects, but they also tell us some things about the word-user.

Another example of connotative meaning involves words that do not report much about the world, but that tell a great deal about the person using them, since they indicate his values, judgments, attitudes, etc. Words that we label as connotative always tell us something of the state of the organism, about the user of that word.

There are words such as "good," "desirable," "likeable," "unpleasant," and "beautiful." These words are very closely tied to the people who use them; the meanings we have for them therefore vary greatly among people. These words cause us trouble in communication. We use them frequently because we want to put *ourselves* in our messages; however, if we are not careful, we fail to communicate our intentions precisely to the receiver. Words such as these do not tell the receiver what the world is like. They do not tell the receiver what certain events mean to him. They tell him only that the source likes or dislikes certain events—that the source thinks they are good or bad. Many times this is not the source's purpose. If it is not his purpose, he should avoid use of such terms. If he does intend to communicate his own attitudes and feelings, he must carefully choose words which not only have certain evaluative meanings for him, but which he thinks have similar meanings for others.

Connotative terms do not refer primarily to the quality of an object, they refer to the state of the organism, the responses of the individual perceiving that object. When we say "that is a good show," we are not describing the show. We are saying that *we felt good* when we saw the show. When we say that someone has an unpleasant personality, we are not describing that person. We are saying that *we felt unpleasant* when we were with him.

One reason for the privateness of connotative meanings is that they describe our own private, internal feelings when in the presence of an event or object external to us. Connotative meanings in part are statements about how we feel, what we believe—as related to a physical object.

In recent years, many psychologists have tried to measure people's connotative meanings.[1] Someday, we might even have a connotative dictionary. Even now, we have some good hunches about the general connotations of certain words. One dimension of connotation is an evaluative dimension: are words "good" words or "bad" words? We are referring to this kind of meaning when we say that a politician should be in favor of motherhood and against sin. "Motherhood" is a "good" word; "sin" is a bad one. Advertisers and speech writers occasionally actually measure people's connotative meanings for some of the words that are used frequently in speeches and advertising copy.

In communicating, we often choose to use words which have heavy connotative meanings. In doing so, we must be careful to choose words which communicate our intent, or we will risk being misunderstood. You might even want to test some of the connotative words you use frequently. See if other people's meanings are at all similar to yours.

Denotative and connotative meanings are not different in kind; they differ only in degree. Denotative meanings are simply connotative meanings on which we all agree. I can provide, if I work at it, referents for the term "democratic." When I do, I am surer that my receiver will mean the same thing that I mean. When I do not, I am less sure.

One group of semanticists has coined the term "ladder of abstraction" to talk about this problem.[2] The ladder of abstraction refers to a continuum. Words can be placed along this continuum. Where you place a word depends on its distance from the physical object it refers to. A name like "President Eisenhower" is close to one end of the continuum. A name like "teacher" is toward the middle of the continuum. A name like "professional" is close to the other end of the continuum.

---

[1] Charles E. Osgood, George J. Suci, and Percy Tannenbaum, *The Measurement of Meaning*. University of Illinois Press, 1957.

[2] S. I. Hayakawa, *Language in Thought and Action*. Harcourt, Brace, 1949, pp. 167–170.

The term "President Eisenhower" denotes a specific object (a person) in the physical world. We can agree about the object, we all would apply the term to the same object, we would "know it when we see it." The term "teacher" also denotes people, but a large group of them. It also denotes behaviors which these people perform. Because of the size of the group, and particularly because of the large number of behaviors attributable to members of that group, we are not as clear about our referent for the word "teacher."

People whom you might refer to as teachers might not be the same ones that I would refer to as teachers. You might refer to employees of a school, and I might be referring to individuals who stimulated learning in others. These are not equivalent. If we do not check our meanings for the term, we might talk together about "teachers" and not be talking about the same objects—but we would not know it because we used the same word to name the two things we were talking about.

In communicating, we often are faced with a dilemma. If we are highly specific, if our terms are closely related to their referents, we are accurate and precise—but our messages are lengthy and often hard to understand. On the other hand, if we are vague and general, if we are far removed from the physical world, we lose accuracy and precision—but we gain time, and maybe interest. Each source has to make decisions like this every time he communicates. What are some of his criteria in making these decisions?

1. How important is it that the receiver knows precisely what I mean?
2. How much time-space do I have?
3. What is the motivational level of my receiver? How interested is he?

In summary, we have labeled a "connotative" dimension of meaning, and we have talked about it as a relationship among words, objects, and people. Connotative words often can be traced back to specific object referents, if we search long and diligently. We talk about them as having sign-object-people meaning; however, connotative meaning can be distinguished from denotative meaning in that connotation is more personal and varies more among people.

In communicating, we utilize all three dimensions of meaning. Take a sentence such as "My mother is alive." What is our *meaning* for the word "mother"? Well, we can say that it is a noun. This is a formal meaning, and is derived from the word's place in the sentence. A second meaning, which we can label as denotative, is the person who bears a highly specific biological relationship to us. Finally, our connotative meaning for the term "my mother" is the sum total of all of our previous experiences with (a) our own mothers, (b) other people's mothers, and (c) all of the situations in which we have used or heard the word "mother."

We can all pretty well agree on the first (structural) meaning, and most of us would agree on the denotative meaning. *It is, however, impossible for us ever to agree completely on the connotative meaning.* Our experiences always differ from those of other people. It is inconceivable that I would have exactly the same connotation for the term "mother" that you do.

Take a term such as "politics." Most of us would agree that this is usually used as a noun. We have trouble agreeing on the referent (denotative meaning) for the term. We can explain this by isolating the position of "politics" on the ladder of abstraction. It is a highly abstract term, far from physical reality. With discussion we can come to an understanding of what another person is denoting when he uses a term such as "politics," though this might require some time. The connotative meaning is another story. Again, this is a unique meaning for each individual, a residue of every experience he has had, linguistic or otherwise, in which the term "politics" or his referents for it were involved.

This has been a brief exposition of at least some of the approaches to a meaning for "meaning." Obviously, much more could be said —books have been written, whole careers dedicated to the questions we have raised. We have been neither exhaustive nor all-inclusive.

At times, we have distorted theoretical positions somewhat in the hope of increasing the clarity and perceived utility of our discussion. What have we said?

1. We have many meanings for the word "meaning."
2. Meanings are found in people, not in words.
3. We learn meanings, just as we learn other things.
4. In communicating, we hope to elicit meaning, to change or emphasize the meanings of our readers.
5. Meanings are not transmittable. All we can transmit is a message, and meaning is not in the message.
6. We can abstract at least three dimensions of meaning: the denotative, the structural, and the connotative.
7. In choosing terms to denote objects, we must be precise if our receiver is to attach the same meaning to our message that we have "given" it.
8. In constructing sentences, we must sequence our words so that their structure reflects our meanings for the relationships among the elements denoted by the words.
9. We must be aware that we can never be completely denotative (objective). Who and what we are enters into everything we see and report. Some part of our meaning for anything remains personal and private, and cannot be duplicated in others.
10. The dimensions of meaning are not independent, they are interrelated as parts of a process. Denotative-connotative distinctions are based on a public-private continuum. There is a structural dimension to all meaning. We impose structure on our perceptions even before we name them.

In communicating, we should remember that our word and sentence arrangement choices affect meaning in at least three ways. Syntax has utility in that it communicates structural relationships among words, and gives us contextual clues as to which of several meanings is the one intended by the writer. Many of our words denote certain objects for the reader. Other words have little denotative meaning, but are primarily connotative, in that they elicit personal experiences, often judgmental in nature.

When we emphasize denotative meanings and careful structure, we can be more hopeful that we report accurately. When we emphasize connotative meanings, we must realize that other people's meanings are *always* slightly different from our own—often, radically different. The fidelity of our communication decreases as connotation increases, but often the readability and interest of our messages go up.

Suggestions for Thought and Discussion

1. If a friend of yours told you that he was afraid to use a word in a certain sense because it did not appear in the dictionary in that sense, but that he felt sure he was right, what would you tell him (assuming you wish to help him understand the concept of meaning more fully)?

2. Suppose you were to get in an argument about a matter of usage with someone who looks on grammar as prescriptive, not descriptive. What would be your approach to winning your argument? List as many approaches as you can.

3. Discuss the concept of denotative meaning; supply examples to illustrate your points.

4. Discuss the concept of structural meaning; supply examples to illustrate your points.

5. What are the possible advantages and possible disadvantages of message redundancy for the receiver?

6. Why is contextual meaning called a "hybrid kind of meaning"?

7. What is connotative meaning? In what ways does it differ from the other types of meaning we have identified? Why is it referred to as "primitive meaning"?

8. Consider the statement "The dimensions of meaning are not independent, they are interrelated as parts of a process. Denotative-connotative distinctions are based on a public-private continuum. There is a structural dimension to all meaning. We impose structure on our perceptions even before we name them." Discuss each part of this statement, giving several examples to illustrate each part.

9. As a group project with others who are interested, prepare your own dictionary entry for one of the following words, or for a word that you choose: *book; issue; lot; record; concern.* First, develop a plan for collecting all the "meanings" suggested by the word to all the people in the group. Then summarize these "meanings" as briefly as you can without loss of significant differences, arranging your summary in some order which you can defend.

CHAPTER 9

Observations and Judgments

THE STRUCTURING OF PERCEPTION

So far we have talked about three kinds of meaning: denotative, structural, and connotative. In this and the following chapter, we will extend our discussion of meaning to larger language sequences—sentences. We will try to compare various kinds of sentences, to sort out differences among sentence types. The thesis to be defended is that sentences can be separated as to (a) purpose, (b) the kinds of meanings they emphasize, and (c) methods of checking up on their adequacy.

When we communicate, we construct sentences to express our intentions. In doing this, we have an infinite number of choices in selecting and arranging the words in those sentences. Each of us has a personal set of choices that we make. We refer to these choices when we talk about a communicator's *style*. For any given intention or objective, we can treat our message by constructing one or another sentence type. The question is, are there different sentence types? If there are, how do they differ from each other? How can you know one type when you see it? When do you use it?

Let us look at four sentences.

1. It costs $10 to join the Michigan State University Chess Club in 1960.
2. If all college students are human, and if all humans are mortal, then all college students are mortal.
3. The sun will rise tomorrow.
4. Brigitte Bardot is a beautiful woman.

How do these sentences differ? Would we be willing to say that they all are true? Are some of them false? Can we attach a label of true or false to all of them or only to some of them? Are these sentences facts? Statements of fact? Do we check up on the adequacy of these four sentences in the same way, or in different ways? These illustrate the kinds of questions we can ask about sentences or propositions.

Let us start at the beginning, and be sure that we have common meanings for the words which we will use in the discussion. The first words we need to define are "true" and its antithesis, "false." What do we mean when we say that something is true? What are the "somethings" that we say are true or false?

Are facts true? We might be tempted to say that facts are true, but this gets us into trouble. For example, was it true that the world was round in 1491, or was it false? This raises the further question, what do we mean by a fact? Let us assume for the moment that facts are neither true nor false; facts just *are*. Facts are aspects of physical events—some part of an entity-process that exists in physical reality.

For example, would we say that a table is true? Is it false? No, it is neither; it just is. Are you true? False? No, you just are. Let us look further. Given a table, if I say "That is a table," is the sentence true? Yes. Given a person named John Smith, if you say "That is John Smith," is the sentence true? Yes. If you say, "That is Bob Jones," is the sentence true? No, it is false.

Facts are found in the world, in physical reality. Facts cannot be called true or false. Facts can only exist or not exist. It is meaningless to say that the roundness of the world is true or false. The world either is round or it is not round; how we vote on it will not change its shape.

The sentence "The world is round" is a different matter. We can label that sentence as true or false. Most of us would say, with certain limitations, that the sentence is true. Sentences of a certain kind can be said to be either true or false. Not all sentences are true or false, only sentences of a certain kind.

In Chapter 8, we said that there are different kinds of meanings. There also are different kinds of sentences. We can separate at least three kinds of sentences. *The first kind is a statement of fact—which we can call an observation.*

Observations

An observation is a sentence which we can label as either true or false. If we cannot label (now or later) a sentence as either true or false, it is not a statement of fact.

Of our four sample sentences, one was a statement of fact—an observation: "It costs $10 to join the Michigan State University Chess Club in 1960." This sentence may be true or it may be false—but it must be one or the other. In short, the terms "true" or "false" are properties of sentences which are observations—statements of fact. All observations are either true or false—no other types of sentences can be said to be true or false.

We need to consider two things about observations. First, how do you know one when you see one? Second, how do you know whether an observation is true or false?

We will take the second question first: how do we know whether a statement of fact, an observation, is a true statement of fact or a false statement of fact? Let us look at our sample sentence. It says (1) there is a university named Michigan State, (2) there is a Chess Club at that University, (3) the Chess Club offers memberships, (4) each member pays $10 to join, and (5) all of this happens in the year 1960. How might we determine whether this sentence is true?

We might do it in this way:

1. We check to see if there actually *is* a university named Michigan State.
2. We *go* to that University, and *look for* an organization called the Chess Club.
3. We *look at* the membership list of the organization.
4. We *look at* the 1960 financial records of the organization. We *find* that there is a $10 item for each member, and that the financial record lists the term "membership fee" beside each of these $10 items.
5. We say that the sentence is true.

Some might argue that this procedure is too complicated, too detailed. Others might want to go further before saying that the sentence is true. For example, the Chess Club treasurer might be altering the books, and the sentence might actually be false. Whether you would follow these specific procedures or not, this kind of procedure is necessary before we can say that a sentence is true or false. If, in any of our four steps, we had found that there was not a correspondence between one of our sentences and the state of events in the physical world, we would have said that the sentence was false.

What, in general, do we mean by "true"? Aristotle said: "To say of what is, that it is, or of what is not, that it is not, is true; to say of what is not, that it is, or of what is, that it is not, is false."[1] This is a tongue-twisting definition, but a good one for our purposes. In other terms, we can say that a sentence is true if and only if (a) the sentence says something about the state of events in the physical world (is an observation), and (b) the state of events in the world *is* what the sentence *says* it is. We check on the truth or falsity of a sentence by first making sure it is a statement of fact, and then by going outside the sentence into the physical world and *verifying* or not *verifying* it. *Verification is the test of an observation.*

In beginning our discussion, we asked two questions: (a) how

[1] Aristotle, *Metaphysics* (Richard Hope, trans.). Columbia University Press, 1952, Book III.

do you know an observation when you see one, and (b) how do you know whether an observation is true or false? We now have answered both questions in part. The definition of an observation is related to our earlier discussion of meaning. We said that words which have specific referents in the physical world are words for which we have denotative meanings. Now we have said that we must check (verify) an observation by going into the physical world and seeing whether the world (fact) is what the sentence (statement of fact) says it is.

If we are to verify a sentence, the words in the sentence must all relate to things in the physical world, or to each other. Statements of fact include two kinds of words: (1) words for which we have denotative meanings—words that name objects in the physical world, and (2) words for which we have structural meanings—words that relate names to other names.

If a sentence includes both of these kinds of words, and only these kinds of words, it is a statement of fact, an observation. If, in addition, the objects that the words denote are related in the way that the structural meanings we have for words say they are related, it is a true statement of fact. If they are not so related, we have a false statement of fact. *Observations emphasize denotative meanings.*

In summary, an observation is a sentence that includes only words for which we have denotative or structural meanings. Both need to be present. If some of our words do not denote objects in the physical world, or are not structural words, we do not have a statement of fact at all—either a true or a false one. If all our words denote objects in the physical world or are structural words, but the structure of the physical world *does not* correspond to the structure of the sentence, we have a *false* statement of fact. If all our words denote objects in the physical world, or are structural words, and the structure of the physical world *does* correspond to the structure of the sentence, we have a *true* statement of fact.

An observation then is an attempt to translate some aspect of the physical world into a code, a language. It is a *report*. In fact, some men who do it for a living are called reporters. In communicating, few of us have the time or the opportunity to verify personally the statements of fact that we communicate. Sometimes we do make our own observations. At other times we rely on the observations of others. In any case, when we intend to report we must be sure that our messages are restricted to statements of fact—statements that say something about how physical reality *is*. We also should be satisfied that the verification process has taken place at some time; that our observations are true statements of fact.

Why do we encode observations? To use the police expression, when we "want the facts, only the facts." A report does not attempt to interpret a fact; it does not attempt to tell us whether something is good or bad. It simply attempts to state what *is;* to make accurate statements about events in the world. A report is a map; a guide to some territory that exists in the physical world.

As we all know, it is difficult to make accurate observations. Lawyers face this problem in getting testimony from a witness. Witnesses notoriously cannot distinguish between observations and other kinds of sentences. Hayakawa gives us an amusing example of this inability in the following fictional cross-examination:

WITNESS: That dirty double-crosser Jacobs ratted on me.

DEFENSE ATTORNEY: Your honor, I object.

JUDGE: Objection sustained. (*Witness' remark is stricken from the record*.) Now, try to tell the court exactly what happened.

WITNESS: He double-crossed me, the dirty, lying rat!

DEFENSE ATTORNEY: Your honor, I object.

JUDGE: Objection sustained. (*Witness' remark is again stricken from the record*.) Will the witness try to stick to the facts.

WITNESS: But I'm telling you the facts, your honor. He did double-cross me.[2]

We often face the attorney's problems when we ask someone to give us the facts. To the witness, it was a "fact" that Jacobs double-crossed him. The witness was not making statements of fact, but he thought he was.

It is hard to be accurate, to restrain ourselves from slipping away from observations and into other things. We constantly try to inter-

[2] S. I. Hayakawa, *Language in Thought and Action*. Harcourt, Brace, 1949, pp. 43–44.

pret what we observe, to judge it—not to describe it. Many professional teachers and editors believe that one of the hardest tasks for the student or apprentice communicator is to learn to delay conclusion-reaching; to just "give the facts," without interpretation or conclusion-drawing.

There are at least two difficulties in our attempts to be objective reporters in communicating. First, in making our own observations, we often interject interpretations and evaluations. Second, we often have to take the word of others—and this, as we have seen, is subject to error.

A third difficulty in making observations is the limit of our own ability to perceive, remember, and report completely and accurately. Yet we all try to be objective. All of us remember the story of the six blind men and the elephant. Most of us pride *ourselves* on the fact that we are objective, accurate reporters. We do not fall into a trap with our own elephants.

We also remember the story about the doctor, the lawyer, the clergyman, and the automobile mechanic. All four were standing on a street corner. An accident occurred. When asked about the accident, each observer gave a different report. The doctor noticed the injuries, how "serious" they were medically, etc. The lawyer noticed the positions of the automobiles and paid careful attention to the assessment of liability for the accident. The clergyman noticed especially the physical condition of the people in the accident and noted whether they were in need of spiritual assistance. Finally, the mechanic observed the condition of the automobiles and estimated the cost of repair and the difficulty of getting the cars back in running condition. Each observer saw "facts" in terms of his own past experiences and interests. Each selected from the total event the aspects he thought were significant. We cannot determine who "really" saw the accident, or what "really" happened. Each observer structured the event in terms of his own background or interests.

Our prior experiences inherently determine the characteristics of our observations. As communicators we spend much of our time encoding reports, trying to translate what we have seen into observations. We must take care—it is not easy. *What we see is partly what is there. It is also partly who we are.* Everything that we observe we observe through our own senses, our own experiences. We do, we must, observe the world from our own point of view, and we report it that way. If our receiver has not shared a good deal of our point of view, we will mislead him or he will not understand us. We can never be completely objective. All that we can do is work toward it. In attempting to make objective and accurate observations, we need to:

1. Be sure to emphasize words for which we have denotative meanings.
2. Take precautions to keep ourselves at a minimum in reporting on the world, so that others can reproduce our observations if they want to.
3. Try to see as the receiver sees. Try to observe from the receiver's point of view, and then communicate that way.

Let us spend a moment on the third point. All of us have asked someone for instructions on how to get somewhere in a strange town. Have you ever been told something like this?

> Go straight for a while. Turn left by the three oak trees. Keep going for a short distance and turn right. After you get to the house with the red chimney, turn left and go straight until you reach the fork by Jane's place. Bear left until you get where you're going.

Such instructions are almost always followed by "You can't miss it." Why? The reporter observed from his point of view, not ours. Instructions are a frequent kind of reporting task. Instructions such as the one I have mentioned are additional examples of Dale's "clear only if known" fallacy; i.e., the report helps only if you did not need it in the first place.[3] The "clear only if known" fallacy is eliminated when we take a receiver orientation, when we try to put ourselves in the other person's shoes.

[3] Edgar Dale, "Clear only if known," *The News Letter,* Bureau of Educational Research, Ohio State University, Vol. XXVII, No. 6, 1957.

Let us summarize what we have said about observations:

1. Observations emphasize words for which we have denotative meanings.
2. Observations are sentences that are statements of fact—they must be verifiable.
3. Observations can be said to be true or false.
4. Observations are difficult to make because:

   a. Our ability to see and remember is limited.
   b. We have to rely on the observations of others, and this produces error.
   c. We make observations only through our own senses, and therefore cannot ever be completely objective.
   d. We tend to interpret and evaluate what we see, rather than merely to report it.

Up to this point, our discussion has been limited to observations, statements of fact that are verifiable and that emphasize denotative meanings. Of our four sample sentences, we have used only the first: It costs $10 to join the Michigan State University Chess Club in 1960. Observations are not the only kind of sentences we can construct. Reporting is not the only kind of affecting purpose that we can have, denotative meaning is not the only kind of meaning that can be emphasized. We can turn our attention to a different kind of sentence, illustrating a different kind of affecting purpose.

Judgments

The fourth sentence that we used at the beginning states that "Brigitte Bardot is a beautiful woman." What kind of a sentence is this? It is a *judgment*. *Judgments are sentences that emphasize connotative meaning.* They emphasize *words* that are connotative: "good," "likable," "pleasant," "beautiful," etc. These are words which have sign-to-object-to-person meaning relationships.

Judgments do not tell us a great deal about physical reality. They tell us a lot about social reality. Specifically, they tell us a lot about the person who makes them. If I say that Brigitte Bardot is beautiful, you learn something about me. If I said that Brigitte Bardot is ugly, you would get a different impression of me.

Judgments are *not* empirically verifiable. Many judgments can be translated into denotative observations and tested factually; however, we do not say that a judgment itself is true or false. *We say that judgments are believed or not believed.* When we check on an observation we try to *verify* it. When we check on a judgment, all we can do is determine whether or not it is *acceptable* to people—do they believe it or do they not? Acceptability is the criterion for testing a judgment.

We can define one kind of judgment as a sentence in which the source says that something is good or bad; i.e., the source tells us whether he approves of something or not. Some judgments are statements of value. We use the term "value judgment" sometimes in place of "judgment" alone. When we see "good-bad" words we know that the source is telling us whether he thinks something is (in a broad sense) good or bad, that the source is telling us about *himself,* not the object.

We need not spend a great deal of time talking about judgments. Most of us are highly competent in making them—if by "competent" we mean that we are judgment-prone. It is not hard to get people to make judgments. Most of us are quite willing to make them instantaneously. We do not have to talk much about the nature of judgments and how to recognize one when we see it.

We have outlined the nature of a judgment. It is a sentence that states an opinion about the value of one thing or another. It emphasizes words that have connotative meanings: words that relate to objects but that emphasize the source's relationship (attitudes, feelings, emotions, etc.) to his words and to the objects about which he is communicating.

We use judgments when we intend to communicate our own attitudes. We should *not* use judgments when we do not intend to communicate our own attitudes. Judgments are not observations; however, we can mistake judgments for observations, as did the witness in Hayakawa's court scene. The witness thought he was constructing statements of fact—observations. Actually, he was constructing judgments. Quite often, we think we are reporting when in actuality we are judging.

Some sentences which emphasize connotative meanings are not judgments. At times we simply use words which are fuzzy in their denotations; words such as "short," "small," "big." These are not judgments. They often are imprecise observations. By judgments, I mean sentences such as these:

1. All farm boys and girls should join 4-H clubs. It's *good* for them.
2. Everyone should see that movie—it's *tremendous.*
3. *Fortunately,* we have secured the services of Bill Johnson as our main speaker.
4. You just can't *trust* that fellow—he's no *good.*

Each of these sentences is a judgment. Each tells us something about the source. When we see words such as "should," "good," and "fortunately," it is almost certain that we are looking at judgments. If we do not recognize judgments when we see them, we get into trouble. Have you ever attended a movie or a play because some friend told you it was "good"? Did you like it? If not, did you chastise the friend because he was "wrong," because what he told you was not "true"? Truth is not a property of a sentence such as "That is a good show." The sentence is not an observation. It is a judgment.

When we read or hear judgments, we have to interpret them in light of what we know about the writer or speaker. What is "good" to you may not be "good" to me. If we make judgments which our receivers misinterpret as observations, we may reduce our effectiveness. If you tell people that they will "like" something or that they will "enjoy" something, and they do not like it or enjoy it, your own effectiveness is reduced.

What are the responsibilities of the communication source in making judgments? I do not mean to imply that we should never make judgments. I do mean to imply that we should know we are making them when we make them—and that we should make them intentionally.

Judgments are intended to gain acceptance of an idea, to create changes in attitude, to win votes for a new practice, etc. The name most frequently given to the purpose that produces judgments is *persuasion*. We can define the purpose of persuasion as an intent to secure belief on the part of the receiver, as an attempt to gain acceptance.

Judgments are statements of belief, statements of acceptance or rejection. They are not objective statements about reality, they are subjective. They express the position of the individual with respect to physical objects or events. They are voting behaviors, statements of the order "I like it" or "I don't like it," "I believe" or "I don't believe."

The purpose of an observation is to translate the physical world into language statements—statements of fact. The intent of a judgment is not to translate, but to vote. Its aims are persuasive, to affect behavior by making statements of value about the world.

Observations intend to report, judgments intend to conclude. Observations emphasize denotative meanings, judgments emphasize connotative meanings. In Chapter 8, distinctions were made between denotation and connotation; however, it was pointed out that they do not differ in kind, but only in degree. The same kinds of comparisons can be made between observations and judgments. They, too, do not differ in kind, but only in degree.

Observations and Judgments: Similarities and Differences

In developing our communication ability, one of the most important distinctions we need to make is that between fact and opinion, between making reports and making value judgments. In a democratic society, questions of opinion or value, questions of belief, may be decided by majority rule. Questions of fact should not be determined by popular referendum. The method of majority voting as a test for belief or acceptability differs from the method of empirical verification used as a test for statements of fact.

This point is well illustrated by the story of the little girl in kindergarten who asked her teacher whether baby bunnies came from little girl rabbits or little boy rabbits. The teacher, having been trained in "inductive" teaching, avoided answering the question and asked the entire class to decide. There was considerable discussion about the question, and both possible answers received some support from the five-year-olds. Finally, the teacher asked the children how they could decide whether bunnies came from girl rabbits or boy rabbits. One little girl raised her hand and said that she knew how they could decide. She suggested that the class vote on it and let the majority rule.

Clearly, a "bunny" question is not decided by popular voting. Girl rabbits are going to continue having bunnies, whether our group of five-year-olds votes that way or not. In analyzing propositions, it is useful to determine whether a particular proposition is a "bunny" question or a "voting" question. We do not analyze them in the same ways, we do not use the same methods for testing the adequacy of the proposition. Facts are not opinions, and opinions alone do not determine facts.

What has been said has merit; yet, if we leave the discussion at this point, we would develop a somewhat distorted picture of the relationship of language to reality. We said earlier that any observation presumes at least two things: something has been observed (the objective dimension) and someone has done the observing (subjective dimension). We can make judgments that are completely independent of physical reality, completely subjective. We cannot make observations that are completely independent of our own organisms, completely objective. *There is a judgment dimension in all observations. There is no such thing as complete objectivity.*

The traditions of Western civilization include an assumption that has been labeled a "two-valued" orientation; i.e., an "either-or" point of view. As we shall show in Chapter 10, much formal logic is based on this assumption, derived from Aristotle's thesis that an event either is *A* or is not *A*.[4]

4 Aristotle, *op. cit.*

Actually, Aristotle did not intend his thesis to include all objects or all events. Interpreters of Aristotle imposed this generalization on his principle of thought. Nevertheless, the belief has lingered that all events can be classified as one thing or another. The concept of rigor has included the notion that all things can be categorized and that these categories can be mutually exclusive, independent from each other. This view is denied by the concept of process; however, it also can be denied by an analysis of the steps in observing, of the ways in which we arrive at our observations—and of the basis for attaching labels of "true" or "false" to a statement of fact.

The scientist is well aware of the fact that all his observations are influenced by himself, that he can make no reports that are completely independent of his own knowledge, his own attitudes, his own cultural and social background. Science is often described as a method that produces complete objectivity. This is not the case.

Science does not assume that observations can be completely objective. In fact, one of the underlying assumptions of science is that observations can never be completely objective. That is why we need the methods of science when we make observations. In other words, science cannot be defended on the grounds that it is objective and other methods are not. Science is defensible on the grounds that nothing can be objective, but that we should approach objectivity as well as we can, knowing full well that we can never attain it.

On what grounds can complete objectivity be denied? One ingredient in any observation is the composition of the physical world. But the physical world must be perceived by a human organism if it is to be reported, if statements of fact are to be made. In order to report on the world, the human must organize his perceptions, must impose a structure on the sense data he receives. He must name things, and he must impose a structure in order to apply names. This introduces subjectivity in two ways.

First, the number of possible perceptions, possible observations, is infinite. We never can observe everything, or all of anything. We must select. *Perception must be selective if it is to be reported.*

All the factors that have been discussed as ingredients in the communication process help to determine what aspects of the physical world will be selected. Depending on our own cultural background, the ways in which we have been trained to look, we will find what we are looking for. Some men may boast that they believe only what they see, that you "have to show me" before I believe. It is just as valid to argue that *we see what we believe,* that our beliefs determine what we see.

There is bias in perception, introduced by the expectations we have about the nature of the physical world and the values we use in determining our own purposes. We perceive to affect. What we perceive and how we perceive it depends on the kinds of effects we intend to have, the kinds of purposes we have been taught to expect.

We perceive some things, and do not perceive others. We make judgments about what will be perceived, and what will not be. We structure our perceptions to fit those judgments. Our own prior experiences, our own values, are inextricably woven into our judgments—and into the perceptions produced by them.

Subjectivity of judgment is introduced into our observations in a second way. Given certain perceptions which we have structured and named, we relate these perceptions, we impose a structure on them as well. There is no "right" or "true" way to put concepts together, to relate one set of perceptions to another. There are only various ways to develop these relationships.

When we discussed the concept of roles, it was pointed out that we could group certain behaviors (structured perceptions) and give each group a name. Depending on our purpose, we might group one set of behaviors one time, and a different set of behaviors another time. There was no correct way to do this. It depended on our purpose, and on the utility of our groupings in accomplishing that purpose.

Clearly, purpose, the way in which we hope to affect the environment, determines the way in which we group concepts, the kinds of observations we make. Purpose is also subjective, also dependent on the personal, social, and cultural backgrounds from which we come. Again, we make judgments on what is important and unimportant, what is valuable and what is not. These are subjective, part of the observer rather than part of what is observed.

Voting is part of any observation, part of verifying any statement of fact. Even the "bunny" questions have to be voted on—by somebody. In discussing social reality, the domain of belief, it has been said that, "What is real to you is real—to you." This is so. Each of us defines his belief system in terms of his own goals, his own intentions to affect his environment and himself. The same statement can be made about physical reality as well. It, too, is voted upon.

Social reality, the area of beauty, elegance, value, is determined by man, is constructed by man. *Physical reality also has to be constructed, not discovered.* As MacLeish pointed out in his article on "The Poet and the Press," the poet and the journalist are in the same business. Both try to construct a reality, rather than to discover it.[5]

The concept of structure is vital to art, but it also is vital to science. The artist, dealing in the area of social reality, can be viewed as trying to impose a structure on the hazy perceptions we have of the world. He creates reality in the process. The scientist, dealing in the area of physical reality, also imposes a structure on our hazy perceptions—and creates reality in the process.

We have to distinguish carefully between facts and opinions, between observations and judgments. What is important is that we remember that this distinction is one of degree, not of kind. Acceptance is determined by voting, but so are statements of fact. Truth emerges as the result of a vote, just as does belief. All observations are both objective and subjective, involving both the nature of the physical world and the values and judgments of the observer. The criteria for voting differ, the definitions of a qualified electorate differ—but the basic process is the same.

Scientists are aware of this. It is for precisely this reason that they impose such severe restrictions on their behavior, attempting to

[5] Archibald MacLeish, "The poet and the press," *Atlantic Monthly,* 203: 40–46, 1959.

reduce their own involvement in the observations they make. The scientist develops rigorous procedures for constructing physical reality, both in creating his concepts and in relating them to each other. He specifies his criteria for acceptance of a proposition, including both structural rigor and empirical rigor.

He checks his observations against the observations of others, he develops nonhuman machinery to make as many of his observations as possible, he specifies the operations he performed so that others can attempt to duplicate them and see if they reproduce his results. Finally, he imposes a physical criterion of prediction. He makes statements about the physical world in areas where he has not yet observed, and then sees if his predictions describe the physical world accurately. In other words, he predicts physical events and verifies his predictions at a later time.

Denotative and connotative meanings can be differentiated on the basis of a public-private agreement on referent, and on the existence of physical events that can serve as referents. Observations and judgments can also be differentiated on the basis of public-private agreement on their truth value, and on the existence of referents in the physical world.

Many judgments do not have an observational dimension. All observations have a judgmental dimension. At some point, belief and acceptance is placed in a statement of fact. It then is called true. That belief may be withdrawn the following moment. Truth is neither absolute nor final. It is a property assigned to sentences of a certain type (statements of fact) that are useful in accomplishing our purposes: prediction, description, explanation, control. All of these purposes are related to the basic purpose of communication: affecting the environment and oneself.

In summary, we have described two kinds of sentences: observations and judgments. Observations emphasize denotative meanings, have specific relationships to events in the physical world, lie in the domain of physical reality, can be said to be true or false. Judgments emphasize connotative meanings, do not have to have specific relationships to events in the physical world, lie in the domain of social reality, and can be said to be accepted or not accepted.

The purpose of an observation is to report. The purpose of a judgment is to persuade. Both observations and judgments are used to affect, to influence. Just as denotation and connotation are not independent, observations and judgments are not independent. There is a judgmental dimension in all observations, in determining which perceptions will be structured and named, and how these perceptions will be organized or related to other perceptions.

Truth is a label assigned to certain observations, by vote of a "competent" electorate, people who are trained to vertify certain kinds of propositions. If the purpose of a judgment is to persuade, it follows that there is a persuasive dimension in all observations.

Statements of fact have in part a persuasive purpose. They direct attention, they structure perception, they suggest a particular way of viewing physical reality. All language utterances have a persuasive dimension. *No statements can be said to be nonpersuasive.*

The man who defends his messages on the grounds that they are completely objective, who asks for special privilege because he is an impartial, nonbiased commentator—that man is to be held suspect. He either is naive in his analysis of the functions of language in describing physical reality, or he is dishonest in his statements of purpose. *There is a persuasive bias in opinion. There also is a persuasive bias in knowledge.*

Suggestions for Thought and Discussion

1. Prepare four sentences that are *observations*. Justify, for each sentence, the label "observation." Trace for one of the sentences a step-by-step process of testing whether the statement of fact is a true statement of fact or a false statement of fact.
2. Prepare four sentences that are *judgments*. Justify, for each sentence, the label "judgment."
3. Prepare a concise outline of the differences between observations and judgments, in two parallel columns.
4. Secure a copy of a newspaper, a copy of a weekly newsmagazine, an advertisement incorporating a substantial amount of written copy, a report of a scientific experiment (available in most scientific books and periodicals), and a copy of a political address (available

in the *Congressional Record* or in published volumes of speeches). Prepare a list of observations and a list of judgments from these sources. Undertake a count of observations and judgments in two of the sources, preferably in one that on initial sampling seems high in observations and one that seems high in judgments; prepare a tally sheet listing in order of appearance *j, o, o, o, j, o, j, o, o,* etc. Keep in mind that not every sentence will be one or the other; some will be neither. What general inferences are you tempted to draw from your brief study? What are some of the factors limiting the inferences you can draw?

5. Discuss: "There is no such thing as complete objectivity." What are the implications of such a statement for science, for arbitration of disputes in the U.N., for decision-making in everyday affairs by rational people?

6. Discuss: "Physical reality also has to be constructed, not discovered." Read the Archibald MacLeish article "The Poet and the Press," and comment on its implications for communication.

7. Discuss: "There is a persuasive bias in opinion. There also is a persuasive bias in knowledge." Assuming that one wishes to be a good communicator, both as a source and as a receiver, what does he do about these biases, in himself and in others? What are some of the factors limiting what he can do?

8. Write a careful analysis of *the structuring of perception*. Examine its implications in communication situations involving: (a) two adults discussing a third person that one of them likes but the other does not like; (b) a teacher attempting to help several students learn subject-matter they have already studied unsuccessfully in earlier stages of their formal education; (c) a person trying to grasp a way of looking at his own values and goals that is both unfamiliar and at least in part unpleasant to him—such as a man facing retirement before he really wants to retire; (d) a person reading a rather difficult book when he would rather be doing something else.

CHAPTER 10

Inference

THE APPLICATION OF
STRUCTURAL RIGOR

THE concept of structure, the assembling of elements into a group, is pertinent to both observations and judgments. All uses of language require the structuring of perceptions, regardless of the purpose of the source. Reporting implies the selection and arrangement of perceptions. Judgment implies the relating of our perceptions to our own value structures.

Many of our affecting intentions go beyond reporting and judgmental sentence types. Man desires to do more than translate the physical world as he sees it and vote on its desirability. He wants to *interpret* events, to talk about the implications of one event for another event, to reach conclusions about the unknown, to make generalizations about events and predictions about future events. We want to construct sentences in which we use words like "because," "consequently," "therefore," "if . . . then," "probably," and so forth.

One of our intentions to affect requires us to predict, to make statements that are not themselves verifiable, at least at the time we make them. In trying to reduce uncertainty, we argue, we deduce.

In short, we make inferences, we tell our receiver what a certain event *means* to him.

When we make inferences, we are constructing sentences that talk about unknown events, based on other events that are known. We are introducing new knowledge, new understanding, without directly verifying our statements. *Inferences are the results of analyses of the structural relationships among sentences.*

In analyzing structure, we have need for the application of rigor. We need a set of procedures that we can use in developing or checking structural relationships. We need to make these procedures explicit, so that they can be checked by others, reproduced by others who are trying to arrive at the same inferences.

The methods of logical analysis are the methods of structural rigor. Logic, like mathematics, is a structural discipline. It is not concerned directly with physical reality. It is concerned with the reality of form. We can define logic as a set of principles and operations that we can use to manipulate words to form sentences, and to manipulate sentences to form new sentences.

This definition of logic is analogous to our definition of grammar. Grammar is not as rigorous, in that it describes procedures for combining elements of a dynamic referential language. Logic is rigorous, in that it describes procedures for combining elements of a static language. The elements of logical propositions are not concerned with a dynamic physical world, but with form only. Both grammar and logic are concerned with describing possible relationships between one sign and another sign. Both are related to our discussion of structural meaning.

Logic in language is concerned with two kinds of questions:

1. If we have encoded one sentence, what other sentences are *necessarily* implied by it?
2. If we have encoded one sentence, what other sentences *might* also be encodable which have a high *probability* of being true?

When we construct a message that answers either of these two questions, we have made an inference. One kind of inference deals with structural *necessity*. The other deals with structural *probability*. Both are intended to reduce uncertainty.

Where applicable, principles of structural necessity attempt to eliminate uncertainty completely. They state absolutes. Principles of structural probability never eliminate uncertainty completely, they only reduce it in varying degrees.

In making inferences, we use certain words that we might label "function words" or "structure words." These words do not denote objects in physical reality. Our meanings for them are structural, not denotative. They relate words that precede them to words that follow them.

Function words include terms such as "and," "or," "but," "however," and "because." A prescriptive grammar separates these words into classes, labeling them as prepositions, conjunctions, and the like. These are not very meaningful categories when we analyze inferential structure. We are more interested in the *functions* performed by this type of word.

In our discussion of structural rigor we will refer to several of these function words. Some of them are related to the principles of logical implication. Others are related to the principles of logical probability. In the first instance, we are making what have been called deductive inferences; in the second instance, inductive inferences.

In beginning our discussion, we can return to our four sample sentences at the beginning of Chapter 9. The second one was a deductive inference: *"If* all college students are human, *and if* all humans are mortal, *then* all college students are mortal." The words italicized are function words. They relate parts of this sentence to other parts.

Let us go back to our sample sentence in Chapter 8 and change it slightly. Suppose we had said: "All smoogles have comcom." Are any other sentences *necessarily* true if that sentence is true; in other words, does that sentence necessarily imply any other sentences? Several other sentences can be generated from that sentence. For example, if we say that all smoogles have comcom, we also have said that if we were to meet a smoogle, he certainly would have comcom. We also said that if we were to meet something that did not have comcom, it would not be a smoogle.

These examples demonstrate *deductive implication* or inference. Let us use another example. Suppose we were to say to our boss that, "All Democrats are communists." At this point, suppose our boss said quietly, "I am a Democrat." We would probably blush, gulp, stammer, or resign. Why? When we said that all Democrats are communists, and our boss said that he was a Democrat, it follows logically (is implied) that our boss is a communist. We "said" our boss was communistic. It was implied in another sentence we had constructed.

In encoding, we need to be careful that we really intend the implications contained in our sentences. We can analyze our sentences to see what other sentences we said at the same time—sentences with which we might not agree. In decoding, we need to be aware of the logical implications of the source's message. We need to check the validity of arguments. When we observe or analyze communication, we need to understand the methods of inference, the nature of *argument*.

One meaning for "argument" is the development of a conclusion that is related to certain premises; i.e., the construction of one sentence, given two other sentences. When the relationship between the premises and the conclusion meets certain tests, we say the argument is "valid." When the relationship does not meet our tests, we say the argument is "invalid." The criterion for accepting a statement of fact (an observation) is its truth—its verifiability. *The criterion for acceptance of an inference is its validity.*

Argumentative validity and observable truth are independent. The conclusion of an argument may be valid and yet not be true. For instance, suppose I were to argue like this:

(premise) Abraham Lincoln died before he was thirty.

(premise) A man cannot be President of the United States unless he is thirty-five or over.

(conclusion) Therefore, Abraham Lincoln was never President of the United States.

We know that the first premise is an observation—a statement of fact. We also can verify this sentence, and find that Lincoln did not die before he was thirty; in other words, the sentence is a false statement of fact. Nevertheless, the conclusion is valid, because *the validity of an argument does not rest on the truth of its parts.* It rests solely on the internal consistency of the relationships between the parts.

Clearly, we are not interested in encoding or accepting false conclusions, even if they are valid. We want to communicate valid arguments with true conclusions. The importance of deductive inference is this. If we have two observations (premises) that are true, *and a conclusion that has been deduced validly from these premises, then we can be sure that the conclusion is also true, even though we have not verified it.*

What need do we have to understand something about the meaning of internal consistency—validity? There are several needs, including:

1. The ability to analyze our own conclusions to see if they are valid.
2. The ability to test other people's arguments to see if they are valid.
3. The better understanding of our meaning for structure and the logic words we use, so that we use them in such a way that they will not mislead us.

What are some of the principles of deductive implication? How can we know that an argument is internally consistent? Let us look at some of the elementary principles of deductive logic, learn how to use these rules or principles, and then apply them to our own communication.

The Syllogism: A Test of Structural Implication

We can test an argument for logical adequacy by first reducing its components to one of four logical types of sentences. Once we have reduced a sentence to one of these four types, we can manipulate it logically. The four types are:

1. All X is/are Y.
2. No X is/are Y.
3. Some X is/are Y.
4. Some X is/are not Y.

In each of these four types, X refers to the subject of the sentence and Y refers to the predicate. Let us look at an example for each sentence type.

1. All X is/are Y.	All students are intelligent.
2. No X is/are Y.	No students are intelligent.
3. Some X is/are Y.	Some students are intelligent.
4. Some X is/are not Y.	Some students are not intelligent.

In each of these sentences, we substituted the word "students" for X and the word "intelligent" for Y.

It is hard to remember our four sentence types. It is hard to keep them apart and to distinguish among them. A helpful device is to think of each sentence as the relationship between two circles. One circle is X and the other circle is Y.

For example, take the sentence that says that all X is Y. We can represent this by two circles. The small circle is X and the large circle is Y. All of the small circle (X) is contained in the large circle (Y). All of Y may or may not be included in X. We cannot tell from the sentence.

Take the sentence that says that no X is Y. Again, two circles can represent X and Y. This time, the two circles do not touch at all. Each is independent of the other.

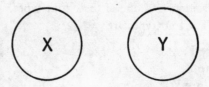

The third sentence states that some X is Y. In this case, our two circles overlap in part, but not necessarily in total.

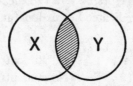

Finally, we have the sentence that says that some X is not Y. We represent this by two circles as well; however, this time we make sure that at least part of the X circle lies outside the Y circle.

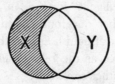

These four sets of circles are useful in keeping the four sentence types clearly in mind. Each of these four sentence-types has a name, based on two things: (1) Whether it talks about all of X or only some of X, and (2) whether the sentence is phrased in the affirmative or in the negative.

When we say that all X is Y, we speak about all of X, and we speak in the affirmative; therefore, the sentence-type, "All X is Y," is named a *Universal Affirmative*. When we say that "No X is Y," we again speak about all of X (we say that all of X is not Y), but this time we speak in the negative; therefore, the sentence-type, "No X is Y," is named a *Universal Negative*.

When we say that some X is Y, we speak about some of X, and we speak in the affirmative; therefore, we call the sentence-type, "Some X is Y," a *Particular Affirmative*. Finally, when we say that some X is not Y, we speak about some of X, and we speak in the negative; therefore, we name the sentence-type, "Some X is not Y," a *Particular Negative*. We can match these four names with the four logical-type sentences.

Sentence types	Sentence-type names
1. All X is/are Y.	1. Universal Affirmative
2. No X is/are Y.	2. Universal Negative
3. Some X is/are Y.	3. Particular Affirmative
4. Some X is/are not Y.	4. Particular Negative

We now have to introduce another technical term: *distribution. When we refer to all of something, we say that the something is distributed. When we refer only to part of something, we say that the something is nondistributed.* For example, when we say that all X is Y, we are talking about all of X; therefore, X is distributed. We are not talking about all of Y, necessarily; therefore, Y is nondistributed.

Let us use an English sentence. When I say that all boys are people, I am distributing my comment about boys over all boys; therefore, "boys" is distributed. I am not distributing my comments over all people; therefore, "people" is nondistributed.

In general, whenever the entire class of X *or* Y *is involved, the term* X *or* Y *is distributed. Whenever the entire class is not necessarily involved, the term* X *or* Y *is nondistributed.* The subject and predicate of each logical type of sentence can be said to be distributed or nondistributed.

In the Universal Affirmative, "All X is Y," X is distributed, Y is nondistributed. In the Universal Negative, "No X is Y," both X and Y are distributed. In other words, in order to say that no X is Y, we have to know about *all* of X and *all* of Y and to say that none of either is the other.

In the Particular Affirmative, "Some X is Y," neither X nor Y is distributed; we are not talking about all of either. Finally, in the Particular Negative, "Some X is not Y," X is nondistributed but Y is distributed. In other words, when we say that some X is not Y, we are *not* talking about all of X. We *are* talking about all of Y. We are saying that out of all of Y, some X's are excluded.

In summary:

Sentence type	Name	Rules of distribution	
		(X)	(Y)
1. All X is Y.	Universal Affirmative	Distributed	Nondistributed
2. No X is Y.	Universal Negative	Distributed	Distributed
3. Some X is Y.	Particular Affirmative	Nondistributed	Nondistributed
4. Some X is not Y.	Particular Negative	Nondistributed	Distributed

We have discussed what we mean by an argument, how to reduce sentences to one of four logical types, and the rules of distribution for the subjects and predicates in each type. We are now ready to analyze an argument and check its validity.

Let us take an elementary argument, called a syllogism. The syllogism consists of two sentences that we call *premises* and a third sentence, derived from the first two, that we call the *conclusion*. Here is an example:

> All college students are human.
> All humans are fallible.

(therefore)
> All college students are fallible.

This elementary argument or syllogism consists of two sentences (called premises), and a conclusion. *The conclusion explicitly states a connection that exists implicitly between the premises.* Let us reduce the above argument to logical-type sentences. Let A represent college students, let B represent humans, and let C represent fallibility. Our argument now reads as follows:

> All A is B.
> All B is C.

(therefore)
> All A is C.

We can look at the argument's validity more clearly when we have replaced our words with nondenotative symbols (A,B,C). This, of course, is part of the value of using mathematical or logical symbols in testing our own arguments and working out our own problems. It is a method of increasing our objectivity. As we eliminate denotative meaning, it is easier to perceive and analyze structural relationships.

We have one more concept to define: *the middle term*. The middle term is that subject or predicate which appears in both premises, but not in the conclusion. The middle term in our sample argument is *B* (humans).

We now can analyze the validity or internal consistency of this syllogistic argument. There are four rules to follow in testing its validity. For any syllogism to be valid:

1. The middle term must be distributed at least once.
2. Any term that is distributed in the conclusion must also be distributed in the premises.
3. If the two premises are negative, no conclusion can be drawn.
4. If one premise is negative, the conclusion must be negative.

If a syllogism violates *any one* of these rules, where applicable, it is invalid.

Let us look at our argument again:

> All *A* is *B*.
> All *B* is *C*.

(therefore)
> All *A* is *C*.

Let us go through the steps of validity testing. First, the middle term must be distributed at least once. The middle term is *B; B* appears in both premises but not in the conclusion.

Is the middle term distributed at least once? In the first premise, *B* is the predicate of a Universal Affirmative; therefore, it is not distributed. In the second premise, *B* is the subject of a Universal Affirmative; therefore, it is distributed. We have satisfied our first rule.

Let us turn to the second rule: a term that is distributed in the conclusion must also be distributed in the premises. Are there any distributed terms in the conclusion? *A* is the subject of a Universal Affirmative; therefore, it is distributed. By our rule, *A* must also be distributed when it occurs in the premises. It occurs in the first premise, again as the subject of a Universal Affirmative; therefore, it is distributed. Since *C* is not distributed in the conclusion, we have satisfied our second condition.

The third and fourth rules do not apply to this argument. There are no negative premises.

In summary, we have tested our argument and found that all the rules that apply were followed; we can conclude therefore that our argument is valid.

Its validity does not mean that our conclusion is necessarily true. We must first find out if our premises are true. *If both premises are true and the argument is valid, the conclusion* must *be true.*

In most of our messages, we do not use complete syllogisms. We usually omit one of the premises. In our example, we probably would not have constructed the entire argument: all college students are human; all humans are fallible; therefore, all college students are fallible. What we probably would say is something like this: college students are fallible *because* they are human. We let the receiver fill in the missing premise (all humans are fallible).

Such a shortened argument is an "enthymeme"; a syllogism in which one of the premises (or the conclusion) is not stated explicitly. We use enthymemes frequently—and we should. If we detailed all of the premises on which we base our conclusions, our messages would bore our receivers. Yet, there are at least three points which we should keep in mind when we use the enthymeme. These include:

1. Be sure in our own analysis that we are presenting only conclusions that are sound. Do not accept an enthymeme when we cannot supply the missing premise. Do not accept a conclusion unless (a) we can supply the missing premises, (b) we are willing to accept the premises as true, and (c) we test the validity of the complete argument.
2. When encoding, make sure that our receiver can fill in the missing premise when we omit it. If this is impossible, at least

be sure that the receiver would be willing to accept the conclusion if he decoded the complete argument.

3. In choosing words to encode in our messages, be sure that we are not misleading our receiver by using words that imply argument, when we are only stating an opinion—without basis. In other words, when we say "because," we should be sure that we are presenting an enthymeme based on a valid syllogism, with true premises. When we say "therefore," we should be sure that we are concluding a valid syllogism, with true premises.

Sometimes our conclusions are too complex to be covered in one argument. We might have to develop the argument through several syllogisms, with the conclusion of one syllogism becoming a premise in another, and so on. This kind of multi-syllogism is called a *sorites*. We will not talk about sorites here, but we should be aware of them in analyzing our arguments. The same principles operate. It just requires more work to check through the entire argument.

We can summarize what has been said about the use of deductive reasoning in improving our communication ability.

1. Through deduction, we can generate sentences that have been implied by other sentences.
2. The concept of logical validity is independent of the concept of truth.
3. Argument is not related to denotation. It makes no statements about physical reality.
4. All we mean by validity is that an argument is internally consistent; certain formal arrangements have been preserved.
5. If a sentence can be deduced from the relation between two other sentences, and if the two other sentences are true, then the deduced sentence is true.
6. There are a few formal rules of deduction that can help us in testing the validity of arguments. Use of these rules will help us:

    a. Test our own statements before we make them.

    b. Analyze the statements of others before we accept them.

7. We often present enthymemes, or perhaps only the conclusions of arguments. In such cases, we should be able to:

    a. Reconstruct the entire argument and be sure of its validity.

    b. Predict the extent to which our receivers can reconstruct the argument for themselves or will accept the conclusion without reconstructing the argument.

It should be pointed out that we have by no means exhausted the methods of logical implication. The logic of deduction is quite extensive and complex. The syllogism is the most elementary kind of deductive manipulation. It has been used only to demonstrate the kind of procedure that is involved in the development of deductive argument.

Syllogisms are elementary arguments. Although the concept of argument is complex, understanding and application of the syllogistic tests are useful when we are concerned with an argumentative message.

Some of our messages are argumentative, but we may well use another kind of inference called "generalizing" even more in our day-to-day living. Generalizing also requires a set of logical rules and arrangements which we refer to as principles of inductive logic.

Inductive logic differs somewhat from deductive logic, but not nearly as much as we might believe. Many of us learned that to deduce is to go from the general to the specific; to induce is to go from the specific to the general. In one sense this is meaningless. Any inductive inference can be cast in the form of a syllogism. In fact, it is useful to do this. We see much more clearly the kinds of assumptions that are required if we are to make our generalizations.

Inductive inference does differ from deductive inference in one major way. The conclusions of deductive logic are completely certain, if the premises in deductive logic can be said to be true or false. The conclusion of a valid syllogism with true premises *must necessarily be true*. Inductive generalization can never be said to be *necessarily* true, since generalizations rest on *probabilities*—on premises which are more or less probable, rather than true or false.

In discussing the nature of observations, it was suggested that the truth or falsity of any statement of fact is arrived at eventually through a voting process. In stating that any sentence intending to describe physical reality is true, we recognize that we cannot be certain about this. We may change our designation to "false" tomorrow, we may modify the sentence somewhat to retain our designation of "true."

There is no meaning to the concept of *absolute* or *necessary* when we are talking about physical reality. With this in mind, it becomes clear that deductive logic cannot produce certainty when its premises are statements of fact.

In using the principles of structural implication, such as the syllogism, we can be certain of the validity of our form. Our confidence in the truth value of our conclusion, however, is limited by our confidence in the truth value of our premises. This confidence is never absolute; therefore, we never derive statements that are necessarily true from deductive reasoning. If we have true premises and a valid syllogism, we have a true conclusion—but we never can be certain that our premises are true.

The point is this. Historically, deduction and induction have been separated on the grounds of necessary vs. probable truth. This is not a meaningful distinction. Neither can produce necessary truth. The difference is that, while both start with probabilistic premises, the structural principles of deduction are certain but the structural principles of induction also are probabilistic.

Principles of induction introduce probability at two levels: the probability that the premises are true, plus the probability that the inference is valid. Principles of deduction introduce probability at only one level. The inference is either valid or invalid—there is no middle ground. There are only probabilities that the premises are true. When we are trying to explain physical reality, structural rigor can never produce certainty—only probabilities of various values.

One reason why deduction cannot produce certainty is that the premises of the syllogism, when they are statements of fact, are themselves the products of inductive inference. We structure our perceptions inductively when we name them. A concept, a name, is arrived at through grouping perceptions, making generalizations about those groupings, and operating on these generalizations. In this sense, deduction and induction are not separable at all. When the premises of a syllogism are statements of fact, they have been arrived at through the use of inductive principles. Only after imposing structure on our perceptions inductively can we apply the principles of deductive logic, the structural rigor of logical necessity.

In structuring the physical world, we can be inductive without being deductive. We *cannot* impose deductive structure without also imposing inductive structure. The principles of induction are central to any development of structural rigor.

Induction: The Development of Structural Generalization

Our discussion of induction will attempt to tie together several previous references to the concepts of structure and uncertainty. In many ways, it can be used as a basis for earlier treatments of the process of communication, in terms of the establishment and utility of terms like role, social system, culture, etc.

In order to understand what is meant by induction, we need to assume and make use of much of the prior discussion. We will not talk directly about the methods of structuring perception; however, everything that is said applies at any level of induction. We will restrict the discussion of induction to the sentence level; to a discussion of how we can use true statements of fact to help us encode other sentences that have a high probability of being true.

At this level of analysis, the basic data of induction are true statements of fact: observations that have been verified. Induction attempts to take one or more statements of fact and relate them in such a way as to produce a prediction, a hypothesis about fact which has not been verified. This can be done in either or both of two ways. Induction can produce a specific prediction, a statement of fact that can be verified in the future. Induction can also produce a more general statement which cannot be verified in itself, but that serves as the *name* for a *group* of statements of fact that can be verified in the future.

For example, it is a true statement of fact to say that the sun rose yesterday. It is a true statement of fact to say that the sun rose the day before yesterday, the day before that, etc. From these statements of fact, through use of the principles of induction, we can make an inference: the sun will rise tomorrow (example number three in our original four sentences of Chapter 9). This is a prediction about fact. It cannot be said to be true or false today—it *can* be verified tomorrow.

Another inference that can be made is that the sun will rise every day. This statement can *never* be verified completely—at least not until the Day of Judgment. The sentence, "The sun will rise every day," is the name of a group of sentences, including the one that says the sun will rise tomorrow, the next day, etc.

Both of these sentence types are inductive inferences. One is a specific factual prediction, the other a general prediction. One can be verified directly, the other cannot. Both are produced through the imposition of structure that relates historical statements—statements of fact from the past.

In communicating, we are prone to say that the sentence, "The sun will rise tomorrow" is true. If we say this, we clearly have a meaning for "true" that is different from the one used in making observations. We have not *verified* the rising of the sun tomorrow. We *cannot* verify it now.

We are misleading our receiver if we lead him to believe that he can have as much confidence (truth value) for the sentence, "The sun will rise tomorrow" as he can have in a sentence of the order, "Columbus discovered America in 1492." Our confidence in an inference can vary according to the truth of the statements of fact on which it is based, and on the adequacy of the structural development of the inference itself. In no case can our confidence in the truth value of an inference be as high as it would be for a verified statement of fact. To believe otherwise is to be misled.

How is this structure imposed? How can we go from the sentence, "The sun rose yesterday" to the sentence, "The sun will rise tomorrow"? This process of inductive reasoning rests on several assumptions. They include the following:

1. There is continuity in the events of the physical world; you may not be able to step in the same river twice, but often the differences in you and the river do not make a significant difference or can be taken into account.
2. The continuity of Nature permits the imposition of an orderly structure on physical events.
3. Given continuity and structure, we can predict that the future will be very similar to the past. Rare or disruptive events will not occur. What happened once in a given set of circumstances will happen again under similar circumstances.

Induction rests on these assumptions. They are not statements of fact, although there is a basis for them. The assumptions of inductive inference cannot be verified, although evidence can be accumulated that supports them. They are *believed,* they represent a *value* necessary to the making of inductive inferences. They are accepted in part on faith.

In making an inference, we start from exactly the same position as does the new-born infant. The world is a "blooming, buzzing confusion." When we attempt to make predictions about the future, we are engaged in exactly the same process that was described earlier in discussing how the infant learns meaning. We organize, we structure, we learn meanings—following the same principles of learning that were used to explain how all meanings are learned. The difference is that a more conscious attempt is made to impose rigor on our structuring, to develop and follow an explicit method of structuring. In short, we impose a formal structural model on our observations, a model of probabilities.

The key to grasping the nature of induction is an understanding of the structural model that is imposed on observations. This model is used as the justification for prediction. There are several models of structure that can be imposed. In our discussion we will refer only to the one that is used most frequently, the normal probability model; however, it should be kept in mind that this is only one way to impose structure. There are others.

To illustrate the use that is made of the inductive assumptions, and the applications of a probability model, let us take an example of a set of events and make inferences from those events. Suppose we have an ordinary United States coin, such as a penny. If we flip this coin in the air, it can come down on one side or the other (we rule out the possibility that it may land on its edge).

Suppose that we flip our penny ten times and observe that it lands "heads" five times and "tails" five times. We can make a true statement of fact: the coin landed on each side the same number of times. Assuming that there is a continuity of events, we might predict that flipping this coin in the future would also produce an equal number of heads and tails.

If we do this, we have made a prediction, but we have *not* imposed a structural model. We have merely hypothesized that future flipping will produce *exactly* the same result that we observed. Obviously, if we were to repeat our flipping, we might obtain a different result. We might get six heads and only four tails, or three heads and seven tails, or even ten heads and no tails. In order to make an inference about the results of future flipping, we need to construct a probability model that we can incorporate into our prediction.

In developing such a model, we begin by denying for the moment our assumption of continuity and assuming that there is *no* order in the physical world. If events do not go together, it follows that any single event is just as likely to occur as is any other event. It would follow that there is no rhyme or reason to the occurrence of events, they just happen. This is the assumption underlying the normal probability model.

If all events are equally likely to occur, we cannot make any predictions about which event will occur. We just have to wait and see. We do realize, however, that each event would occur about the same number of times—in the long run. This is part of what is meant by the statement that each is equally likely to occur.

At any given time, any event can happen. Over a number of trials, however, all events should occur the same number of times—*by chance*. The term "chance" names the assumption that there is no order in the occurrence of events.

We can apply this assumption to our penny. If heads and tails are equally likely to occur, we should get an equal number of each if we flipped our coin an infinite number of times. We recognize that we cannot flip the coin an infinite number of times, however, and that on any given number of flips, we may get more heads than tails or vice versa. We need to take this into account in developing our model.

In flipping a coin, two events can occur: a heads or a tails. If we have no basis for a prediction of which will occur, we have to assume that they are equally likely to occur. As a definition of probability we can say, given events which are equally likely to occur, that *the probability that a given event will occur is equal to the number of ways that event can occur divided by the number of events that can occur.* In our example, a head can occur only one way, and two events can occur (heads and tails); therefore, the probability that a head will occur is ½ (.50)—by chance. Correspondingly, the probability that a tails will occur is also ½—by chance.

Suppose we flip our coin twice. What events can occur? We can get two heads, two tails, or one head and one tail. Following our definition of probability, we might be tempted to say that the probability of getting a head and a tail is ⅓, that there is only one way in which the event "head and tail" can occur, and there are three possible events.

If we do this, we are making an error. The event "head and tail" can occur in two ways. We can flip a head the first time and a tail the second (first way). We also can flip a tail the first time and a head the second (second way). Specifically, four events can occur when a coin is flipped twice: heads-heads (HH), heads-tails (HT), tails-heads (TH), and tails-tails (TT). The probability that we would flip two heads is ¼; the probability that we would "head and tail" is 2/4; the probability that we would get two tails is ¼.

We can say this in another way that provides greater insight into the nature of induction. Suppose we are about to flip our penny two times. Before flipping it, we assume that it is just as likely to come up heads as tails on any given flip (the hypothesis assumes no structural relationship between flipping and the side of the coin that comes up). Under this assumption or hypothesis, the best guess we can make is that we will get one head and one tail. On any given set of two flips, we have a 50-50 chance of being right in our guess—and a 50-50 chance of being wrong. We could get two heads, or two tails—*even if our hypothesis is true that heads and tails are equally likely*. In other words, we can make the statement that heads and tails are equally likely to occur, observe that one occurred more frequently than the other, and still be correct in our original assumption—because of the chance probabilities of occurrence.

Suppose we flipped the penny three times. What events could occur? We could get three heads one way (HHH). We could get two heads and a tail three ways (HHT, HTH, THH). We could get one head and two tails in three ways (TTH, THT, HTT). We could get three tails only one way (TTT). Now, assuming that heads and tails are equally likely, the probability that we would get three heads on three flips is ⅛ (there is one way to get that event, and there are eight possible events). The probability of two heads and a tail is ⅜, as is the probability of one head and two tails. The probability of three tails is ⅛.

If we add our probabilities for all possible events, we arrive at the figure ⅝ or 1. In other words, if we flip a coin three times, the probability that we will get three heads, two heads, one head, or no heads is 1—certainty. In computing probabilities, "1" is the largest figure obtainable. To use probability terms, if we say that a particular event is certain, is necessary, is inevitable, we are saying that the probability that it will occur is 1. This is important in understanding that inferences can never produce certainty—can never permit probabilities of 1.

Suppose we flipped our penny a million times. It would require more pages than are contained in this book to list all of the possible events which could occur. In total, the number of events would equal the figure we would get if we multiplied "2" by itself one million times, $2^{1,000,000}$, or "2" to the one-millionth power. It is simple to determine the probability that we would get one million heads—under the assumption that heads and tails are equally likely. If this assumption is correct, the probability that we would get a heads on every flip is $\frac{1}{2}^{1,000,000}$. This is an extremely small fraction, but it is an actual number. We can draw two conclusions about it.

First, if we were to get 1,000,000 heads on 1,000,000 flips of the coin, we probably would question seriously our original assumption—we would begin to believe that the coin was loaded and that we were wrong when we said that heads and tails were equally likely.

On the other hand, we could get 1,000,000 heads—by chance— *even if our assumption were true*. In other words, if we get 1,000,000 heads on a million flips, we would reject our assumption that heads and tails were equally likely—but we could be wrong in rejecting it.

We could not be certain that we were right, because there is a chance, however slight, that the result we obtained would be obtained from a "true coin." This demonstrates the impossibility of certainty as a result of the use of the principles of induction or probability.

Inferences are predictions made about the unknown, based on a sample of what is known. Any given set of observations can help us in making such predictions; however, any given set of observations can lead us to make correct or erroneous predictions—and we can never be certain whether we are correct or in error, we only can be highly confident or not so confident.

With this introduction, we can return to our original concern with the process of induction. We make inductive inferences by imposing a structural relationship on events. We do it in order to reduce our uncertainty about the unknown, to increase our predictive accuracy. In making inferences, we can be rigorous or not. It is quite possible to make predictions without any deliberate attempt to develop a criterion of structural adequacy for these predictions. Such predictions are not rigorous, do not follow principles of probability inferences, and are more likely to be in error. If we attempt to impose rigor on our structures, we need to perform several operations.

The basic data for inductive inferences are statements of fact. We observe the flipping of a coin and notice that heads came up ten times in a row. We want to make an inference about this coin. We want to say that it is "loaded," that heads and tails are not equally likely to occur. *The methods of inference do not permit us to check the validity of this inference directly. We must check its validity indirectly, by hypothesizing its opposite.*

We hypothesize that the coin is a "true" coin, and that heads and tails *are* equally likely to occur. Under this hypothesis of no difference between heads and tails, we determine the probability that the event we observed would occur. In our example, the probability of getting ten heads in ten flips if the coin is true is equal to $\frac{1}{2}^{10}$, or $1/1024$. This is an extremely low probability, indicating that the event we observed must have been a *rare event,* if the coin is "true."

We have stated that we do not believe in rare events, and that we will reject the inference that the coin is a "true" coin. In rejecting this hypothesis, we give support to its opposite, that the coin is "loaded." The methods of inference do not permit us to support our inferences directly. In order to be rigorous, we have to set up a "straw-man" inference, usually the inference that there is no relationship between events. Testing the validity of an inference involves trying to destroy the straw-man inference, and thereby indirectly supporting our own prediction.

Inductive inference is a negative method, not a positive one. We can never say that our inferences are correct, only that the opposites of our inferences appear to be incorrect. Induction permits us to reject hypotheses, or to fail to reject hypotheses. Induction does not permit us to accept hypotheses.

The probability model on which validity-testing is based requires this kind of approach. The usual assumption, called the null or zero hypothesis, is that nothing is related to anything else, that all events are equally likely to occur. In order to make inferences that say things *are* related, in order to impose a structural relationship *between* two kinds of events, we attempt to disprove the null hypothesis, to reject the inference that A and B are not related.

If we demonstrate that the events we observed are unlikely under the no-structure (null) hypothesis, we reject it and accept an alternative inference—the one we believed to be the case from our observations. If we do not demonstrate that the observed events were rare, unlikely, we cannot reject the hypothesis of no-structure, and we are forced to continue believing that events in the world are unrelated.

We can demonstrate this more clearly by moving from coin-flipping to a different inference: that the sun will rise tomorrow. In making this inference, we have a large number of observations at our disposal. We know, or can determine, that the sun has risen every morning for the last 100 days. We can predict, on the basis of this information, that the sun will rise tomorrow, because we believe that there is a continuity in the events of the physical world (first assumption).

In order to check the validity of our inference, we set up a straw-man inference, the null hypothesis. Using this hypothesis, we state that the sun rising or the sun not rising are equally likely events (second assumption—imposing of structure). In other words, the probability that the sun will rise on any given day is $\frac{1}{2}$; the probability that it will not rise is also $\frac{1}{2}$.

Under this null hypothesis, we compute the probability that the sun would have risen every day for the last 100 days. This example is just like coin-flipping. The event "sun up every morning" could have only occurred in one way. The total number of events, the total number of possible "sun up" and "sun not up" combinations for those 100 days is equal to the number 2 raised to the one-hundredth power, or 2^{100}.

Under the null hypothesis, the probability that the sun would have risen 100 straight days by chance is equal to $\frac{1}{2}^{100}$. This is an extremely small probability, indicating that we must have observed an extremely rare event (sun up 100 consecutive days) if the null hypothesis is true.

We do not accept rare events (third assumption), and we therefore reject the null hypothesis. In rejecting this inference, we give support to our original inference, and we say that it is valid to infer that the sun will rise tomorrow—recognizing that we may be wrong, and that actually we might have witnessed a very rare event.

This is the process of rigorous induction. It is the method used by the scientist in generalizing from the results of experiments. It is the method used by the logician in generalizing from specific events. It is a method that is available to any one if he is willing to learn the kinds of requirements imposed by the application of inductive rigor, and the factors that can affect the validity of his inferences.

We have not discussed the concept of the "rare event." Some decision must be made as to what events will be labeled "rare" and what events will be labeled "normal," under the null hypothesis. After imposing our probability model that assumes that all events are equally likely, we compute the probabilities of events that have occurred.

If we observe that a given event (such as the sun rising or heads coming up) has occurred significantly more often (or less often) than we would expect by chance, we reject the null hypothesis as a basis for inference. We make an alternative inference to the effect that there *is* a structure in the physical world, that things do go together. The question is, what level do we choose for significance, how far must an event's probability deviate from the chance expectation of a 50-50 split before we call that a "rare" event and use it to reject the null hypothesis.

There is no "right" answer to this question, no "correct" figure which can be given. *The determination of the cutting point between normal and rare events is a matter of judgment, not of observation or inference.* The values of the person making the inference determine where he will draw the line. Questions of value cannot be separated entirely from problems of inductive inference, or for that matter, from questions of fact.

The value basis for this decision is related to two principles we have discussed earlier: the concept of reward and the principle of the conservation of energy (principle of least effort). In making an inference, we put aside temporarily our belief that the world has structure. We assume, for purposes of inference, that the world is disorganized, that the null hypothesis is true.

In checking this assumption against our observations, we have two alternatives. We can decide to (1) *reject* that assumption and make an inference about how the world *is* organized, or (2) *not* reject the assumption and make *no* inference about how two events are related.

We can take either alternative. Whichever we take, two consequences are possible: (1) we can be correct in our decision, or (2) we can be incorrect. These decisions, and their correctness, can be grouped into the four alternatives of inference.

We can reject the statement that A and B are not related (tomorrow and the sun rising are not related) and be right. This is desirable. We can fail to reject the statement that A and B are not related (rainfall in Kansas and price of tea in China are not related), and be right. This is desirable. We can forget both these two alternatives for the moment, and concentrate on the two kinds of errors we can make in induction, as illustrated by the other two alternatives.

We can reject the statement that A and B are not related and be wrong. We can fail to reject the statement that A and B are not related and be wrong. In both cases we have made an inference that is not correct. We have erred, but our errors under the one alternative are quite different from our errors under the other. In the first case, we have denied the complete uncertainty assumption. We have stated that there is a principle of structure which connects two events when there really is not. In other words, we have added to our supply of predictions when we would have been better off without any prediction at all. In the second case, we have decided not to reject the uncertainty assumption when we really should have rejected it. We have missed an opportunity to add to our prediction supply, we have missed a chance to contribute knowledge which would be rewarding in the future.

When we erroneously reject the uncertainty hypothesis, we expend energy in the hope of receiving a reward—but the reward is not forthcoming. When we erroneously refuse to reject the uncertainty hypothesis, we conserve our energy—but in so doing miss the reward we could have achieved if we had been willing to make a prediction. Again, the fraction of decision is pertinent to the discussion.

The decision on defining a "rare" event is determined by the relationship between expected reward and expected energy to be expended. In making inductions, we operate under both kinds of expectations. As an example, we can analyze the job of the scientist. The scientist basically is conservative. He assumes that the world is random until he gets evidence to cause him to infer otherwise. He has a value called the principle of parsimony.

Parsimony is a conservation-of-energy principle. It states that we should never use more concepts or assertions about concepts than are absolutely necessary to predict an event. The principle of parsimony also encourages the scientist to not "clutter up" his view of the world by including predictions that are not valid—by not rejecting the null hypothesis when it is true.

The principle of parsimony exerts force on the definition of "rare event." If we use it to conserve energy, we require the event to be extremely rare before the null hypothesis is rejected. Carried to its limit, the conservation of energy principle would never permit inductive inferences at all. It would cause us to prefer no additions to our supply of predictions—because they require the expenditure of energy.

On the other hand, the scientist is rewarded if his prediction turns out to be correct. The consequences of correct predictions enable him better to organize physical reality, to be more able to affect his environment. If the principle of expected reward were carried to its limit, it would cause us to make inferences constantly

—on the flimsiest of observational evidence. It would define all events as "rare" events and constantly deny the principle of no structural relationship, the null hypothesis.

The actual decision on definition of a rare event is a function of both of these pressures. To the extent that we are in need of some kind of prediction to help us organize the world, we will define "rare" as pretty close to "normal," as events with high chance probability. To the extent that we have many predictions at our disposal and desire to conserve our energy so that we can use it to explore only useful predictions, we will define "rare" as very far from "normal," as events with low chance probability. No matter where we place our definition, we are subject to error. *Error can never be eliminated entirely from inductive inference.*

Our coin flipping can serve as an illustration of these points. We flip a penny four times. We get a heads each time. The question is, will we reject the hypothesis that this is a true coin, and infer that it is loaded in favor of heads, or will we fail to reject the null hypothesis, and continue to operate as if this is a true coin.

Our decision depends on the point at which we define events to be "rare" or "abnormal." We first assume the null hypothesis to be true, and determine the probability of getting four heads under that assumption. There are sixteen possible events that could have occurred (2^4). The event "HHHH" could only occur one way; therefore, the probability of getting four heads in four flips, under the null hypothesis, is $\frac{1}{16}$, or .0625. In other words, if we flipped a coin four times, the odds are 16 to 1 that we would not get four heads—if it is a true coin.

To put it another way, suppose we repeated our coin flipping for 100 trials, each trial consisting of four flips of the coin. Out of a hundred trials (each requiring four flips of a coin), we would expect that six of those trials would produce "HHHH" by chance; the event we observed would occur 6.25 percent of the time by chance. Is 6.25 percent a probability sufficiently small for us to call it a "rare" event, or is it large enough to include it as a "normal" event and assume that it had happened by chance?

We have to decide. Whichever way we decide, we might be

right—and we might be wrong. We can never be sure. Most social scientists choose what they call the 5 percent level as their cutting point. In other words, they decide that if an event would have occurred 5 percent of the time or less by chance, they will call it a rare event and reject the null hypothesis. If the event would have occurred more than 5 percent of the time by chance, they will not call it a rare event and will retain the null hypothesis, attributing the event they observed to chance.

For purposes of illustration, we can adopt this 5 percent cutting point. If we do, we will conclude that the event we observed, "HHHH," would have happened more than 5 percent of the time by chance. We will not reject the null hypothesis, we will not make the inference that this is a loaded coin. We might be right. On the other hand, the coin may actually be loaded—but we did not say so.

Suppose we had set our cutting point at 10 percent instead of 5 percent. Under these circumstances, we *would* have defined "HHHH" as a rare event. We would have rejected the null hypothesis, and made the inference that this coin was loaded in favor of heads. We might have been right. On the other hand, the coin may actually have been a "true" coin, and we may have made an inference that was not correct.

What are the chances that we will reject the null hypothesis when we should not? The probability of making an error of this type is set by the cutting point we choose. If we make 100 sets of observations and reject the null hypothesis every time, using the 5 percent level as a cutting point, we will make an inference 5 times when we should not have made one. We do not know *which* five times, but we do know that five times out of a hundred this will be the case. We can know how often we will make this error. We cannot know which times we made it.

What are the chances that we will fail to reject the null hypothesis when we should reject it? We cannot tell. It depends on a great number of factors, such as the care with which we made our observations and the adequacy of our inferential ability.

The determination of a rare event is a question of judgment.

In making this judgment, we are subject to two kinds of errors. We may go ahead and make an inference when we should not. We may refuse to make an inference when we should have made one. We cannot eliminate the chances of either of these errors if we are going to make inductive inferences. We cannot make predictions that are rigorous about future events if we do not make inductive inferences. Any prediction, rigorous or otherwise, is subject to error.

Rigorous predictions are less subject to error than are less rigorous ones, but even a careful and thorough application of the methods of inductive rigor will produce error on occasion. *There is no justification for certainty of prediction, when we are predicting events in physical reality.*

In summary, we have said that inductive inferences are predictions about unknown events, based on observations and the application of the techniques of rigorous induction. In making an inference, we perform the following steps:

1. Impose a probability model, usually the model involving the null hypothesis that states that events A and B are independent, that there is no structural relationship between them.

2. Define the cutting point between "rare or abnormal" events and "normal" events, in terms of the probability of occurrence under the null hypothesis.

3. Calculate the probabilities of occurrence of the events we have observed, under the null-hypothesis definition of probability.

4. Decide whether the events we observed fall on the "rare" side or the "normal" side of our cutting point.

5. If the events fall on the "rare" side, reject the null hypothesis (because we do not believe in rare events) and make an inference about how A and B are related.

6. If the events fall on the "normal" side, do not reject the null hypothesis and refuse to make an inference about any relationship between A and B.

7. Remember that we may have been in error, whether or not

we made an inference. We might have done so when we should not have, we might have refused to make one when we should have made one.

Inferences are arrived at through a negative process. We do not say that we believe A and B to be related. We can only say that there is evidence to reject the assumption that A and B are not related. Again, many of us were raised in a culture which did not teach us to distinguish between "true" and "not-false." They are not equivalent expressions. When we say we have reason to believe that A is false, it does not always follow that the negative of A is true. When we reject the assumption of no structural relationship, we cannot accept completely the assumption of a structural relationship. Particularly, we cannot accept completely the assumption of a specific structural relationship. Inferences are always tentative, never absolute.

One additional comment about inferences. An inductive inference can always be interpreted as a statement about an entire population, based on a sample from that population. When the Gallup poll makes a prediction about the outcome of an election, it is making an inference about how the population will vote, based on a sample of voters. When we infer that a coin is loaded, we are making a prediction about an infinite number of flips of a coin—based on a sample number of flips that were observed. When we say that the sun will rise every day, we are inferring something about all days—based on our observations for a limited number of days.

Generalizations are statements about a whole, based on observation of a part. In making such inferences, we need to take into account at least three kinds of questions:

1. HAVE THERE BEEN A SUFFICIENT NUMBER OF OBSERVATIONS?

It is difficult to determine whether a sample of observations has been large enough. It is easier to determine that it has been too small. American advertising has exposed us to large numbers of inductive inferences that are based on insufficient sampling. We all have heard the suggestion that we should try a certain headache powder, because "three out of four doctors recommend it." When we analyze these statements we often find that the evidence is based on a sample of exactly *four* doctors—three said yes and one said no. This sample is not large enough to permit a generalization to the effect that 75 percent of doctors favor that headache powder.

Another example can be taken from the publicity brochure of a private Eastern college. This brochure stated that 33 percent of its undergraduate girls married college professors (this not only is an inadequate sample, it very probably is a weak argument for encouraging girls to attend that school). Examination revealed that *exactly* three girls had registered as students in this school in its entire history—and *one* had married a college professor. Would it be safe for a girl to infer that she had one chance in three of marrying a professor if she attended that college? Obviously not.

We all hear statements of the order "everybody believes such and such," or "everybody knows that such and such is the case." Whenever we hear such a statement we can recognize it for an inductive inference—frequently based on a sample of one or two people.

For an illustration of just how an insufficient sample can affect our inductive decisions, we can return to the example of flipping a coin four times. Suppose we were trying to decide whether that penny were loaded, and we chose a 5 percent level for our definition of a rare event. This means that we would have to observe an event that could happen 5 percent of the time or less, by chance, before we could reject the null hypothesis.

If we had flipped the coin only four times, the most extreme event that could occur would be "HHHH," or "TTTT." The probability of either of these occurring is $\frac{1}{16}$, or 6.25 percent. In short, we could never reject the null hypothesis if our sample only included four flips, and our definition of "rare" was set at 5 percent —no matter how "loaded" the coin actually was. We did not make a sufficient number of observations to permit a decision on the nature of our inductive inference. We had asked a question. We did not have enough observations to permit making an inference.

As Mowrer has pointed out, when we say that "Tom is a thief," we have made an inductive inference.[1] We have observed that Tom took money that he had not earned. On the basis of this single observation, we generalized to the entire population of Tom's behavior. We predicted that Tom would steal again. A word like "thief" not only makes an observation—Tom has taken money that was not his—it also predicts that the same event will occur again under similar circumstances. Clearly, this is not a justifiable inductive leap. The fact that we make such leaps is a continual burden on the backs of the one-error ex-convict.

2. Is the Evidence Representative?

When we generalize from a sample, we not only must be sure that we have enough evidence, we also must be sure that our evidence is representative; in other words, that we do not have a *biased* sample.

We have all heard generalizations based on nonrepresentative sampling. As an illustration, take the political candidate who infers that he will win an election because "everybody I talk to says he is going to vote for me." The problem is that the candidate does not talk to a random sample of people. He is much more likely to talk to people who intend to vote for him—his sample is biased in his favor and does not represent the population as a whole.

The same deficiency exists in the reasoning of an actor who infers that his work is appreciated because "all of the people I meet tell me how much they like my work." It is quite possible that the actor just does not know people who do not appreciate him. They leave him alone.

As a third illustration, take the editor who makes an inductive inference that his magazine, book, or reports are easy for his

[1] O. H. Mowrer, "The psychologist looks at language," *American Psychologist* 9, 11, pp. 660–694, 1954.

readers to understand because "I have my entire staff read the entire thing, and they find it easy to understand." An editorial staff usually is not a representative sample of the population of readers. They are a biased sample. Their attitudes, knowledge, communication skills, and social position are not an accurate reflection of the same factors as they exist in the whole population.

Again, we can find the basis for the need of a representative sample from our coin-flipping example. Suppose a coin had been flipped ten times, and heads had occurred five times, tails five times. Suppose we only observed five of these flips, and all five were heads. An inference based on these five observations would lead us to reject the null hypothesis and predict that this was a loaded coin. If we had observed all ten flips, we would not have rejected the null hypothesis.

A representative sample can be defined as one in which any given element of the population has the same chance of being selected as does any other element of the population. All other samples have bias—are not completely representative. One of the leading magazines of the 1930's, the *Literary Digest*, forgot the importance of this. In the 1936 election, the *Literary Digest* sampled the political attitudes of the American public. On the basis of its results, the magazine predicted that Mr. Landon would be elected President.

When the population was polled on election day, the inference was demonstrated to be in serious error, in overwhelming error. The magazine lost a great deal of prestige because of this. It went out of business shortly thereafter.

What caused such an error in prediction? The sample was drawn from people who had a telephone in their house and from people who drove automobiles. This was not a representative sample. Republicans were significantly more likely than were Democrats to have telephones and automobiles; therefore, the sample produced a significant bias in favor of the Republican candidate. A simple error, the selection of nonrepresentative evidence, produced a serious consequence.

3. Is There Conflicting Evidence?

If a person makes a generalization based on his observations, we sometimes can confront him with negative evidence—observations contrary to his generalization. When we do this, his usual reply is "Well, the exception proves the rule."

Many people actually believe that evidence contrary to an inductive generalization strengthens the confidence we should have in the validity of the generalization. This belief develops from a mistranslation of one key word, *probat,* in a Latin maxim: *Exceptio probat regulam.* This adage has often been translated as "The exception *proves* the rule." A more accurate translation would be "The exception *tests* the rule."

Contrary evidence reduces the probability that we will reject the null hypothesis. In our coin-flipping experiment, if we observe "HHHH" on four flips, we are more likely to reject the null hypothesis than we are if we observe "HHHT." Conflicting evidence increases the likelihood that the events we are observing are not structurally related and are only chance fluctuations consistent with the null hypothesis.

4. Has Causality Been Suggested from Inductive Inferences?

We often make statements of the order, "*A* is the cause of *B*," or, "*B* occurred because of *A*." Inductive inferences never permit the use of the term "causal," if by causal we mean determined.

All we can do with an inductive inference is to make statements of relationship. The direction of that relationship is not determinable, at least not through induction. For example, there are many advertising executives who have stomach ulcers. Suppose we reject the null hypothesis that says there is no relationship between being an advertising executive and having stomach ulcers. We make an inference that these two events are related.

The temptation is great to say that the pressures of advertising *cause* ulcers, or that Mr. Jones got ulcers *because* he was the vice-president. This is dangerous. Assuming that men in high places do have ulcers more frequently than do other men, it is just as plausible to argue that the men most likely to get ulcers are also those most likely to work hard enough to achieve fame and high status. We could argue that ulcer-proneness causes success, that success causes ulcers, or that some third event causes both ulcers and success. Induction can never provide an answer to that kind of question. *Causality can never be inferred inductively.*

These are four of the questions we need to ask ourselves in analyzing inductive inferences. There are others we could ask as well. It should be pointed out that this has not been intended to be a thorough discussion of the nature of the inductive process. That is a highly complicated process, requiring considerable skill, knowledge, and experience on the part of the individual who tries to apply structural rigor to his inductive inferences.

Much of the training of scientists is in the principles of induction and deduction. Clearly, we have only touched the surface here. All that has been intended is an illustration of the complexity of the process and of its use as a tool in improving communication.

One final word about the concept of "rare event." This concept dominates a good deal of our communication activity, particularly in the inferences we make. When we analyze human behavior, we utilize in particular the concept of the rare event—whether or not we do it consciously. Terms such as "mentally ill" imply that a cutting point has been placed on observations of behavior. Behaviors that occur less frequently than the cutting point permits are called "psychotic." Behaviors that occur more frequently than the cutting point are called "normal."

The labeling of the mentally ill is determined by the cutting points imposed by the culture. A person who is "mentally ill" in one culture may be quite "normal" in another—it depends on where we draw the line.

The same thing applies whenever we make statements of the "abnormal" variety. A doctor has his cutting points when he labels a man as overweight. A supervisor has his when he fires a man for incompetence. A parent has his when he punishes the child for misbehaving. Overweight, incompetency, mental sickness, misbehavior, abnormal traits do not exist in the physical world. They are words which name the structures we impose on our perceptions, to better accomplish our purposes.

Some cutting points are useful, justifiable. Others may not be efficient or effective. It is useful to determine the extent to which we set our own cutting points in a meaningful way. We often merely accept those suggested by others—and they may or may not meet our own needs.

Science and Structure

Many times we have referred to science or scientists in our discussion of the dimensions of meaning and the functions of language. We can look on science as a kind of communication situation and analyze it from a communication point of view.

The scientist communicates in order to affect his environment. In order to do so, he makes observations, he makes inferences (both deductive and inductive), and he makes judgments. The scientist's basic purpose is the reduction of uncertainty, the development of structure.

There have been arguments over whether science utilizes deduction or induction. Our discussion implies that it utilizes both, that both are essential to the development of scientific laws. The scientist is concerned with constructing a physical reality that is useful. In doing this, in gaining an understanding of his environment, he constructs three kinds of sentence-types. He tries to describe, explain, and predict events in the physical world.

Obviously, the scientist's own values determine which aspects of the world he will perceive, and how he will perceive them. Clearly, too, value judgments are inherent in the methods of inference themselves. Recognizing this, we can concentrate for a moment on the relationship between explanation and prediction, from a scientific point of view.

Scientific descriptions are simply statements of fact that have been verified. Scientific predictions are inferences about unknown events. Scientific predictions can be developed deductively or inductively. Let us look at each alternative in turn.

If the scientist restricts himself to deduction, he can deduce hypotheses about physical reality completely independent of physical reality itself. This is not an adequate basis for science for two reasons.

First, his original perceptions were inductive, if they had any relationship to physical reality. Second, his checking of the validity of his predictions requires the use of inductive principles, if he is to have any confidence that his predictions are related to physical reality. Clearly, the scientist *can* restrict his inferences to deduction, but he will not progress in his understanding of physical reality if he does so.

What about induction? Can the scientist restrict himself to induction? The answer again is that he can, but he will not be very productive if he does. All he can learn from induction is the relationship of events. He cannot make statements of causality, he cannot *explain* why things go together or do not go together.

In order to explain events, in order to develop his predictions from a causal base, he needs to deduce his predictions. An explanation of a prediction can be defined as a statement of the premises from which that prediction can be deduced and of the methods of deduction which produce the prediction.

Predictions are arrived at through the use of both deductive and inductive procedures. When a prediction is made totally by induction, and later events verify that prediction, we say that science has uncovered new evidence. When a prediction is made from both induction and deduction, and later events verify it, we say that science has developed a law of nature.

Scientific laws are inferences about future events that are based on (1) observations of past events, and (2) the principles of deduction that permit the inference to be deduced as well as induced. Deduction is a valuable tool for scientists. Most of the scientists who have been acclaimed by their colleagues are those who deduced hypotheses, rather than those who merely made observations and induced inferences from them.

Again, we are not suggesting an either-or process. Both deduction and induction are essential to science. Science is a process involving (a) organizing perceptions of the physical world and providing definitions of those perceptions, (b) making observations based on the conceptual definitions, (c) organizing those observations and deducing hypotheses, and (d) testing those hypotheses by applying the principles of inductive rigor, redefining, reobserving, rededucing, reverifying, and so on.

Scientific descriptions are statements of fact. Scientific predictions involve both induction and deduction. Scientific explanations are deductions. Scientific laws are derived from the use of all the methods of verifying and inferring that have been discussed—plus a great deal more.

The concept of structure is vital at all stages in the scientific process. At the inferential level, we differentiate sciences on the basis of their relative uses of deduction and induction. A highly theoretic science such as physics makes relatively few observations. It has collected enough true statements of fact to permit physicists to concentrate on trying to structure these statements of fact deductively. This is why we call physics a highly theoretic science.

The behavioral sciences, on the other hand, are still primarily inductive in nature. They still spend a great deal of time making observations, developing true statements of fact. There are few (if any) scientific laws in the behavioral sciences. There will not be any until behavioral scientists are able to insert their findings into a deductive model and manipulate their knowledge in order to deduce hypotheses.

Both deduction and induction are necessary to any science. As the operations of a science permit increased use of deduction, we say that the science has progressed—has become more theoretical. This is not to say that deductive sciences are not practical. As Kurt Lewin—a leading "theoretical" psychologist—said, "there is nothing so practical as a good theory."

This brief description of the role of structure in science has been made for two reasons. First, science as a method of seeking knowledge has come to dominate our attention to the point where we need a better understanding of the methods of science in order to interpret our environment. The thesis suggested here is that most of the procedures of science are linguistic. They seek the construction of reality through the development of true and valid propositions.

The second reason for mentioning science is to point out that it is a process, just as communication is. Science is a way of looking at the world, a way of imposing structure on our perceptions. Science is not something restricted to the scientist or the laboratory. It is a method of analysis, a method of imposing structure. All that we have said about communication is intended to approach the analysis of human behavior from a scientific point of view.

The process of communication dictates a particular point of view about science as a whole; namely that the scientist, like the artist, is in the business of constructing reality. The principles of communication analysis are the principles of scientific analysis. The study of communication has as one of its benefits an increased understanding of the characteristics of human behavior.

An understanding of communication, like an understanding of science, is intended to increase man's ability to cope with his environment, to structure it to fit his needs, to determine his needs more rationally. As the Polish-American scientist Korzybski pointed out in *Science and Sanity*,[2] the ways of science may well be the ways of sanity, assimilation of scientific approaches to problems may increase our ability to be rational. If any segment of our environment needs scientific scrutiny as a tool of rational understanding, our communication behavior is one such segment, our language behavior is one such segment.

The study of communication, as represented here, is a scientific study. At the same time, the study of communication can provide insights which are helpful in improving the methods of science as well. The concept of structure as a tool to reduce uncertainty is

[2] Alfred Korzybski, *Science and Sanity: An Introduction to Non-Aristotelian Systems and General Semantics*. Science Press, 1941.

central to an understanding of either communication or science. Both are processes. Both involve the imposition of structure on hazy perceptions, in order to create a reality that is compatible with the needs of man.

Suggestions for Thought and Discussion

1. "Argumentative validity and observable truth are independent. The conclusion of an argument may be valid and yet not be true." Discuss this statement. What are the meanings for valid and true that make this an accurate statement? Why is it important to remember a sentence such as this?

2. Analyze a message which is argumentative in nature. In doing this, perform the following operations:

   a. Reduce an argument to logical-type sentences and check its validity.

   b. Find examples of enthymemes. Reconstruct a syllogism from the enthymeme, selecting a premise which would make the syllogism valid. Determine whether the premise you developed is true or not; that is to say, determine whether you would have accepted the argument as valid if all of it had been presented to you.

3. Find as many examples as you can of faulty deductive reasoning. Discuss why this reasoning might have been faulty, and what could have been done to make it valid.

4. What are the limitations of the syllogistic form of reasoning in our every-day affairs? Why cannot we use it to check all our conclusions?

5. What is the essential difference between a deduction and generalization? How are they similar? Which is more important in developing our knowledge? Defend your answer.

6. Why is a concept of probability necessary to the development of rigorous induction? Discuss the nature of the inductive process, and try to answer the following questions:

   a. Why can we never be certain of our generalizations?

   b. What is meant by the statement that induction is a negative method?

   c. How do we define the concept of the "rare event"?

   d. Why can we not make statements about causality from induction?

7. Discuss the relationship between science and structure, with emphasis on the differences between description and explanation. What is the role of logic in science?

8. Compare and contrast observations, inferences, and judgments. What do they have in common? How do they differ?

9. On the basis of the material in Chapters 7, 8, 9 and 10, develop a definition of the "rational man." What do we mean when we say that a man is rational? irrational?

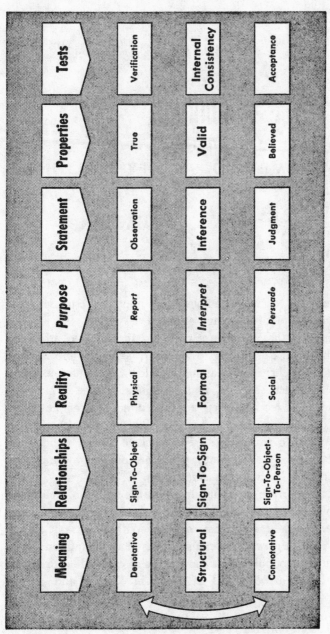

A model of the relationships among meaning, reality, and sentence-types.

CHAPTER 11

Definition

AN ATTEMPT TO SPECIFY MEANING

COMMUNICATION elicits meanings, the internal responses that people make to the message stimulus as well as the internal stimulations that these responses produce. In order to affect his receiver, the source attempts to discover, arrange, and present symbols that will elicit the meaning intended. Such attempts never meet with complete success, and occasionally meet with little success at all. The receiver often is confused, not sure of the meaning intended. This state usually produces the response, either verbal or tacit, "What do you mean?" The sensitive source, upon being asked what he means, attempts to specify his meaning more clearly. The method he is likely to use is *definition*.

There is no shortage of discussion about the nature of definition. For example, if we return to Aristotle, we read that definition is the statement of the essence of a concept.[1] Within the same framework, the *Encyclopaedia Britannica* states that "definition [is] a logical term used popularly for the process of explaining, or giving the meaning of, a word."[2] Text books in English and Speech

[1] Aristotle, *The Posterior Analytics,* Book II, Chap. 3-10. In: *The Basic Works of Aristotle* (Richard McKeon, ed.). Random House, 1941.

[2] Encyclopaedia Britannica, Volume 7, p. 138.

usually refer to definition. Williams defines definition as "one of the essential components of good exposition . . . a process of setting a limit."[3] McBurney and Wrage describe definition as "a statement of the meanings of a term."[4] Additional references will be found on pages 305-307.

We can find discussion of definitions that are intensional or extensional, inclusive or exclusive, nominal or real, complete or incomplete, essential or partial, hortatory or linguistic, informative or conceptual, and so on. In one of the more exhaustive treatments, Leonard[5] suggests as many as seventy-two different types of definitions. In spite of all this, it might be argued that the average intelligent individual remains hazy about the nature of definition, its purpose, the way one can tell when he has a good definition or a bad one, and—possibly most important of all—the process of choosing a method of constructing a good one. Many people's meaning of definition is restricted to "that's what you find in the dictionary," or "a definition tells you the real meaning of a word."

Most of these statements are relevant to definition. They vary with respect to the point of view taken about the location of meaning (in words or in people). It seems fair to say, however, that the person interested in a useful answer to the question, "What do you mean?" might not be helped appreciably by such statements. One is reminded of Dale's "clear only if known" fallacy. How do we give the essence of a concept, or is it even possible to do so? How does one go about setting the limits of meaning? How can we state the meanings of a term, or the meanings intended by a source for a term? These are the fundamental questions of definition, from the point of view of communication. The intent behind this chapter is to present a point of view about definition which it is hoped will be (1) consistent with the general view of meaning presented earlier, and (2) of some value to the individual faced with the problem of explaining his meanings with greater specificity.

[3] Arnold Williams, *Modern Exposition*. Crofts, 1942, p. 71.
[4] James A. McBurney and Ernest J. Wrage, *The Art of Good Speech* Prentice-Hall, Inc., 1953, p. 155.
[5] Henry S. Leonard, *An Introduction to Principles of Right Reason*. Henry Holt and Company, 1957, pp. 271-404.

What Is a "Good" Definition?

In discussing definition, we start by determining a criterion for definition. A definition is a statement about some symbol, attempting to specify or delimit the meanings for the symbol held by the person using it. It certainly is fair to say that "a definition should depend upon the purpose for which it is made and the person for whom it is made."[6]

In constructing or analyzing a definition, it is dangerous to believe that definitions are true or false, right or wrong, good or bad. Definitions are not statements of fact, they do not describe the physical world, they have no moral value, they cannot be considered correct or incorrect. Definitions are expressions that suggest the meaning a person intended to attach to a word or other symbol. They have only one criterion of adequacy: they are useful or they are not useful. *A definition is a "good" one to the extent that it is useful.* The question to be asked is, did the definition do what it was intended to do, did it accomplish the purpose it was intended to accomplish?

Arguments over whether a particular definition is true or not, whether it is proper or not, whether it is correct or not, are meaningless. Most of these arguments are based on the fallacy of believing that a given word or symbol has a meaning of its own, and that definition is a procedure to state the *real* or *right* meaning of the symbol. As shown earlier, words do not have meanings. Meanings originate in people; therefore, words cannot be said to have a single or right definition. *We define symbols to meet our purposes.*

What is the purpose of definition, and how do we assess the utility of a definition? Definitions are adequate if and only if they (1) elicit a clearer meaning in the receiver than was elicited by the term being defined, and (2) elicit a meaning that corresponds to the meaning intended by the source. A communication source attempts a definition in the presence of confusion on the part of the receiver. The definition should reduce this confusion. Also, it

[6] Progressive Education Association, *Language in General Education*. D. Appleton-Century Co., 1940, p. 139.

should reduce it in such a way that the receiver approaches the source's meaning for the symbol being defined.

A definition that is useful in one situation may not be useful in another; a definition that is beneficial to one receiver may not be beneficial to another. In constructing a definition, we need to take into account (1) the meaning we intended by a particular term, (2) the need that the receiver has to understand the term, and (3) the meanings that the receiver has for other terms available for use in the definition.

INTENTIONS OF THE SOURCE

The first question to ask in constructing a definition is, *why* the definition? To what use will it be put by the source? How will the term being defined be used? As we shall discuss later, the method of defining, the choices of terms within a given method, should be determined by the purpose of the definition, the way in which the term being defined is to be used. If, in defining a term, you intend to find out whether there are any objects in the physical world that correspond to that term, that is one thing. If you intend to classify the term as part of a group of other terms, that is something else. If you intend only to express your own internal connotations in the use of that term, that is something else again. In short, the dimension of meaning being utilized by the source, and the use to which he intends to put the term, will determine the kind of definition to be constructed.

NEEDS OF THE RECEIVER

When the receiver asks for clarification of a term, the source may err by misperceiving the nature of the receiver's confusion. A definition can fail to accomplish its purpose if the source assumes that he knows what the receiver is confused about—and is wrong in his assumption. A story that illustrates this concerns the mother of a five-year-old girl. The mother was quite concerned about explaining the process of child-birth to her daughter. She read diligently all of the excellent source books on this particular communication problem and felt prepared to answer any of her daughter's questions. One day the little girl came in very excitedly, after talking with other children about where they had come from. She had been asked where she had come from, and had not known what to say. She asked her mother to tell her. Deciding that the time for a careful definition of reproduction had arrived, the mother proceeded to discuss some of the physiological processes involved. When she finished her five- to ten-minute narrative and asked her daughter why she wanted to know, the daughter explained that one of the boys had said he came from Chicago and had asked her where she came from.

Clearly the mother had not taken the needs of the receiver into account and had made the error of assuming that the daughter's confusion over the meaning of a phrase was of one kind when it actually was of another.

Existing Meanings of the Receiver

We are all familiar with definitions of the following type: "Honesty may be defined as the state of being honest." One deficiency of this type of definition is that a form of the term to be defined is included in the definition. Analogous problems arise whenever we use terms of any sort that are just as foreign as the term being defined. In the definition of "honesty," the receiver's lack of meaning for the word "honesty" (which assumedly produced the need for definition) probably is accompanied by a similar lack of meaning for the terms "the state of being honest."

In giving definitions for one term, we often use terms that are even more difficult for the receiver than the original one. If we do so, we have failed to accomplish our purpose—specification of meaning. Examples of this are contained in each of the following definitions, both illustrative of utterances often encountered:

1. The carburetor is the thingamajig on the whatsis that is part of the engine.

2. Electric organ: an organ with an electrophonic rather than a mechanical or pneumatic action.

In both cases, although for quite different reasons, the receiver's meanings for the terms used "in definition" are as obscure as those for the problem terms (carburetor, electric organ).

Definitions that are useful utilize the existing meanings "possessed" by the receiver. They attempt to elicit reasonably precise meanings for the term being defined, by using terms for which the receiver already has reasonably specific meanings.

In summary, a definition can be constructed effectively only when we take into account:

1. The specific purpose of the source—what he intends to do with the term being defined.
2. The specific confusion in the mind of the receiver—what it is that he does not understand or that he wants to know about.
3. The existing meanings of the receiver that can be used in constructing a definition—meanings which increase the chances that he will respond as intended by the source.

Kinds of Definition

With these points in mind, we can consider various kinds or types of definitions. As suggested earlier, many different methods of classifying definitions are available. Within the context of our discussions, definitions are related to meaning. It seems useful to group definitions according to the three types of meaning suggested: formal, denotative, and connotative. Each of these meaning dimensions is related to a kind of definition.

FORMAL MEANING: THE *Genus et Differentia* DEFINITION

The traditional kind of definition that is related to formal meaning is familiar to all of us. A term is defined by placing it in its proper class (*genus*) and then by distinguishing it from all other terms in that class (*differentia*).

As an example of the *genus et differentia* type of definition, we can take the statement "man is a rational animal." "Man," the term being defined, is placed as a *member of the class* of animals. "Animal" is the *genus* of man, the class name that includes all men. After being so placed, the term is *separated from all other members of the class* of animals by the statement that man is rational. "Rational" is the *differentium* of man, the characteristic that distinguishes man from all other members of the class of animals.

It is easy to see the analogy between our earlier discussion of logical inference and the class membership or *genus et differentia* definition. The process of definition under this method consists solely of procedures for locating a symbol as a member of a class of symbols and then separating the symbol from all other members of that class. It is purely a relationship between one sign and other signs. It specifies formal meaning.

The *genus et differentia* definition often is contrasted with a definition constructed by describing the *properties* of an object denoted by the term being defined. This is not a definition of a different kind. We can look at properties (blondness, rationality, redness, taste, etc.) as the names for classes. When we attribute certain properties or characteristics to a term we are suggesting that there are certain classes or sub-classes of a genus, and that the word being defined is a member of one of these sub-classes. *Definition by class membership and definition by assigning properties are equivalent methods*. To do one is to do the other. Each satisfies the following criteria:

1. The term being defined and the definition itself must be mutually interchangeable; in other words, wherever you can use one you must be able to use the other.
2. The term should be included in a class that includes all instances of the term (all men must be members of the class of animals).
3. The term should be distinguished from all other terms in that class (all men must be rational, and no other animal must be rational).

The other considerations to be taken into account in constructing formal definitions need not be listed, since the intent here is merely to point out the basic characteristics of this type of definition and to relate it to an appropriate dimension of meaning.[7]

Prior to the development of relativity theory in physics and the corresponding philosophic interest in the importance of process and the empirical basis for knowledge, the *genus et differentia* procedure was regarded as basic to all definition. Even today it is valuable when our purpose is to classify a particular symbol as a member of a group of other symbols or to develop a shorthand for another set of symbols. There are three major disadvantages to this type of definition, however, which need to be taken into account. The three criticisms suggest that classificatory definitions (1) are static rather than dynamic or relativistic, (2) imply universal application rather than application only in particular situations, and (3) ignore relationships between the terms being defined and the objects in the physical world to which the terms might be intended to refer. We can discuss each of these criticisms in turn.

STATIC VS. RELATIVISTIC

The *genus et differentia* definition requires us to place terms in classes and sub-classes. It requires us to fix our meaning for a term and to assume that our meaning is not relative to space, time, and the fluctuating point of view of the person constructing the definition. For example, if we define "Murder" simply as "the taking of another person's life," we must classify all behavior as either "murder" or "not-murder." Things either are something or they are not; they are black or they are white. There is no room for grays, for doubt or questioning as to relative degrees, for meeting continual and inevitable change.

This kind of thinking, often referred to as a "two-valued orientation" by critics of the classical method of definition, causes serious trouble. One problem relates to the decisions we make. For example, most of us were taught as children that "murder is murder." At

[7] See, for example, Henry S. Leonard, *loc. cit.*

the outbreak of World War II, the need arose to alter this meaning. Many of our young men were highly disturbed by this and could not distinguish between "murder" and patriotism, which was defined as "killing the enemy." Some men refused to join the Army. Others joined, but could not make the distinction and were released. More unfortunately, some did not learn to make the distinction, but changed their entire meaning for both terms. In other words, for them "murder" became "not murder," and killing became something of value, even after their return home after the war. Most, of course, learned that it depends—on the situation, the purpose, and so on. They had escaped from the "two-valued orientation."

We can find many examples of the problems caused by this two-valued orientation, produced in part by our value for the *genus et differentia* definition. It has helped us justify the burning of "witches," avoid the study of Communism as an "evil" viewpoint, condemn the youngster who made one mistake because a "criminal is a criminal." When we hear people say that something either is or is not, that something either is good or is bad, that A is a such-and-such, no matter how you look at it—we can predict communication problems.

A partial cause of such problems can be traced to our misuse of the *genus et differentia* definition, particularly our tendency to use it to classify all terms as either A or not A, as either members of a specific genus or not, as either differentiated this way or not. If we realize this, take it into account, and avoid use of formal definitions unless we are dealing only with structural meaning, we can avoid the problem. The fact that we do not take it into account, that we have been raised in a culture which applies this kind of definition to names for physical objects, and that we accept in large part the two-valued orientation toward life—this causes a significant proportion of our everyday communication problems.

THE DANGER OF "ALLNESS"

The problem of "allness" or universal application in formal definitions is related to one of the important developments in twentieth-century thinking. Based primarily on research in physics credited to Einstein, our thinking has returned to Heraclitus' classical reminder that you can not step in the same river twice. Einstein demonstrated that physical reality is partly determined by what is perceivable and partly determined by who is perceiving. All observations are relative to both the observed and the observer. We can never perceive all of a thing, and we can never perceive anything exactly as someone else would, or exactly as we would at another point in time, space, and mental state.

What is being suggested is that *any definition has to specify the situation in which it holds. We cannot assume that it holds in all situations.* The *genus et differentia* definition typically uses a form of the verb "to be" in its formulation. We usually define X by saying "X is . . .". Irving Lee, in commenting on definition, pointed out that "when a form of the verb 'to be' connects a noun and an adjective we invariably express a false-to-fact relationship."[8] It is misleading to say that things "are," that there is an "allness" to reality that can be defined.

The names that we use do not refer to things that "are," at least not with the form that we impose on them. Words, and the objects they denote, only follow the classification systems we impose on them. If our system is useful, we keep it. If not, we discard it. When we define, we must remember that we are imposing a classification system on our terms, we are not saying "what is," we are not determining "all" of anything. As Lee[9] suggests, we might profit from substituting the expression "may be classified as" for the word "is," when we make a *genus et differentia* definition. We are only taking one point of view, relating terms in one way. There always are other possible relationships; we have never told all the story.

Referring back to the Whorfian hypothesis (see page 44), the existence of a language form to express being or existence ("is," "are," etc.) encourages us to accept a certain philosophical position about reality. We might argue that we would profit in many ways if we could exclude the verb "to be" from our vocabulary. In any

---

[8] Irving J. Lee, *Language Habits in Human Affairs*. Harper & Brothers, 1941, p. 243.
[9] *Op. cit.*, p. 253.

case, we do not define "all" of what we mean by a definition; we merely use a method of partial classification.

Let us, for example, take a term such as "intelligence." One often hears the question, what is intelligence? The question usually reflects a desire to learn what intelligence *is,* to learn the meaning that can be used correctly at all times, for all purposes, in all situations. It is difficult to explain to the parents of a child who scored very well on one intelligence test, but badly on another, that there is really no such *thing* as intelligence; that often all we mean by the term is a behavior relative to a particular test, a particular index of some forms of human behavior. He who searches for a meaning for *all* of intelligence, or any other term referring to our systems of classification, might more profitably search for the pot of gold at the end of the rainbow.

DEFINITION AND PHYSICAL REALITY

The third criticism of the formal type of definition is probably the most crucial. Actually, it is not a criticism of the definition form itself but of it in the use to which we often put it. We have suggested that any classificatory definition lies in the domain of formal meaning. It is concerned with the relationship between one sign and another sign or signs. *Classificatory definitions cannot relate signs to objects in the physical world. They are concerned only with formal reality.*

When we intend to relate a sign to physical reality we should not make use of the *genus et differentia* definition. We face a basic problem if we fail to realize that classificatory definitions do not relate to the physical world.

Take the following definition: "A centaur is an animal (genus) with the head and shoulders of a man (differentium) and the body of a horse (differentium)." This definition does not state whether there *are* or *are not* any centaurs in existence in the physical world. All it lets us do is substitute the word "centaur" for the much longer phrase "animal with the head and shoulders of a man and the body of a horse." It is a kind of shorthand or abbreviation; we can use it to increase the efficiency of communication. The danger lies in our tendency to assume that there *must* be centaurs because we have defined them. In other words, having used this kind of definition, we assume that centaurs must exist. We forget that such a definition does not say anything about the physical world, but only provides a convention for substituting one sign for a group of other signs.

Probably few of us believe that centaurs exist; perhaps we should consider another example. We can define Democracy as a form of government in which all citizens have an equal voice in decision-making. The danger is that we assume that there must *be* democracies because we have a word for them, when in actuality there may be no situations in the physical world which correspond to one in which "all citizens have an equal voice in decision-making." This illustrates what the modern logician refers to when he says that we often talk "nonsense." What he means is that there often is no relationship between our statements and physical events which can be sensed. Our statements have no empirical base; they are non-sensory.

No classificatory definition bears any necessary relationship to physical reality. We may define our terms with great precision— but not be using them to refer to anything. In doing this, we often fool ourselves into thinking that we are denoting physical events when we are not, but only talking about words.

In summary, the *genus et differentia* and other formal definitions are very useful when we are attempting to classify terms as members of classes and separate terms from other terms that are members of the same class. The criticisms made are not leveled at the definition form itself but only at our sometimes unfortunate uses of it for purposes it is not adequate to serve. The formal definition is useful as a shorthand technique to improve the efficiency of our communication, and as a tool of logical analysis which enables us to manipulate terms and propositions carefully and precisely. It can be used when we are talking denotatively, but only when we are certain that there are physical events corresponding to our terms, and when we are not concerned about securing great precision of meaning.

When we are concerned only with formal reality, or structural meaning, formal definitions are quite adequate, even most desirable. When we are talking about physical reality or denotative meaning, we need a different kind of definition.

Denotative Meaning: The Operational Definition

We often are faced with the problem of helping someone determine what it is that we are referring to or denoting in our use of a symbol. As we have said (see pages 192-93), the best way of reducing ambiguity or confusion within the receiver is to find the object being denoted by a term and point to it while using the term. In other words, we demonstrate the sign-object relationship in denotative meaning by encoding the sign and pointing to the object at the same time.

Pointing behavior is ideal. As Hayakawa suggests, we can profit if we "keep definition to a minimum and point to extensional levels wherever necessary . . ."[10] Unfortunately, pointing usually is not available to us. We may be separated in time or space from our receiver—we can not point. The objects which we are trying to denote may not be around—we can not point.

Alternatives to pointing are known to all of us. The use of examples and illustrations to help define a term denotatively is as old as the use of language itself. In the last fifty years, a more formal approach to denotative definitions has been developed. This development stems from inadequacies in the traditional *genus et differentia* definition, and in the consequent rigid beliefs and conclusions reached about the nature of the physical world. Because of the work of Einstein and others, it was discovered that many of the key physical concepts defined by formal definitions did not seem to refer to the physical world with precision. Some such terms actually denoted nothing at all. A crisis in science developed over the apparent need to change radically our attitudes toward nature. The question was raised, can we ever be sure that we are making progress in understanding physical reality? Will we need to continue changing our attitudes toward nature?

[10] S. I. Hayakawa, *Language in Thought and Action*. Harcourt, Brace and Co., 1949, p. 173.

In analyzing the crisis in science, several theorists thought they saw a solution to the basic problem. "There is no need to revise our attitudes toward nature if we accept that a proper definition of a concept is not in terms of its properties but in terms of actual operations."[11] When Bridgman wrote this, he typified the concern of the modern scientist to relate our use of words to physical experience. Bridgman argued that any "concept is synonymous with the corresponding set of operations . . . that is, the concept . . . involves as much as and nothing more than the set of operations by which [it] is determined."[12]

The methods of the operational definition are very simple. If we try to define a term, we specify a set of operations. If these operations are performed, the consequence will be the experiencing of what is referred to by the term. Rapoport puts it another way when he says that "the syntactic structure of an operational definition involves an imperative form of a verb (do so and so) and a predictive assertion (you will find . . .)."[13]

The operational definition always assumes a given point in space and time, and specifies what one must do if he is to (1) identify, (2) create, or (3) experience the event named by the term being defined. As Bridgman points out, "if the concept is physical, the operations are actual physical operations; if the concept is mental the operations are mental operations."[14]

We can find operational definitions easily. The modern cookbook is one example. If you ask the home economist what she means by a cake, her answer might well begin with the phrase "take the whites of six eggs," etc. She gives you a list of ingredients, a set of instructions for mixing the ingredients. When you have done everything she told you to do the thing you have is a cake. You perform a set of physical operations. The result is the object referred to by the term "cake."

We might argue that that is not the *real* meaning of "cake," or

[11] Percy W. Bridgman, *The Logic of Modern Physics*. The Macmillan Co., 1927, p. 6.

[12] *Op. cit.*, p. 5.

[13] Anatol Rapoport, *Science and the Goals of Man*. Harper & Brothers, 1950, p. 60.

[14] Percy W. Bridgman, *op. cit.*, p. 6.

that that is not *all* that "cake" means. Of course it is not. The operational definition does not attempt to give *all* of the meaning that the source has for a term. In fact, the *operational definition assumes that one can not give all of the meaning that one has for a term.* All that we can do is to reduce our meaning to that applying in a given situation, and try to express that particular meaning.[15]

The operational definition is useful in our attempts to elicit precise meanings from our receivers. It is specific, and it relates our terms directly to the physical world. It can help us avoid all three problems referred to in the earlier discussion of the formal definition. It is less static, avoids the "allness" problem, and is directly tied to physical reality.

AVOIDANCE OF STATIC THINKING

The operational definition always is restricted to a particular point in space and time. It defines a given term with reference to the point of view of the user of the term, for a particular situation and purpose. By avoiding the permanent assignment of a term to a class, it avoids the tendency to make meanings static and permanent. It permits change easily. For example, when we defined murder as "the taking of another person's life," we tended to fix our meaning. On the other hand, when we specify a set of operations, performed by a given person on another person, at a particular place under particular circumstances—and then attach a name ("murder") to these operations—we reduce the tendency to make our definition static, all-encompassing. Behaviors we choose to call "murder" at one time or place we may not choose to call "murder"

[15] Some theorists avoid using the term "definition" in discussing denotative statements and prefer the term "reduction sentence." In doing this, they reserve the term "definition" for the purely formal technique of substituting one set of terms for another. The distinction between the two methods is of obvious importance; however, from a communication point of view, both seem to meet the criteria for use of the name "definition." See, for example Rudolf Carnap, *Introduction to Semantics* (Studies in Semantics, Vol. I. Cambridge, Mass., 1942) and Carl G. Hempel, *Fundamentals of Concept Formation in Empirical Science* (International Encyclopedia of Unified Science, Vol. II, No. 7, 1952).

at another, and so on. The possible danger here, of course, is that we would never have any predictability of meaning if we carried this too far. Meanings are relative but we do not have the freedom that Humpty Dumpty had with "glory."

If we are trying to encompass all our meanings for a term such as "murder," the operational definition will not do. We need some general classification system. On the other hand, if we are trying to specify the actual operations which occurred (or might occur) in those cases where we apply the term "murder," the operational definition is far superior to the classificatory definition.

In actual practice, we generally move back and forth between a static classificatory definition and a more fluid operational definition. In law, for example, we have a general set of classificatory definitions for "murder." Much of the work of the trial lawyer in a murder case may be to isolate the particular behaviors performed by the accused, which the state has called "murder," and then to try to determine whether these behaviors fit the predetermined classification.

Avoidance of the Danger of "Allness"

The danger of "allness" is related to the danger of static thinking. The syntactic form of the operational definition avoids use of the verb "to be." By avoiding this syntactic form, and its corresponding thought form, we reduce the tendency to assume that our definitions and our thinking apply to every case. We heighten our ability to separate one situation from another. The form of the operational definition customarily begins with a set of "givens." These form a specification of the situation in which we intend to use the term. After the "givens," we list a set of operations. We suggest that "if" one performs these operations, he will conclude by observing (or creating, or experiencing) the referent of the term. No assumptions are made that the same object is or is not related to the same term in another situation, or under a different set of operations.

For an example, we can return to the term "intelligence." A

typical intelligence test can be used as an operational definition of intelligence. Within the context of the age, cultural background, and so forth of the child being tested, the test sets out instructions for its administration. Given a child of a certain age and cultural background, and given that the test has been administered and scored as specified in the instructions, a number can be calculated. This number is labeled as the "mental age" of the child. If the mental age is divided by the chronological age of the child, a quotient is determined. This quotient is labeled as the "intelligence quotient" of the child.

If asked what is meant by intelligence, we can answer by describing the test, the situation in which it is administered, the way it is scored, and so forth. We avoid sentences of the type "Intelligence is . . ." and the accompanying assumption that intelligence "is." All we have is a set of operations, for a given situation, that produce a result. We label this result and call it intelligence. In so doing, we attempt to construct a reality, recognizing that such reality is relative to the observer and to a given situation.

Presence of Denotative Relationship

Just as the absence of a sign-object relationship provides the most crucial criticism of the *genus et differentia* definition, the existence of such a relationship is the chief advantage of the operational definition. Instead of defining man as a rational animal, and leaving it at that, we are forced to specify the physical events referred to by the phrase "rational animal." By so doing, we *reserve use of the term until the operations are performed,* and the events referred to are observed. We have a built-in check to insure that we are actually talking "sense" when we say that man is a rational animal, rather than merely using words that have no referents, or that have referents which have become completely obscured.

We can return to the word "democracy." Suppose that we are forced, when we use this word, to specify the given situation(s), behaviors, and consequences that we are trying to name. Admittedly, our discourse often increases in length, and possibly decreases in human interest. As compensation, however, we protect ourselves from idle chatter and we determine whether there actually is something in the physical world to which we are referring. A list of actual quotations, here reproduced anonymously, illustrates the communication problems in using terms without prior operational definitions.

1. Television is a medium which brings to the American public the opportunity to lift itself beyond the mundane, and to experience the liberation of the intellect.
2. Education is a process of interaction between the teacher and the whole child, in which the intangibles of behavior are just as important as are reading and writing.
3. The X Party stands for those basic American values which are held dear by all citizens: freedom, justice, and decency.
4. Art is a spiritual necessity, essential to the general aesthetic values of man.

It should not be inferred that we have no meaning for sentences such as these, nor that the sources of these quotations could not specify the denotative referents for the terms used. It can be argued, however, that many of us, in the presence of such phrases, overlook the possibility that there may be no physical events which correspond to these linguistic events, and that we may in fact be talking "nonsense" without realizing it. Countless lengthy disputes could have been shortened or avoided if the parties concerned had specified operationally the meanings they had for their terms—or recognized that they had none.

Many of our most cherished terms seem suspiciously devoid of operational significance. What do we mean by terms like free enterprise, the dignity of labor, a liberal education, an enlightened foreign policy, good music, and so on? What are the sets of operations that are equivalent to these terms? To what are we referring when we use such terms? Are we referring to anything?

One often hears arguments about whether the classificatory

definition or the operational definition is the "right" one. The classicist defends the formal definition—at the expense of any alternative. On the other hand, enthusiastic empiricists such as Rapoport have said that "an operational definition can do everything all the others can do and more . . . if one is concerned with communicating meaning, one should use it at the slightest indication that the meaning is otherwise not clear."[16]

The solution does not require a vote for one or the other. Neither can be said to be better for all purposes. It depends. It probably is correct to say that more problems arise from using formal definitions when we should use operational ones than arise from the opposite error; however, both are useful tools for increasing the precision of our meanings. In either case, we can only construct a useful definition if we begin with an analysis of (1) the purpose of the source, (2) the needs of the receiver, and (3) the kinds of meanings with which the receiver comes to the communication situation.

Connotative Meaning: The Semantic Differential

Scholars such as Ogden and Richards,[17] Morris,[18] and others have attempted to isolate connotative meaning so that it, too, can be specified with some precision. Attempts have been made within the last twenty years to develop operational methods for indexing connotation. The most comprehensive attempt has been made by Osgood and his associates at Illinois.[19] Osgood uses the term "meaning" to refer to internal judgments that are made by the individual. In developing the Semantic Differential, the instrument used to index these judgments, he operated under three assumptions:

---

[16] Anatol Rapoport, op. cit., p. 61.

[17] C. K. Ogden and I. A. Richards, The Meaning of Meaning. Harcourt, Brace and Company, 1923.

[18] Charles W. Morris, Signs, Language and Behavior. Prentice-Hall, Inc., 1946.

[19] Charles E. Osgood, George J. Suci, and Percy Tannenbaum, The Measurement of Meaning. University of Illinois Press, 1957. The discussion of a definition of connotation reflects primarily the work reported in this reference.

1. The process of judgment can be thought of as the placing of a concept on a set of continua, each limited by a pair of polar terms (opposites).
2. Many of these continua are highly similar to others and may be represented by a single dimension.
3. A limited number of these meaning continua can be used to help specify the meaning which an individual has for any concept.

Osgood assembled a large group of polar adjective pairs such as good-bad, fair-unfair, strong-weak, and valuable-worthless. He placed each element of a pair at one end of a seven-interval rating scale, and asked people to place a check mark somewhere along each scale, given a particular term. The answers which people gave for many such terms and scales were submitted to statistical analysis, and three major dimensions were discovered. Osgood called these the three dimensions of connotative meaning. Although later work has raised the possibility of additional dimensions, these three illustrate the general procedure adequately for our purposes.

The three dimensions are (1) evaluation, (2) activity, and (3) potency. The evaluative dimension was indexed most nearly by the scale good-bad; the activity dimension by the scale active-passive, and the potency dimension by the scale strong-weak. By using these and other similar scales, one can employ the Semantic Differential to index the internal judgments that people make, given a stimulus. The stimulus may be a word, a phrase, an entire message such as a picture, a name of a person, and so on.

The instrument has been used to predict a considerable number of behaviors, such as voting in an election, the various personality phases of a split-personality subject, images of a particular disk jockey, and so on. An interesting study by Kumata[20] indicated that the existence of these three dimensions is not restricted to citizens of the United States, but that other nationality groups behave in accord with similar dimensions of connotative meaning.

[20] Hideya Kumata, "A factor analytic study of semantic structures across three selected cultures." Unpublished Ph.D. dissertation, University of Illinois, 1958.

The Semantic Differential holds considerable promise for professional communicators. It can be and has been used to test probable reactions to advertising campaigns, the relative attention value of various titles for books or monographs, of the images that students have of their instructors, of educational television, and so on. It undoubtedly will be used for many other tasks of specifying connotations that people have for a given stimulus. A sample use of the Semantic Differential is reproduced below. The concept being rated is "communication." The scales selected represent the three major dimensions.

COMMUNICATION

good ____:____:____:____:____:____:____ bad
      3   2   1   0   -1   -2   -3

valuable ____:____:____:____:____:____:____ worthless

active ____:____:____:____:____:____:____ passive

strong ____:____:____:____:____:____:____ weak

It is interesting to note that the most significant, or powerful, dimension of connotation is the evaluative dimension, relating to our tendency to judge something to be good or bad. This dimension accounts for the largest part of the variability in meanings which we have, and is used increasingly as an operational definition of people's attitudes.

The Semantic Differential represents an attempt to provide an operational definition for connotative meaning. It is not unrealistic to speculate that someday we might have a dictionary of connotative meaning in which are given our most frequent connotations for many of the words in the English language. Reference to this dictionary could help us predict how people would react to a given word, or possibly even a set of words. Further uses of this tool remain to be developed.

SUMMARY

We have examined in some detail the most prominent kinds of definition used in specifying structural and denotative meaning. In addition, we have suggested that the recent work on a measure of connotative meaning, the Semantic Differential, holds promise for analogous specification of connotation. The major purpose of this discussion has been to emphasize several points:

1. The process of definition is essential when we are confronted with confusion or uncertainty about the meaning intended through our use of a term.
2. Definitions do not provide us with knowledge. They are not statements of fact that can be said to be true or false, right or wrong, good or bad.
3. The criterion of a "good" definition is its usefulness in specifying our intended meaning—nothing more.
4. Deciding how to construct a definition depends on:

   a. the intentions of the source—the purpose for construction;
   b. the needs of the receiver—why he is confused, and what he is confused about;
   c. the existing meanings, held by the receiver, that can be used.

5. One vital dimension of purpose is the kind of meaning needed: structural or denotative. Each has an appropriate set of definition procedures, which cannot be used interchangeably.
6. Formal definitions are a kind of shorthand, allowing us to substitute one term for another and to analyze terms logically. The *genus et differentia* definition is the major formal definition.
7. Operational definitions are attempts to relate our terms to objects that exist in the physical world. They help us determine what it is that we refer to, or whether we actually are referring to anything at all.
8. Both formal and operational definitions are necessary. Which to use is determined by purpose. Neither is sufficient alone.
9. Definitions do not give us knowledge. They do, however, enable us to classify and relate knowledge previously obtained (formal) and to determine whether we have the potential for

knowledge with the terms we are using to talk about the world (operational).

In discussing definitions, reference has not been made to the dictionary. The dictionary is not what it often is assumed to be, the repository for "right" definitions. It is useful in our search to specify our meanings, and it would be misleading to conclude our discussion without reference to the role of the dictionary.

The Role of the Dictionary

The well-prepared dictionary is a tool. It is a valuable tool in developing our verbal communication abilities; however, it can be used most efficiently when it is used properly, and when it is not asked to do things it cannot do well. How *is* a dictionary useful?[21]

The dictionary gives us the most frequent published spellings of a particular word. It gives us also one or more frequent pronunciations of the word. Admittedly, both spellings and pronunciations—particularly the latter—vary from one part of the country to another, even from one county to another within the same state. The dictionary cannot legislate either spelling or pronunciation; it is not an arbiter, but a reporter, with a very large newsbeat to cover.

As a reporter, it cannot cover all occurrences, or even keep up with very recent occurrences. It does not have the timeliness of a daily paper, the individualized approach of a small-town weekly. It could, if it chose, attempt to reproduce the most frequent occurrences; but instead it tends to reproduce usage selectively, and thus inevitably it introduces the bias of its point of view. The dictionary is a large national publication, infrequently published, and always (1) out-of-date, (2) superficial in its coverage, and (3) not as relevant to a particular problem as other sources probably would be—including your own experience. The best source for how people

---

[21] One of the more thorough and enjoyable treatments of the use of a dictionary is contained in Donald J. Lloyd and Harry R. Warfel's *American English in Its Cultural Setting*. Alfred A. Knopf, 1956, pp. 458-481.

pronounce, how people spell, how people mean—the best source is people.

What else can a dictionary do? It can give us fascinating insight into the history of language, the relationships among languages, among cultures, among people. Careful study of the etymology of words for many is in and of itself a worthwhile activity, for many an aesthetically stimulating activity. Where do words come from? How are they related to other words, age-old words? The dictionary can help you attack questions of this order.

Etymology also is useful in giving us some hints about the meanings people have for words, based on meanings other people used to have for similar words. The consistencies of meaning through time and space are a testimonial to man's own continuity of belief and judgment. Possibly more exciting are the amazing inconsistencies of meaning through time and space, the radical changes we have undergone in our meanings for words. All of this kind of knowledge and speculation is available through the dictionary. In this sense, we can agree with Lloyd and Warfel when they say that "dictionaries have long been considered . . . the finest single instrument for cultivating the mind."[22]

What about definitions? In one sense, the dictionary does not contain definitions. True, it at times can provide a *genus et differentia* definition for a term—but seldom does so with any precision. True, it at times provides an operational definition for a term that is used in few contexts, including the use of nonverbal illustrations. In general, however, it does not give us either formal definitions or operational definitions. The dictionary lists a large number of words, interesting words, usable words. For each word, it gives another set of words. If we do not have any meaning for a word, we can get hints from the dictionary. In essence, it says to us "if you don't have a meaning for this word, try these."

The dictionary reports relationships among words, instances in which they are used in sentences, differing contexts in which they are employed. All of these provide us hints as to the meanings we

[22] Donald J. Lloyd and Harry R. Warfel, *op. cit.*, p. 459.

might express with a word, or the meanings that a word might elicit from others. Not truth, not certainty, only hints—but very valuable hints indeed.

In recording pronunciation, spelling, etymology, related words, and contexts, English lexicographers have made great progress since the days of Bailey's *An Universal Etymological Dictionary* in 1721, one of the first attempts at an English dictionary. Many modern dictionaries have abandoned the role of prescriber and arbiter of meaning and usage and accepted the linguistically consistent role of recorder and reporter. The modern dictionary is more cautious, more careful, more thorough than its ancestors would have believed either possible or desirable.[23] Unfortunately, many users of the dictionary have not made analogous progress.

The dangers in the dictionary lie in its possible misuse by unsuspecting or submissive users. It is a tool, a carefully developed tool, analogous to a fine-edged spade. As a spade, it can help us uncover fertile ground and open new fields for intellectual cultivation. It cannot replace all other tools and experience, nor especially the ingenuity of the user. Above all, it should not be used to defend the misbeliefs of yesterday against the modern, efficient, and effective tools of modern intellectual farming, reflected by the revolutionary developments in linguistic and communication theory.

Educators deplore the fact that many of our children are not exposed in school to any mathematical concepts that have been developed since the seventeenth century. Regrettably, transmitted information and theory about the nature and use of language often is even more out of date. It is one of the goals of students of language and communication to rectify deficiencies such as these through the development of more systematic knowledge about language, and the accompanying development of methods of transmitting this knowledge in ways that will be understood and accepted. It is probable that the acceptance of such knowledge in many quarters will require the use of even more than what Aristotle referred to as "all" the available means of persuasion.

---

[23] As illustrations of a sophisticated linguistic approach to the construction of a dictionary, see: *The New World Dictionary,* or *The American College Dictionary.*

Suggestions for Thought and Discussion

1. Construct an operational definition for each of the following terms. Try to include operations which would enable someone to "know one when they saw one."

   a. *race:* as in the sentence "He is a member of the *x* race" or "Her mother was of the *y* race and her father was of the *z* race." How might a biologist and a sociologist differ in their definitions of race?

   b. *conservative:* as in the sentence "The majority of the legislature are liberals, but the Senator from my district is a conservative." When you are through, substitute the term "reactionary" for "conservative." How do you distinguish between these two terms, operationally?

   c. *liberal education:* as in the sentence "All college students should receive a liberal education." Specify the *it* that college students should receive. How could one tell whether he was getting a liberal education or some other kind of education?

   d. *arrogance:* as in the sentence "He is arrogant when he is around people; in fact, he possesses a great deal of arrogance generally." When you are through, substitute the term "self-confidence" for "arrogance." How do you distinguish between these two terms, operationally?

2. Collect a number of *genus et differentia* definitions and a number of operational definitions. Compare them. How do they differ? Can you make any statements about their relative difficulty, precision, length, interest, and so on? Did you find any *genus et differentia* definitions that specify meanings for terms which seem to refer to physical events? Can you locate the physical events to which such terms refer, or did you discover a term that actually does not refer to anything but just sounds as if it did?

3. Why are formal definitions necessary for logical analysis of a set of propositions? What deficiencies do operational definitions have when we want to manipulate a concept in a series of logical inferences?

4. Which is more important, formal or operational definition? In what ways is one more important than the other, and vice versa? Within your own professional field of interest, can you find exam-

ples of good and bad (i.e., useful and nonuseful) definitions of either type?

5. What uses could you make personally of the Semantic Differential? Conduct an experiment. Predict the connotations which several of your friends will have for two or three terms. Using these terms and the scales suggested in the text, administer the Semantic Differential to them. Observe their responses and check them against your predictions. If you erred in your predictions, try to explain why. What are the implications of such errors for your own communication ability and success?

SUGGESTED READINGS
IN COMMUNICATION

For the reader who is interested in continuing his explorations in the field of communication theory and process beyond the introduction provided by this book, several possible readings are suggested below. The readings have been selected on two criteria: (a) breadth, and (b) availability to the interested but nontechnical reader. For convenience, the readings are separated into two groups: *communication process* (covering the first six chapters of the book) and *language and communication* (covering the last six chapters).

Communication Process

Chase, Stuart, *The Proper Study of Mankind*. Harper & Brothers, New York, 1948.

Cherry, Colin, *On Human Communication*. The Technology Press, Massachusetts Institute of Technology, Cambridge, 1957.

Festinger, Leon, *A Theory of Cognitive Dissonance*. Row, Peterson and Company, Evanston, 1957.

Hartley, Eugene L., and Ruth E. Hartley, *Fundamentals of Social Psychology*. Alfred A. Knopf, Inc., New York, 1952.

Janis, Irving, and Carl Hovland, *Personality and Persuasability*. Yale University Press, New Haven, 1959.

Katz, Elihu, and Paul Lazarsfeld, *Personal Influence*. The Free Press, Glencoe, 1955.

Mead, George H., *Mind, Self and Society*. University of Chicago Press, Chicago, 1934.

Merton, Robert, *Social Theory and Social Structure*. The Free Press, Glencoe, 1957.

Ruesch, Jurgen, and Gregory Bateson, *Communication, The Social Matrix of Psychiatry*. W. W. Norton Company, Inc., New York, 1951.

Schramm, Wilbur (ed.), *The Process and Effects of Mass Communication*. University of Illinois Press, Urbana, 1954.

Siebert, Frederick S., Theodore Peterson, and Wilbur Schramm, *Four Theories of the Press*. University of Illinois Press, Urbana, 1956.

Smith, Bruce, and Chitra Smith, *International Communication and Political Opinion*. Princeton University Press, Princeton, 1956.

White, David M., and Bernard Rosenberg (eds.), *Mass Culture*. The Free Press, Glencoe, 1957.

Wiener, Norbert, *The Human Use of Human Beings*. Doubleday and Company, Inc., Garden City, 1956.

Language and Communication

Bloomfield, Leonard, *Language*. Henry Holt and Company, New York, 1933.

Brown, Roger W., *Words and Things*. The Free Press, Glencoe, 1958.

Chall, Jeanne S., *Readability*. The Ohio State University Press, Columbus, 1958.

Hall, Edward T., *The Silent Language*. Doubleday and Company, Inc., Garden City, 1959.

Hayakawa, S. I., *Language in Thought and Action*. Harcourt, Brace and Company, New York, 1949.

Hovland, Carl I., *The Order of Presentation in Persuasion*. Yale University Press, New Haven, 1957.

Johnson, Wendell, *People in Quandaries*. Harper & Brothers, New York, 1946.

Lloyd, Donald J., and Harry R. Warfel. *American English in Its Cultural Setting*. Alfred A. Knopf, Inc., New York, 1956.

Meyer, Leonard B., *Emotion and Meaning in Music*. University of Chicago Press, Chicago, 1956.

Morris, Charles W., *Signs, Language and Behavior*. Prentice-Hall, Inc., New York, 1946.

Osgood, Charles E., George J. Suci, and Percy Tannenbaum, *The Measurement of Meaning*. University of Illinois Press, Urbana, 1957.

Piaget, Jean, *The Language and Thought of the Child*. Meridian Books. New York, 1955.

Whatmough, Joshua, *Language: A Modern Synthesis*. St. Martin's Press, New York, 1957.

Whorf, Benjamin, *Language, Thought, and Reality*. The Technology Press, Massachusetts Institute of Technology, Cambridge, 1956.

Zipf, G. K., *Human Behavior and the Principle of Least Effort*. Addison-Wesley Publishing Company, Inc., Cambridge, 1949.

Index